Conceptual Mind and Computing Paradigm

$A = (f(m), I)$

E. Al Galvis

Conceptual Mind and Computing Paradigm (2nd Edition)

The author and publisher make no expressed or implied warranty. No liabilities are assumed arising out of the use of the information or software contained herein, including responsibility for potential errors or omissions. Every effort has been made to provide appropriate trademark information about all the companies and products mentioned in this book.

Printed in the United States of America
ISBN 978-1523816057

In the memory of my loving Mother and grandparents who made this work possible.

TABLE OF CONTENTS

PREFACE

Conceptually, our mind is an entity of beautiful simplicity designed for the single function or purpose of *processing information*. This book is about a Conceptual computing model mimicked from the mind and its application to software engineering challenges.

Concepts are straightforward entities that can be readily grasped. For instance, the concept of messaging represents the interchange of information between individuals like you and me. This book isn't an introduction to programming or software design. It assumes that you are reasonably familiar with at least one programming language and basic software design techniques.

The Conceptual computing model can be implemented using any arbitrary computer language. Concepts are highly reusable entities that can be applied to solve a variety of common problems in the real world. The model can streamline software and make it more flexible, reusable, understandable, timely, and cost-effective. It can improve overall quality while saving a considerable amount of effort and resources dedicated to building complex software applications.

The world around us exhibits inherent solutions and associated design in response to specific problems. Conceptualization entails the extraction of concepts, relevant to the problem domain – both natural and human-made. In doing so, the problem at hand can be effectively solved by mirroring the concepts involved as part of preexisting solution and design. A realistically accurate representation and solution are also achieved.

The book seeks to achieve a healthy compromise between theory and application. The theory is illustrated by presenting plenty of examples and working applications. There is no much in terms of involved mathematical formulations; mainly some demonstrations presented for completeness sake. In agreement with Occam's razor, the Conceptual computing model and the associated paradigm represent entities of striking simplicity:

"Nature does not multiply things [Concepts] unnecessarily; that she makes use of the easiest and simplest means [Concepts] for producing her effects; that she does nothing in vain, and the like." Galileo Galilei.

1

In writing this book, I also tried to pursue Occam's razor as related to content and presentation. Mother Nature always seems to know best. In general, it is probably how good software and writing should be: simple. On the other hand, for the sake of clearness and illustration, certain key ideas are repeated as needed.

For better understanding, the book substantially relies on the reader's intuition and reasonable common sense. While reading this book, we ought to think in conceptual terms, which our minds are perfectly capable of doing. Also, the natural language represents the ultimate tool for conveying information, in the form of concepts, as related to expressiveness, conciseness, and power – a match for the conceptual mind that hosts it.

In order to fully understand certain ideas, you may need to rely on other disciplines such as philosophy, psychology, and cognition. They will be referenced when appropriate. Concepts and the conceptual mind have been studied from many perspectives that can be leveraged while reading the material.

If you would like to provide your expert review of this book, we would love to hear from you. Criticism and comments for improvement are always welcome; especially, in terms of areas that were missed or require additional work. I apologize in advance for any potential mistakes or omissions.

ROADMAP

This book consists of the following main parts:

Realistic Information Model (REAL): describes several relevant aspects behind the Conceptual model including philosophical, psychological, and cognitive aspects.

Information/Conceptual Machines *(A=(f(m),I))*: introduces the Turing-complete mathematical foundation on which the Conceptual model is based upon. The mathematical foundation is straightforward and therefore leveraged to explain ideas and principles covered by subsequent chapters.

Information Family of Concepts: collection of concepts related to information processing.

Conceptual Framework: the Turing-complete Conceptual computing model is leveraged for the specification and design of a comprehensive component framework applicable to the implementation of arbitrary information technologies.

Design Pattern Implementation: covers how the Turing-complete Conceptual model can be leveraged for the reusable implementation of common design patterns.

Distributed Conceptual Model (DCM): the Turing-complete Conceptual model is applied to the design and specification of a comprehensive distributed component/service infrastructure.

Cognitive/AI Architecture: application of the Turing-complete Conceptual computing model to the realm of cognitive architectures and artificial intelligence.

Model Evaluation and Metrics: evaluation of the Conceptual model and related metrics.

It is recommended that you start by reading the introductory chapters: a) Conceptual Paradigm b) Realistic Information Model (REAL) c) Mathematical model d) Physical Foundation

e) Live or Animated Entities and f) Messaging. These chapters should give you a foundation for the understanding of all the other chapters.

The Turing-complete Conceptual model is applicable to a wide range of information technologies. After reading the aforementioned chapters, you will be in a position to start reading specific chapters of interest to you. The information family of concepts represents a substantial portion of the book. You can read them all at once, or one at a time, on as needed basis. Several other chapters make reference to specific concepts in the collection.

If you are interested in the mathematical foundations, you will enjoy the relevant chapters: a) Mathematical Model (Information and Conceptual Machines) b) Information Machine and Turing completeness. They provide the mathematical foundation behind the model.

You may also derive satisfaction from the fact that all the qualities exhibited by the Conceptual computing model are a direct consequence of its straightforward Turing-complete mathematical foundation. The mathematical demonstrations presented require basic knowledge of algebra, set theory, probability, and logic.

After reading the introductory chapters, you can directly dive into the chapter dealing with the Conceptual framework. Most of the applications are built on top of it. The Jt Conceptual framework is a reference implementation of the presented computing model. It supports Java and Android. The complete source code of the framework is part of the accompanying materials. Most mainstream technologies are fully integrated with the framework including Apache Axis (SOA), JDBC, EJB, Java Mail, JMS, Servlets, JSPs, and XML

The sample applications are mainly written using Java and Android. However, the Conceptual computing model and framework can be implemented using any arbitrary computer language. The transparent integration of heterogeneous platforms, technologies, protocols, and computer languages is one key benefit derived from the Conceptual model. A basic knowledge of Java and/or Android is recommended for the understanding of the software examples/applications.

Finally, the universal concept of Logos is discussed in a separate chapter. The appendixes compare the Conceptual computing model in the context of a wide variety of related approaches, theories, studies, and models.

1. CONCEPTUAL PARADIGM

Biomimetics is the examination of nature, its models, systems, processes, and elements to emulate or take inspiration from, in order to solve human problems. The term Biomimetics comes from the Greek words bios, meaning life, and mimesis, meaning to imitate. Applications of Biomimetics have led to innumerable advances in science and engineering. The Computer Science field is no exception. The von Neumann Architecture, on which modern computers are based, took significant inspiration from the human brain.

The human mind represents the pinnacle of natural creation. Nothing else in the known universe comes close. According to cognitive psychology, computer systems are information processors, like our minds [25]. In consequence, computer systems can be significantly improved by mimicking the conceptual paradigm and model leveraged by the mind. Conceptually, the logical mind is designed for a single purpose or function: *logical processing of information.* According to George Boole's remarkable assertions, the laws of thought are mathematical in their form.

"The truth that the ultimate laws of thought are mathematical in their form, viewed in connexion with the fact of the possibility of error, establishes a ground for some remarkable conclusions. If we directed our attention to the scientific truth alone, we might be led to infer an almost exact parallelism between the intellectual operations and the movements of external nature.
Suppose any one conversant with physical science, but unaccustomed to reflect upon the nature of his own faculties, to have been informed, that it had been proved, that the laws of those faculties were mathematical; it is probable that after the first feelings of incredulity had subsided, the impression would arise, that the order of thought must, therefore, be as necessary as that of the material universe. We know that in the realm of natural science, the absolute connexion between the initial and final elements of a problem, exhibited in the mathematical form, fitly symbolizes that physical necessity which binds together effect and cause."   George Boole (!) [1]

Boole's remarkable conclusions, regarding the mathematical (logical) nature of thought, are in harmony with modern logic and recent research in the area of cognition.

"Thought was still wholly intangible and ineffable until modern formal logic interpreted it as the manipulation of formal tokens."
  Allen Newel and Herbert Simon [25]

Logic comes from the Greek Logos, which is a concept with broad polyvalent meaning: word, to reason, to speak, law, rule, and so on. The modern definition speaks about the power of the concept [33]: "thought of as constituting the controlling principle of the universe". The name of multiples disciplines is derived from Logos: logic, biology, physiology, psychology, information technology, neurology, theology, and so forth.

The natural mind is an entity of beautiful and mathematical *simplicity*. Only *three* concepts are involved as part of the mind's 'computing model': information, messaging, and conceptual/information machine. These abstractions also represent a streamlined and complete set of concepts (Turing complete) applicable to the comprehensive implementation of arbitrary information/computing and technologies. The natural concept of messaging is ubiquitous. Realistically, it also represents the only mechanism of communication between the mind and its environment.

In harmony with leading theories, the unified Conceptual model explains and mimics key cognitive abilities including memory, logical reasoning, symbol/language manipulation, learning, and goal oriented behavior. The Conceptual machine (A) that mimics the mind can be expressed mathematically as $A=(\beta(m),I)$. A is Turing complete, fully implementable, and features the same processing power of a computer. Furthermore, based on George Boole's Laws of Thought, the Conceptual machine is also capable of *logical* reasoning. The function/primitive $\beta(m)$ represents logical processing of information, applied to incoming messages (m), as defined by Boole's algebra of logic.

As a consequence of the Conceptual computing model mimicked from the mind, software/information technology is improved in several aspects including overall complexity, mathematical foundations, realistic correspondence, gap between human and machine, encapsulation, reusability, decoupling, interoperability, scalability, quality, cost, and timeframe. Mother Nature solution to the 'software problem' and associated complexity is in character, as expressed by Occam's razor:

"Nature does not multiply things unnecessarily; that she makes use of the easiest and simplest means [Concepts] for producing her effects;" Galileo Galilei

Simplest concepts indeed: $A=(\beta(m), I)$.

6

2. REALISTIC INFORMATION MODEL (REAL)

Our perceived reality is defined by a single concept: *information*. The Latin roots of the term mean "to give form to the mind". In turn, the ancient Greek word for form was used in the philosophical sense to denote the ideal identity or essence of an entity in reality. In other words, information is the 'substance' or essence that shapes our minds and allows us to conceptualize our reality. Our thinking minds and patterns consist of this single concept.

Relevant ideas such as realism (realistic correspondence), reductionism, and Occam's razor have had a prominent impact on science and scientific models. Realistic correspondence is a key aspect while evaluating scientific models. Philosophical realism asserts that reality exists independent of the observer and that the *truth of a representation is determined by how it corresponds to reality (The Correspondence Theory of Truth [30])*.

Information is a fundamental concept, a cornerstone of human activity, societal interaction, and existence. Without the ability to process information, a variety of living beings and specifically people would not be able to cope with reality, adapt, and therefore survive. Critical functions like thinking, moving, walking, talking, reading, hearing, decision making and internal body functions would not be possible.

As mentioned earlier, the human mind represents the pinnacle of natural creation when it comes to information processing. As a consequence of Biomimetic principles, computer systems can be significantly improved by realistically mimicking the conceptual framework and paradigm utilized by the mind.

The Conceptual model, based on the fundamental concept of information, *mimics* reality and seeks to provide an accurate/comprehensive representation of the real world. Nature has already done the work, set the standard, and successfully solved information challenges via proven solutions. The Conceptual model attempts to faithfully examine and mimic nature's information model, processes, and solutions.

In particular, it attempts to understand and mimic the conceptual paradigm used by the mind, part of the natural realm. A realistic information model includes the following *concepts*, mimicked from nature: information, messaging, and information machine. Information machines interact with each other (interchange information) via messaging within the context of information processes. Software components can implement the information machine abstraction: such components are called *Live or Animated Components.*

The ubiquitous concepts part of the realistic model can be found everywhere: communities, organizations, companies, human body processes, and applications consisting of local or distributed components working cooperatively through messaging. The aforementioned concepts can be organized into more complex entities represented by the *Group* concept.

Notice that the concept of information machine refers to several classes of physical entities capable of processing information: person, computer system, automated machine, living being, and so forth. In other words, the same concept applies to many different classes of physical entities.

Consider an organization or process where multiple entities work cooperatively to achieve common goals. The survival and development of such organizations have depended on finding solutions for information and process challenges. For instance, communities of individuals have developed sophisticated ways of communication (i.e. messaging). Human speech, and in general communication between members of the same species, would be an example.

The interchange of information (messaging) is vital to the survival of every organization and community. Societies have built sophisticated information infrastructures and frameworks to carry the messaging required for communication and decision making purposes. Communities and organizations have been able to deal with fault tolerance challenges by providing individual, message, and process redundancy.

From a realistic perspective, our logical minds are designed for a single purpose or function: *logical processing of information*. Actually you are doing it right now while you read (process) this document. You are processing information sentence by sentence: each sentence represents the message being processed logically.

Not to mention all the processing of information that has taken place in order for the information to reach its destination: networks, computers, email systems, visual system, nervous system, etc. Each one of these systems is conceptually an information system (information machine) designed for the single purpose of information processing.

Ideally, complete results can be achieved when the overriding design mindset, abstractions, principles, and goals are governed by the deliberate and faithful pursue of a model (i.e. realistic model) that mimics reality without any artificial deviations, which generally result in shortcomings, weaknesses and/or inefficiencies.

The absence of the messaging concept would be an example. Artifacts are in direct conflict with natural concepts. Tight gear meshing of procedure calls (artifact) must never be confused or mischaracterized as real messaging. The natural concept and the artifact are *different*. Messaging is the *real* thing, so to speak.

Nature is wise, its processes present many qualities: simplicity, completeness, accuracy, robustness, efficiency, versatility, and so forth. Other critical aspects are also part of natural processes, including redundancy and fault tolerance. A realistic model that mimics nature should absorb such traits and characteristics – in agreement with Biomimetics. There is no need to reinvent the wheel so to speak. As a consequence, software engineering methodologies and techniques can be improved by mimicking the models, abstractions, processes and solutions found in nature and the real world.

The terms object and component are often used interchangeably hereafter. Conceptually speaking, a component, like a CPU chip, also represents an object. Physical objects often become components of more complex structures (car part or arm).

From an information perspective, the fundamental aspect is whether the object or component is able to process information in the real world. If so, the object or component is called a Live/Animated component. In reality, most entities are unanimated objects or components, unable to process information.

On the other hand, we should distinguish between the concept use to represent the entity, inside our minds, and the entity or physical object being represented. Although tightly related, they are two separate and decoupled entities. Concepts as mental representations are based on information and separate from the actual entities or physical objects being represented: Kant called it the "thing-in-itself" or the "thing per se" [30]. For instance, the physical entity called 'mind' is able to process information. The mental representation ('mind') cannot, since it only exists inside our mind. The mental representation and the actual entity are separate.

The position stated in the previous paragraph does not contradict a *moderate* realistic position. It is also consistent with a compromised approach known as *conceptualism*, which presents itself as a middle ground between nominalism and realism: asserting that universal concepts exist, but they exist in the mind, rather than real entities existing independently of the mind. 'Exaggerated' realism holds that universal things exist in nature which is viewed as going against common sense.

The Turing-complete Conceptual approach explains and mimics key cognitive abilities including memory, logical reasoning, symbol/language manipulation, learning, and goal oriented behavior (see Cognitive/AI architecture). The Conceptual model is in close correspondence with and/or supported by leading research, theories, and disciplines related to the mind: computational theory of mind (CTM), The Language of Thought Hypothesis (LOTH), cognitive psychology, psychology, psychological associationism, neurological engrams, Unified Theories of Cognition (UTC), Physical Symbol System Hypothesis (PSSH), philosophical reductionism, conceptualism, and realism (see appendix on Related Theories, Studies, and Research). Such relevant research, theories, and disciplines will be leveraged when appropriate, in order to fully describe and/or support the Conceptual model.

3. MATHEMATICAL MODEL (Information and Conceptual Machines)

"The truth that the ultimate *laws of thought are mathematical in their form*, viewed in connexion with the fact of the possibility of error, establishes a ground for some *remarkable conclusions*. If we directed our attention to the scientific truth alone, we might be led to infer an almost exact parallelism between the intellectual operations and the movements of external nature." George Boole [1]

"My contention is that machines can be constructed which will simulate the behavior of the human mind very closely."   Alan Turing

There are three (3) main concepts involved as part of the mathematical computing model, which was originally introduced as a collaborative paper [8].

Information Machine (A): An automatic machine able to perform computations via the information primitive which defines the machine's single function (or purpose). The machine A is defined by a two-tuple A= *(processInformation(message)*, I). A is Turing complete. It can also be expressed as $A = (f(m), I)$, where f represents any computable function.

a) **Message (m):** incoming information is processed in the form of messages (m), also called information packets or chunks (IC). A message (m) is expressed by an n-tuple $m = (b_1, \ldots, b_n)$ where $b_1, \ldots, b_n$ are symbols in a finite set of symbols (alphabet $(\sum)$).

b) **Information (I):** Information machines include a memory subcomponent able to store and retrieve information. The information stored (i.e. known) by the machine is represented by $I = (IC_1, \ldots, IC_n)$, where $IC_1, \ldots, IC_n$ are information chunks (or packets). $IC_i = (b_{i1}, \ldots, b_{in})$; $b_{i1}, \ldots, b_{in} \in \sum$; $i \in [1..n]$.

c) **Information primitive:** *processInformation (message)* represents a function $f: \sum^* \rightarrow \sum^*$

To be rigorous, $\sum$ needs to be included as part of the machine definition: $A = (f(m), I, \sum)$. For simplicity sake, it is usually excluded. Information machines (with memory), also known as A-machines, are Turing complete. Additionally, information machines can have several modalities.

a) **Information Machine/Component:**

$A = (f(m), I)$. The machine may consist of a group of Animated/Live components (ACs) working concurrently:

$A = \{AC_1, \ldots, AC_n\}$. Each individual component can be represented using the information component abstraction as well: $AC_i=(f(m), I)$. The same mathematical concept (A) is recursively applicable to the machine and all its components which may in turn consist of subcomponents.

b) **Information Machine without memory:**

$A = (f(m))$. No information (I) is stored by the machine.

c) **Conceptual Machine:** machine able to process conceptual information (C). For processing purposes, messages $(M = (b1, \ldots, bn))$ are transformed into its equivalent (C) representation.

d) **Boole's Conceptual Machine:** conceptual machine capable of logical reasoning as defined by the deductive approach. It can be expressed as $A=(\beta(m), I)$, where the function $\beta(m)$ represents logical processing of information, applied to incoming messages (m), as defined by Boole's algebra of logic (Laws of Thought!). It consists of a single main component, logical engine (LE), whose function $\beta(m)$ has been substantially simplified (i.e. narrowed) in terms of its scope. Logical capabilities provide the foundation for other cognitive abilities including language learning/processing, decision making, and problem solving.

Information itself (I) can be classified into two categories: conceptual (C) and non-conceptual. The following definitions apply to conceptual information.

a) **Concept construct (C):** conceptual information expressed by a single language construct, $C = (a1,a2, \ldots ,an)$ where $a1,a2, \ldots ,an$ are information associations.

b) **Information association (a):** a_i is an association of the form (x_i, y_i), meaning that x_i is equal or associated to y_i ($x_i = y_i$) where x_i and y_i are defined as follows.

    - $x_i = (b1, \ldots, bn)$; $b_i \in \sum$; $i \in [1 .. n]$, or x_i represents a concept as defined by C.

- yi = (b1, ..., bn); $b_i \in \Sigma$; i $\in$ [1 .. n], or yi represents a concept as defined by C.

c) **Language (L):** Conceptual machines process messages that are constructed based on a Language (L) which consists of a set of symbols (i.e. words) and their associated definitions. L = {(symbol1, Definition (symbol1)), ... , (symboln, Definition (symboln))} where each symbol is an information chunk (or packet) as defined above: $symbol_i$ = (b1, ..., bn). The meaning (i.e. semantics) of each symbol is provided by its lexicographic definition: Definition (symbol) represents a function f: $\Sigma^* \rightarrow \Sigma^*$

d) **Sentence (S):** a sentence in the language (L) is a concept (C): S = (a1,a2, ...,a_n) where a1, a2, ...,a_n are information associations.

e) **Procedure (P):** a procedure is a concept (C) defined as a sequence of steps to be executed: P = (S1, ..., Sn) where each step (or statement) is expressed in the form of a sentence (S) in the language (L).

f) **Conceptual Knowledge (K):** The conceptual portion of the information contained in the memory subcomponent can be expressed as K = {C1, ... , Cn}. Each chunk of conceptual information (IC = (b1, ... ,bn)) is transformed into its equivalent (C) representation. K consists of all the concepts known to the machine including procedures (P), and language information (L).

In summary, the model consists of following three (3) main concepts: information, messaging, and processing of information as defined by a single mathematical function $(f(m))$. It should become obvious why information is the fundamental concept behind the model.

A complex problem has been reduced, via conceptualization, to a complete and streamlined set of implementable concepts as part of a straightforward solution. Computer software based on traditional computing models is unnecessarily complex since nature's conceptual mind, as modeled here, is beautifully simple – which is consistent with Biomimetics and Occam's razor.

Messaging is tightly intertwined with the concept of information. Through the concept of messaging, information is transferred and the machine is able to interact with its physical environment.

Conceptual information introduces several additional entities: Language (L), Sentence (S), Procedure (P), Conceptual Knowledge (K), and concept construct (C). Notice that all of them represent concepts themselves. Therefore they can be represented using the (C) construct.

To visualize the natural concepts involved you may want to think about the human mind and the associated entities. Obviously, since the model attempts to mimic the mind, there is a realistic *one-to-one* correspondence. Notice that the mind serves a dual purpose and it is able to manipulate both non-conceptual and conceptual information. Non-conceptual information consists of entities like images, sounds, smells, flavors, and tactile sensations that do not carry conceptual information.

For instance, the image or sounds associated to a familiar pet. On the other hand, images and sounds often carry concepts (C); for example, in the case of written/spoken sentences. In such case, the message (image/sound) needs to be transformed into its conceptual representation (C) during processing by the mind.

Obviously, the ability to process conceptual information is highly developed in human beings. It makes us unique since animals lack such level of cognitive abilities. As usual, nature is leading the way in terms of a paradigm for computing and information processing: *conceptual paradigm*.

Due to its simplicity and expressiveness, the mathematical model is being introduced early to facilitate the explanation of the subsequent chapters. It is also very intuitive, based on abstractions that everyone can relate to and readily grasp.

The information machine represents a *model* of the mind. It should be stated that scientific *models* do not need to be exact in order to be valid, but approximately true (see Models in Science [30]). Multiple valid models of the same natural phenomena are also feasible. Consider the weather models, for instance. Regardless of how closely the Turing-complete Conceptual *model* mimics the mind, it presents a wide range of measurable qualities applicable to information technologies and computer software (see Model Evaluation and Metrics).

The Turing-complete mathematical model is in agreement with and/or supported by well-known theories and disciplines related to the mind: computational theory of mind (CTM), The Language of Thought Hypothesis (LOTH), cognitive psychology, psychology, psychological associationism, Unified Theories of Cognition (UTC), Physical Symbol System Hypothesis (PSSH), and philosophical conceptualism/realism (see Cognitive/AI Architecture and appendix on Related Theories, Studies, and Research).

4. PHYSICAL FOUNDATION (Concept of Energy)

"I believe computer science differs little from physics, in this general scientific method, even if not in its experimental criteria. Like many computer scientists, I hope for a broad *informatical* science of phenomena- both manmade and *natural*- to match the rich existing physical science." Robin Milner [29]

"Computer science is the study of the phenomena surrounding computers ... an empirical discipline." Newell, A. and Simon, H. [25]

Physics comes from the ancient Greek meaning "the natural things". It is also the name of Aristotle's treatise on nature. Physics is defined as the scientific study of *mass* and *energy* and how they interact with each other. The following discussion is carried out at a conceptual level, from the standpoint of computer science.

The main purpose of this section is showing that the Conceptual computing model has a solid physical foundation – therefore realistic, in agreement with the Correspondence Theory of Truth [30]. Such concrete physical foundation is less abstract and complementary to philosophical basis being presented (conceptualism and realism). It cites related empirical and cognitive research that is in close correspondence with the model and its mathematical foundation.

As a consequence of Einstein's special theory of relativity, Mass and Energy are equivalent. This result lies at the core of modern physics (see Equivalence of Mass and Energy [30]). Mass can simply be viewed as a form of Energy and vice versa. Hereafter, both forms of the same entity will be employed interchangeably. Thus, Energy is the 'universal concept'. All entities in the known physical universe are made of it.

The mathematical laws of physics (i.e. nature) govern the interaction between all forms of Energy, which include gravitational and atomic forces. Energy can also be mathematically modeled, quantified, analyzed, and studied using concrete empirical methods. Sense the environment around you. A quick empirical verification illustrates that everything that being perceived by our minds is made of Energy.

"Everything is made of atoms [Energy]. That is the key hypothesis. Everything that animals do, atoms do. There is nothing that living things do that cannot be understood from the point of view that they are made of atoms [Energy] acting according to the laws of physics." Richard Feynman

"An object (or concept) is said to be *reducible* to one or more objects if all statements about it can be transformed into statements about these other objects." Rudolf Carnap [52]

Excuse the liberty of using [Energy] to stress a point. Notice that thinking or 'mental computing' is also part of what human beings do. It should be stated that reductionist hypothesis has been accepted by a great majority of scientists, although the limitations of a purely reductionist approach (i.e. greedy) need to be acknowledged as well [35]. Therefore, a compromised position between reductionism and holism makes sense, in which both *complementary* perspectives are beneficial [35]. There are several key aspects that serve as motivation for *reductionism* [52]. Among them:

a) Unification of science.

b) Minimization of terms and concepts used by theories in order to encourage theoretical simplicity and eradicate redundancy (Occam's razor). This aspect should make science more accessible and easier to learn (learning curve).

c) Filling in of gaps and elimination of contradictions between theories.

d) Enabling researches to see the big picture of the sciences to avoid gaps or contradictions.

"Present account of models of computation highlights several topics of importance for the development of new understanding of computing and its role: natural computation and the relationship between the model and physical implementation, interactivity as fundamental for computational modeling of concurrent *information processing systems* such as living organisms and their networks, and the new developments in logic needed to support this generalized framework.

Computing understood as *information processing* is closely related to natural sciences; it helps us recognize connections between sciences, and provides a *unified* approach for modeling and simulating of both living and non-living systems." Gordana Dodig-Crnkovic [36]

"William of Occam opposed the proliferation of entities, but only when carried beyond what is needed --procter necessitatem! ... But computer scientists must also look for *something basic* which underlies the various models; they are interested not only in individual designs and systems, but also in a *unified theory of their ingredients.*" Robin Milner [29]

When it comes to computing, information represents the basic and fundamental concept. According to Landauer, Information is physical [33]. Information is Energy – the 'matter' of Nature: "Everything is made of atoms ...". The Latin roots of the word mean "to give form to the mind", which seems quite accurate.. The mind is constantly interacting with the environment via messages (information) received through the senses. Such messages represent forms of Energy: sound, visual image, smell, tactile sensation, and taste.

"Information is not a disembodied *abstract* entity; it is always tied to a physical representation ... This ties the handling [processing] of information to all the possibilities and restrictions of our real physical world, its laws of physics and its storehouse of available parts." Rolf Landauer [33]

In close correspondence with the Conceptual computing model, recent empirical studies on animals have showed that memories are physically encoded inside the brain [50]: the information stored inside the mind (I) also represents Energy. By activating a small cluster of neurons through ontogenetic, the animal subject is forced to recall a specific memory. By removing these neurons, the subject would lose that memory. It is highly likely that human brain functions in the same way [50]:

"This is the rigorously designed 21st-century test of Canadian neurosurgeon Wilder Penfield's early-1900s accidental observation suggesting that mind is based on matter [Energy]....The main significance here is that we finally have proof that memories (engrams, in neuropsychology speak) are *physical* rather than conceptual."

The German evolutionary biologist Richard Semon coined the term engram. He proposed the idea that experience is encoded on a specific web of brain neurons. Related studies have demonstrated how the eye encodes information to be transferred to the brain [51]. The empirical findings are in agreement with the Turing-complete Conceptual computing model. Information (I) is stored in memory as a group of Energy packets or chunks.

Modern theories of cognition also support the physical nature of the human mind [32]. "Theories of human cognition are ultimately theories of *physical,* biological systems. Our ability to describe human cognition in one way rather than another rests ultimately on the *physical* and biological nature of human beings." As discussed earlier, it is widely accepted that *everything* in nature is constrained by the laws of physics [33, 35]. Thinking and the information (i.e. Energy) stored inside the mind are not exceptions.

According to reductionism, science, and computer science in particular, can be reduced to physics. In consequence, we can define (i.e. reduce) computing using concrete and objective physical terms: in terms of Energy. Computing can be defined as transformation or processing of Energy (i.e. information). It describes the transformation that happens within a computer – or the mind while thinking, in agreement with recent empirical findings and cognitive psychology. An information machine $(A=(f(m),I))$ – like the mind, computer, or component – is a processor of Energy.

The concept of messaging can also be defined in physical terms: transference of Energy (i.e. information) – in the form of messages (packets of Energy). It is tightly intertwined with the concept of information machine which interacts with its environment through messaging.

"Computation is inevitably done with real physical degrees of freedom, obeying the laws of physics, and using parts [Energy/Atoms] available in our actual physical universe." Rolf Landauer [33]

In summary, the Conceptual model presents physical and realistic foundations (Correspondence Theory of Truth [30]). It should be fairly obvious that the information (messages) received through our senses are forms of Energy. On the other hand, it is assumed that the empirical findings on mammals match the behavior and physical structure of the human brain, which is likely [50]. Such findings are also in agreement with prevailing thinking in the realm cognitive psychology [25] which views the human mind as an information processor (i.e. computer). Cognitivism asserts that cognition represents *information processing.*

In correspondence with reductionism, the Turing-complete Conceptual computing model has been reduced to physics *(A= (f(m), I))*: the concept of information (i.e. Energy) and processing thereof. Per Milner's hopes, computer science can be reduced to an *informatical* science of phenomena matching the existing physical science [29]. In consequence, the Conceptual computing model, based on a single concept, is straightforward and shows the aforementioned reductionist qualities: *Reduction brings forth simplification (parsimony), unification, and elimination ('shaving') of redundancy. Through simplification, reductionism aims to make science more accessible and easier to learn: filling gaps and minimization of terms/concepts in scientific theories.*

According to the Conceptual model, the mind behaves like a integrated device or computer for recording, searching, recognition, and retrieval of information (.i.e. Energy) based on a straightforward set of operations: record (write), play/remember (read), and logical processing. For instance, when you are able to 'replay' a song or voice previously heard (i.e. recorded). The same applies to a procedure or task previously learned which can be 'replayed' inside the mind.

Multisensory capabilities are present in the mind allowing for the integrated manipulation and recognition of multiple forms of Energy: sight, smell, sound, touch, and taste. Modern computers and multiple electronic devices present some multimedia capabilities: recording and playing of sound or video. Some advanced systems incorporate recognition capabilities: voice and face recognition, for instance. However, it must be emphasized that the mind operates in a unified fashion *(A=(β(m),I))* in harmony with the integrated conceptual computing model and unified theories of cognition (UTC) [32] (see Cognitive/AI architecture): A single unit for the sole purpose of processing packets of information (i.e. Energy): conceptual (C) and non-conceptual. All the information in memory (I) is also Energy.

In a Universe made of Energy, it is only fitting that an Energy processor, like the mind, is able to understand it and adapt to it. In a sense, through the mind the Universe also understands itself. It is also fitting that our ideas and thought patterns be made of Energy. Paraphrasing Galileo, Mother Nature is simple and does not multiply a thing; that she makes use of the universal concept of Energy, and its law(s), for producing all her effects.

In general, idea, thought, symbol, message and even information are entities hard to define in precise terms. They may often seem vague and 'abstract'. By *reducing* and relying on the physical concept of Energy, the matter becomes more clear and concrete. In the physical world, all these entities exist in the form of Energy, or aggregates thereof, which corresponds with the Conceptual mathematical model. Therefore, they can be defined in precise mathematical and physical terms (concrete). Keep in mind that most of our logical thinking (thought, idea) happens in the form of Sentences (S) which can be represented using the concept construct (C). Sentences also represent aggregates or packets of Energy.

Many physicists and philosophers assert that the concepts of time and space do not exist in physical reality (see Time [30]). They represent useful illusions (mental constructs) only within the mind: modes or concepts by which we think. Notice the Conceptual computing model relies exclusively on the concept of Energy (information) and processing thereof. Human-made mental constructs (abstractions) can be represented and manipulated as part of the information stored (I) by the information machine, using the concept construct (C).

"Time and space are modes [concepts] by which we think and not conditions in which we live." Albert Einstein

5. LIVE OR ANIMATED ENTITIES ($A=(f(m), I)$)

5.1 Intent

Live or Animated entities are able to process information and exhibit independent behavior – a "life of their own", so to speak. This abstraction encapsulates functionality, information, and processing mechanism required to provide the entity with its independent behavior. In particular, it relies on its own independent processing mechanism and implements the Turing-complete information machine abstraction, part of the Conceptual computing model: $A=(f(m),I)$. Information is represented using the concept construct (C).

Live/Animated entities improve decoupling, encapsulation, reusability and scalability while at the same time reducing overall complexity. Functionality, processing/treading mechanism, and messaging mechanism are decoupled entities, independent of one another.

Messaging allows the interchange of information (i.e. messages) between the Live/Animated entities. Although decoupled and independent of one another, processing mechanism and component functionality are completely encapsulated within a single entity (A).

5.2 Applicability

This abstraction can be applied in a wide variety of scenarios. Live or Animated entities are all around us in the real world. Living beings, computers, automated systems, machines and subcomponents of these entities represent a few examples. All these entities are able to process information (information processors), exhibit an independent behavior, and therefore can be modeled as *Live* or *Animated* entities.

Messaging is the mechanism of communication between Live/Animated entities and their external environment, including other entities, systems, and applications. This approach is not only realistic; it also handles many of the complexities associated with the implementation of traditional multithreaded and distributed applications.

From an information standpoint, Live/Animated entities represent information processors (information machines). In consequence, all these entities can be modeled using a common and straightforward mathematical abstraction, part of the Turing-complete Conceptual computing model: information machine - $A=(f(m),I)$.

Most of this section will be dedicated to Live/Animated *components* which represent a software implementation of the information machine abstraction. Because they share the same concepts, the Turing-complete mathematical model applies to all levels of organization: a component, a process, an application, a system, a computer, an architecture, and arbitrary groups of these entities. It provides a complete mathematical foundation for every level. The Turing-complete Conceptual model reduces computing/*information* technology to the concepts of information (Energy), messaging, and information machine (see Physical Foundation).

A component can be modeled using its precise mathematical definition (Live/Animated entity): $A=(f(m),I)$. So can a full-blown computer $(A=(f(m),I))$. A process, system, application, or architecture can be modeled as a collection of these Live/Animated entities working concurrently and communicating via messaging: ($\{A_1, , A_n\}$ where $A_i = (f_i(m), I_i)$).

5.3 Motivation

The implementation of traditional multithreaded and distributed applications is a complex undertaking which usually becomes costly, time consuming, and prone to error. Quality defects related to multithreading are often encountered (thread management, synchronization, race conditions, deadlocks, etc). These software defects are difficult to avoid, reproduce, and isolate.

Large multithreaded applications and/or implementation teams complicate the problem even further. The degree of complexity and risk considerably worsens as the number of threads and their interactions increases.

When computers, smartphones, cars, and computerized systems in general, apparently experience random failures, it should not come as a surprise if the root causes are associated with complex multithreading defects. The quality issues become crucial when the software happens to be controlling mission critical applications.

Traditional multithreading and 'gear meshing of procedure calls' are widely employed as part of software applications. For instance, a banking application may need to model a teller component able to process multiple banking transactions concurrently. There will probably be several distributed teller components or threads running independently within the context of a banking application.

Consider the following quote: "We can note in passing that one of the **biggest problems** in the development of object-oriented SW architectures, particularly in the last 25 years, has been an enormous over-focus on objects and an under-focus on messaging (most so-called object-oriented languages *don't really* use the looser coupling of **messaging**, but instead use the much tighter *gear meshing of procedure calls* – this hurts scalability and interoperability)." Alan Kay et al.

Another real world example would be a highly interactive smartphone application able to concurrently speak, recognize voice, play music, manage the graphical user interface while performing other operations (phone calls, text messages, notifications, alarms, GPS, etc). Multiple threads of execution are required. No single thread is allowed to monopolize the CPU for long periods of time, otherwise the offending thread may be forced to stop.

The conventional solution for general purpose applications, and in particular for the examples presented above, is based on multithreading and gear meshing of procedure calls. As mentioned earlier, multithreaded applications present a wide variety of challenges and problems including:

a) Complexity dealing with thread management, synchronization, race conditions, and deadlocks.

b) Strong coupling which ties the solution to a specific platform, multithreading technology and/or application language; specifically in the context of multithreaded or distributed applications.

c) Lack of encapsulation since the threading mechanism is usually implemented as a separate object. A single thread may also be 'artificially' associated with multiple objects.

d) Lack of reusability which usually results from strong coupling, lack of encapsulation, and the inability to provide reusable threading functionality as part of a framework.

e) Complex quality issues brought about by the previous challenges which get compounded and harder to manage as the number of threads and/or team members increases.

f) Scalability and interoperability limitations.

g) Quality/testing Issues. Testing of traditional multithreaded applications can be a complex and challenging activity. It is fairly easy to introduce bugs. On the other hand, it can be fairly difficult and time consuming to avoid, reproduce, catch, and fix bugs within the context of traditional multithreaded applications. Large multithreaded applications complicate the problem further. Bugs may appear sporadically, under very specific multithreading conditions, that are hard to avoid and reproduce.

Component-based applications consist of a collection of components that interact with each other. To achieve realistic correspondence, these components should be modeled as Live/Animated components: they represent information processors (machines) and exhibit independent behavior. Notice that the teller component should encapsulate the component functionality and the processing mechanism as two independent concerns within the component.

On the other hand, they are both part of a single component (teller) and should not be artificially modeled as separate entities. In general, the implementation of a Live/Animated component calls for one single thread which provides the processing mechanism. Messaging provides the realistic mechanism of communication. Information is represented using the concept construct (C).

A realistic software model capable of providing comparable functionality to arbitrary multithreaded/distributed applications would consist of several Live/Animated components $(A=(f(m),I))$ communicating with each other via messaging. This solution addresses many of the issues associated with comparable multithreaded and/or distributed applications based on gear meshing of procedure calls.

5.4 Participants

a) **Live/Animated component (receiver):** encapsulates functionality and independent processing mechanism which provides the component with the ability to process information and its characteristic independent behavior (Fig. 1-3). Live/Animated components communicate with other components via messaging: components, message and messaging mechanism are decoupled, encapsulated, and fully independent. All forms of messaging are modeled including synchronous (Fig. 3), asynchronous, streaming, distributed messaging, two-way messaging, secure messaging, and combinations of these forms.

b) **Message Sender**: component that sends the message.

c) **Messenger:** intermediary that transfers the message from the sender to the Live/Animated component (Fig. 1). It is often the case that the messenger is not required (Fig. 2). The message can be sent directly to the Live/Animated component.

d) **Message:** any piece of information (i.e. data) that needs to be interchanged between sender and recipient. Two messages are usually involved: input message and output message (or reply message). The reply message is not required. All messages are represented using the concept construct (C).

e) **Asynchronous Message Queue:** internal subcomponent used to enqueue the incoming messages (Fig. 1-2). The component relies on a queuing mechanism to store the incoming messages being sent asynchronously. The component's processing mechanism dequeues the messages and processes them one at a time. A Conceptual framework usually implements the logic required to manage the component thread and the message queue. The component only needs to inherit (i.e. reuse) this functionality from a framework superclass.

5.5 Structure

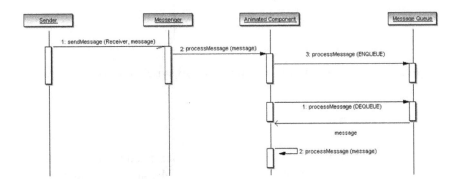

Figure 1. Live or Animated component (with a messenger)

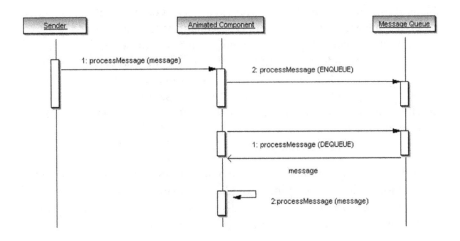

Figure 2. Live or Animated component (without messenger).

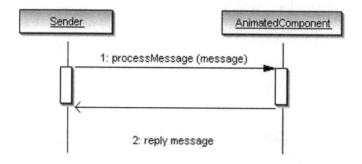

Figure 3. Live or Animated component and synchronous messaging.

5.6 Collaboration

Live/Animated entities rely on messaging which is another concept that seeks to accurately mimic reality (see Messaging): independent Live/Animated entities interact with each other and interchange information (i.e. messaging) within the context of predefined processes (Fig. 1-3).

Messaging is the realistic mechanism of communication. Sender, receiver, message, and messaging mechanism are decoupled entities, encapsulated, and fully independent. Each of these aspects can be changed independently without impacting the others. In reality, information (messages) can take many forms, all of which can be modeled using computer software and the messaging concept: a number, an email message, a document, a spoken sentence, biochemical message, and so on.

Live/Animated components can also be incorporated into distributed applications, since messaging provides transparent access to distributed components as part of a complete distributed component model (Turing complete) – distributed components are treated as local ones.

In the case of asynchronous communication, Live/Animated components require a queuing mechanism to store incoming messages: enqueueMessage(message). A message is sent directly or via a messenger (Fig. 1-2). The Live/Animated component processes incoming messages, one at a time, via its independent processing mechanism. It relies on the information primitive to process incoming messages (Fig. 1-2).

In other words, the Live/Animated component is constantly processing incoming information via its independent mechanism, which mainly waits for incoming messages and processes them by invoking the information primitive (*processInformation (message)*). Consider your short term memory, email system, postal mailbox or message recording machine – as an analogy. Messages can be sent asynchronously and placed in a message queue or pile until you are ready to "process" them.

Live/Animated components are able to mimic this behavior and handle the complexities associated with asynchronous messaging, multithreading, and distributed component access. A teller component, local or distributed, should be able to readily process messages associated to banking transactions (deposits, withdrawals, account balance, etc.)

5.7 Consequences

Encapsulation. Live/Animated components improve encapsulation. Component functionality, information (I), and processing/threading mechanism are encapsulated into a single entity. They should not be artificially modeled as separate objects. It should be fairly obvious that the Live/Animated entity ($A=(f(m),I)$) is a fully encapsulated and independent entity.

Coupling. Decoupling is improved. Component functionality, processing/treading mechanism, and messaging mechanism are decoupled. Each one can be modified independently without impacting the others. Also, the processing mechanism is decoupled from the calling component.

The rest of the components in the system do not need to know how the processing mechanism of the Live/Animated component is implemented. There is no dependency between the calling component and this mechanism.

The processing mechanism can be changed freely without impacting the calling component. Decoupling is also improved as a direct consequence of using messaging as the communication mechanism and abstraction. Each component is a self-contained unit that can perform independently from the rest of the system. Again, it should be obvious that the Live/Animated entity $(A=(f(m),I))$ is fully decoupled from its environment.

Reusability. Live/Animated entities improve reusability. The calling application is able to readily reuse a component that encapsulates functionality and processing mechanism. It does not need to re-implement or become overly concerned as to how processing mechanism and asynchronous messaging are implemented. It also feasible to reuse components based on heterogeneous technologies and languages within the context of the same process. This is possible because Live/Animated components are fully encapsulated entities, decoupled, and independent.

The processing/threading functionality should be implemented within the context of a Conceptual framework which also improves reusability. Live/Animated components can inherit and reuse the framework functionality. There is no need to re-implement it for each animated component to be involved, as opposed to traditional multithreaded applications.

Abstraction level. Live/Animated entities operate at a high level or abstraction close to the reality being represented: conceptual level. It is widely accepted that high level of abstraction is conducive to software improvements [44, 49]. Concise and expressive abstractions are essential in software. High level abstractions reduce "cognitive distance", which is the notion of the intellectual effort required to use a particular abstraction [44].

Traditional multithreaded/distributed applications. Live/Animated components constitute the building blocks required to assemble production quality applications, comparable in functionality to traditional multithreaded/distributed applications.

Component based frameworks and UML/BPM/BPEL tools. Live/Animated components can be readily incorporated into UML/BPM/BPEL diagrams in order to design and implement complex applications. Notice that for components to be incorporated, in a straightforward fashion, they need to share the same interface. Messaging represents such common interface.

Conceptual Component Frameworks. As mentioned earlier, the processing/threading mechanism should be implemented within the context of a Conceptual framework. This is feasible and recommended as a best practice. Management of the threading mechanism becomes responsibility of the framework. It involves thread creation, management, destruction, message queue synchronization, etc. Live/Animated components can inherit and reuse the framework functionality. There is no need to re-implement it for each component involved.

Quality Assurance/Testing process. Live/Animated components facilitate testing and debugging efforts. Components can be tested as independent units by sending messages to the component and verifying the expected reply messages (black-box testing).

Because functionality and threading mechanisms are decoupled, the component functionality can be tested separately via synchronous messaging (single thread). Keep in mind that the main difference between synchronous and asynchronous messaging is the queuing mechanism required.

In general, functionality can be tested without using the asynchronous queuing mechanism, one message at a time. Threading capabilities and testing of such capabilities are usually ensured by the Conceptual frameworks that implements messaging.

In general, only the component functionality, without multithreading considerations, needs to be thoroughly tested. A good Conceptual framework should ensure the quality of the threading and messaging implementation which are reused by the Live/Animated component.

Race conditions and deadlocks. By removing multithreading artifacts/APIs, race conditions and deadlocks are avoided. Keep in mind that the queuing mechanism ensures that messages are placed in the queue and processed sequentially by the Live/Animated component. The queuing mechanism also ensures that access to the shared resource (message queue) is properly controlled.

Fault tolerance. Live/Animated components ($A=(f(m), I)$) can readily emulate state machines. Therefore, they can be extended to provide fault-tolerant capabilities in a very natural fashion by replicating components/messaging and coordinating their interaction via consensus algorithms [6,16] (see Distributed Conceptual Model).

Conceptual paradigm and learning curve. In order to take advantage of the proposed concept, people need to think in terms of realistic abstractions when they model, design, and build software applications; specifically, in terms of information (Energy) and processing thereof. This may require learning time and training. Although a realistic model is natural, intuitive, and consistent with the real world, conventional multithreaded/distributed applications are based on method/procedure invocation (gear meshing of procedure calls) and traditional multithreading capabilities.

Keep in mind that natural concepts have many qualities. Therefore it is challenging to find drawbacks associated with these entities, which is unexpected within the context of design patterns. A similar situation occurs when we look at other natural concepts that may be part of reality, like Gravity and Force.

Based on observation and faith, the Creator has a knack for perfection: "... the wondrous works of the One perfect in knowledge." The proposed abstraction is best studied and understood from the standpoint of concepts where finding trade-offs is not as critical and perhaps unfeasible (see appendix on Related Approaches of Software Reuse).

Overhead. Transferring messages between components and handling a message queue introduces a small overhead when compared with traditional method/procedure invocation. The benefits associated to the proposed abstraction outweigh this performance cost; in particular, the degree of realistic correspondence.

Pool of Live/Animated components. Manipulating large numbers of concurrent Live/Animated components may prove to be computationally expensive if each component is implemented using an independent thread. For this particular scenario, we may need to consider a design based on a pool of Live/Animated components in order to control the total number of threads running concurrently. Live/Animated components can be created and destroyed as needed, in order to limit the total number of these entities running concurrently.

5.8 Known uses

Design patterns: Live or Animated components have been used to implement and/or facilitate the implementation of other well-known design patterns like Gang of Four design patterns (GoF), J2EE Design patterns, Master-Worker and MVC. Consider that Live/Animated entities are present in a variety of realistic scenarios and that many pattern implementations may have to deal with concurrency and asynchronous messaging.

For instance, a Command pattern implementation may need to process concurrent requests coming from several components within a traditional multithreaded application. The pattern implementation can use Live/Animated components as the basis for a realistic and comparable implementation. An implementation of MVC may require model, view, and controller to be implemented as three separate Live/Animated components interchanging messaging asynchronously. Such scenario is common in the context of mobile applications running under Android.

Component/Conceptual Frameworks: Live/Animated components can be used to build reusable component/conceptual frameworks. Again, consider that the Live/Animated entities are ubiquitous in the real world. Applications often require them for a realistic design and implementation. Once the abstraction is implemented (one time) as part of the framework, it can be reused over and over again to provide concurrency and asynchronous messaging capabilities. Such degree of reusability has a positive impact on overall software complexity, cost, timeframe and quality.

Distributed component and service model (SOA): Live/Animated components are well suited for the implementation of a complete distributed component/service model and related distributed applications. Conceptually, communicating with a remote Live/Animated component is not very different from communicating with a local one since messaging is being leveraged.

Actually, the Live/Animated component $(A=(f(m),I))$ does not need to do anything special to support distributed access. The component is the same; no additional artifacts or logic are required. The Conceptual framework provides the communication infrastructure to convey distributed messages to remote components.

BPM/BPEL processes and technologies: Live/Animated components have been readily reused for the implementation of BPEL/BPM technologies, frameworks, and processes. Actually, the set of abstractions provided by the Turing-complete information family mimics the set of entities found in processes of everyday life. They can be reused, in very natural ways, to implement comprehensive BPEL/BPM technologies and processes.

Complex issues related to scalability, concurrency, distributed access, asynchronous messaging, and security are handled by the proposed abstractions as part of a reusable, realistic, and comprehensive information infrastructure.

5.9 Related Patterns

As mentioned earlier, the implementation of several other design patterns may call for concurrency capabilities and asynchronous messaging. A robust/realistic model and implementation should include Live/Animated components to provide comparable functionality. In general, any design pattern participant (component) can be potentially modeled using the proposed abstraction by simply inheriting functionality from a Conceptual framework.

Command, Observer, Mediator, Decorator, Model View Controller (MVC) and J2EE Business Delegate are some examples of design patterns that can benefit from using the Live/Animated component abstraction since it accurately mimics reality. Traditional approaches usually require that their participants reimplement multithreading and/or asynchronous messaging capabilities (see appendix on Related Approaches of Software Reuse).

5.10 Implementation

The separation between the involved concepts (model) and their implementation needs to be emphasized, which is a common characteristic found in related approaches [46], [11]. Thus, multiple valid implementations (i.e. realizations) of the same Turing-complete Conceptual computing model are feasible.

The Live/Animated entity ($A=(f(m),I)$) can be implemented using a component and the messaging interface (JtInterface). The interface consists of a single information primitive to process the input message and produce a reply message. It acts as a universal messaging interface that applies to distributed and local components. It also applies to all modalities of messaging: synchronous, asynchronous, streaming, distributed messaging, two-way messaging, secure messaging, and combinations of these forms. The interface handles any type of message. It returns a reply (of any type).

The proposed implementation is mainly a reference implementation of the Live/Animated entity $(A=(f(m),I))$ and there are other potential implementations of the concept. In Java, the messaging interface can be declared as follows:

public interface JtInterface { Object processMessage (Object message); }

The generic type Object is used which is similar to the implementation of common design patterns (Iterator, for instance). In reality, the component may only be able to process and return specific types of message. In that case, appropriate types may be specified. For instance:

public interface MyMessagingInterface {
  MyOutputType processMessage (MyInputType message); }

The previous interface is also a valid implementation of messaging. Advanced object-oriented technologies provide features like Java generics which allow the types to be parameterized:

public interface JtInterface<Type, Type1> { Type1 processMessage (Type msg); }

Notice that arbitrary modern computer languages can be used to implement messaging, including plain old java objects (POJOs):

public Object processMessage (Object message)

The mathematical concept construct (C) is also straightforward and can be implemented using common data structures supported by modern computer languages: list, array, hash table, etc. (see Concept Construct). Messages are implemented using the concept construct (C) and can be transparently interchanged between Live/Animated components (local and/or distributed).

Live/Animated components also require a mechanism to enqueue messages: *enqueueMessage(message)*. The Live/Animated component processes these messages using its own independent thread: messages are dequeued, one at a time, and processed using the information primitive (*processMessage(message)*).

36

Notice that several execution threads have concurrent access to the messaging queue: the component is able to receive messaging from multiple components concurrently. Therefore, access to this shared resource needs to be controlled. Not every computer language, especially an older one, implements concurrency or is able to deal with it efficiently. The proposed abstraction is best suited for modern technologies and object-oriented computer languages. Synchronous messaging, on the other hand, supports legacy technologies.

6. CONCEPT CONSTRUCT (C)

6.1 Intent

This abstraction allows the conceptualization, communication, and processing of information. A precise definition for the word *concept* can be found in the dictionary: "an idea of something formed by mentally combining all its characteristics or particulars; a construct".

A concept construct (C) is the group of associations (information associations) that represents such characteristics or particulars. The concept construct (C) separates the fundamental information aspect from all other aspects such as how the information is stored, represented, transferred, secured, and processed.

Concepts constructs (C) are also fully decoupled from the entities that process them. Information machine and concept construct (C) are decoupled entities, fully independent. Consider that there is clear separation between information and the mind (information machine) that communicates and processes it. The concept construct (C) realistically mimics human communication and thinking patterns, which are mainly carried out through sentences in the natural language.

As stated before, most of our logical thinking (thought, idea) happens in the form of Sentences (S) which can be represented using the concept construct (C). From a physical perspective, sentences represent aggregates or packets of Energy (see Physical Foundation). In agreement with conceptualism [30], concepts constructs (C) are mental representations based on information and separate from the actual entities or physical objects being represented.

6.2 Applicability

"Concepts are the constituents of thought. Consequently, they are crucial to such psychological processes as categorization, inference, memory, learning, and decision-making." (see Concepts[30]). The mind uses concepts to understand, communicate and process arbitrary ideas – in the form of sentences in the natural language. Every sentence in the language can be represented using the concept construct (C).

Any arbitrary message represents a concept. Therefore, arbitrary messages can be represented using the concept construct (C). Another example would be the concept of a reservation. We can use the concept construct (C) to convey information about multiple aspects: hotel reservation, computer reservation, airplane reservation, parking reservation, etc. The concept of a reservation can be applied in multiple contexts.

Notice that the information related to each particular class of reservation will be different. The information needed for a hotel reservation is not the same as the one required for an airplane reservation, although both scenarios share the *same concept*. The concept construct (C) is versatile and dynamic entity with wide applicability.

6.3 Participants and Structure

In formal terms, the concept construct (C) can be defined as an n-tuple of information associations: $C = (a1, a2, ..., an)$

ai is an information association of the form (xi, yi), meaning that xi is equal or associated to yi ($xi = yi$). A concept construct (C) can be recursively expressed as: $C = ((x1,y1), (x2,y2), ... , (xn, yn))$
- xi represents a concept construct as defined by C or a sequence of symbols in the alphabet: $xi = (b1, ... , bn)$; $b_i \in \sum$; $i \in [1 .. n]$
- yi represents a concept construct as defined by C or a sequence of symbols in the alphabet: $yi = (b1, ... , bn)$; $b_i \in \sum$; $i \in [1 .. n]$

The simplicity of the concept construct (C) can be deceiving. Arbitrary ideas can be expressed as information in the form of a concept construct (C). All the conceptual information accrued until the present day, expressed by spoken or written sentences, can be represented using the concept construct (C).

Stated in plain terms, a concept construct (C) is a group of *information associations* (information aggregate). As indicated earlier, a spoken sentence is a concept that can be expressed using the concept construct (C). Any sentence (S) consists of multiple information associations: S = (a1, a2, ..., an).

Messaging is the abstraction used to transfer concept constructs (C). Our minds receive conceptual information via verbal or written communication in the form of messages (sentences). An arbitrary message (M) is also a concept that can be expressed using the concept construct: M = (a1, a2, ..., an)

As discussed earlier, concept constructs (C) do not have any information processing capabilities. In a sense, they are 'passive' entities responsible for the single purpose of conveying information. Arbitrary aspects can be expressed using a single abstraction or language construct: concept construct (C). For instance, every unanimated physical object modeled by a traditional O-O language can be represented as a concept (C). The attributes of the object can be expressed in terms of information associations (see appendix on Related Approaches of Software Reuse).

On the other hand, representing a concept (like a message for example) using a typical object (O-O) is difficult and restrictive because its attributes are not fixed. The object representation is just not a good fit (correspondence). Messages can have all kind of structures although they correspond to same concept: Message (M).

Concept constructs (C) are similar to the information stored in database tables (rows) although they do not consist of a fixed number of attributes. In general, a third party component or system is required to process the database information. There is a clear separation between the information and the components/systems responsible for processing it.

Composition of concepts (C) follows the well-known principle of compositionality (Frege's Principle) [30]: the meaning of a complex expression (C) is determined by the meanings of its constituent expressions (concepts) and the rules used to combine them. Two concept constructs (C) are said to be semantically equivalent (C1 = C2) if they have the same meaning. For instance, two sentences are semantically equivalent if they meet the criteria.

6.4 Implementation

The sentence "please make a reservation" consists of the following group of associations:

$S = (a_1, a_2, a_3, a_4)$ a1, a2, a3, and a4 are information associations.

S can be expressed as follows:

S=((1,please), (2,make), (3,a) (4,,reservation))

An alternative representation may consist of grammatical associations:

S=((adverb, please), (verb, make), (article, a) (object, reservation))

adverb = please
article = a
verb = make
object = reservation

A third representation may be in the form of a predefined application message intended for a computer component:

S=((operation, make), (what, reservation))

The example can be generalized to represent any arbitrary sentence. Multiple representations are possible. Similar to human and component communication, the main aspect is that the involved parties agree on syntax and semantics.

Arbitrary computer technologies can be used to implement the concept construct (C). Notice that the object abstraction (O-O) is implemented via a language compiler or interpreter. The concept construct (C) can be implemented using similar capabilities.

The concept construct $C = ((x1,y1), \ldots , (xn, yn))$ can be constructed and manipulated using a hypothetical conceptual computer language or technology as follows:

```
C->x1 = y1;
C->x2 = y2;
....
C->xn = yn;
```

The semantics of "->" is similar to "." for Objects. It expresses the information association (or attribute). However, concept associations are dynamic as opposed to fixed object attributes. Additionally, the concept construct (C) represents *pure* information: in reality, it does not need to implement any methods.

For example, consider the sentence "please make a reservation". It can be manipulated using the concept construct (C) as follows:

```
Concept Sentence = new Concept ();
Sentence->proverb = "please";
Sentence->verb = "make";
Sentence->article = "a"
Sentence->object = "reservation"
```

Sentence->verb is the verb associated to the Sentence. Notice that the same concept (Sentence) can be used to represent any arbitrary sentence. Although every sentence is associated to the same concept, sentences can have all kind of structures. They may combine verbs, adjectives, adverbs, prepositions, and so on. There is a large number of possibilities. A similar situation applies to the concepts of reservation and message.

42

Messages can have all kinds of forms. A traditional object, with a fixed number of attributes, is not a good fit to represent such dynamic entities. Like sentences, concept constructs (C) do not consist of a fixed number of information associations. Concepts constructs (C) and objects are two separate abstractions – with different semantics and representation. On the other hand, every physical object can be represented as a concept construct (C). Information associations are used to represent the attributes of the object.

Currently, there is no computer language featuring built-in capabilities to process the concept construct (C). Another suitable mechanism needs to be devised. Due to the clear separation (decoupling) between the concept construct (C) and the entity processing it, a factory component can be responsible for creating (manufacturing) and managing the construct (C). The implementation of the Factory design pattern is suitable for this purpose. The factory needs to provide capabilities to create, read, update and delete information associations.

For convenience, the following primitives should be provided:

```
// Create or Update an information association
factory.setValue (Concept, attribute, value);
```

```
//Read an information association
value = factory.getValue (Concept, attribute);
```

The Sentence example would look like:

```
JtConcept Sentence = new JtConcept ();
```

```
factory.setValue(Sentence, "adverb", "please");
factory.setValue (Sentence, "verb", "make");
factory.setValue (Sentence, "article", "a");
factory.setValue (Sentence, "object", "reservation");
```

The second implementation is not as clear and compact as the one proposed earlier. On the hand, it can be implemented using any computer language.

The factory component will have to handle arbitrary concept constructs: $C= ((x1, y1), \ldots , (xn, yn))$. There are several potential implementations depending on the target language and the data structure chosen for the representation of the group of associations: array, list, hashtable, etc.

No internal processing mechanism is required. A concept construct (C) can be visualized as 'pure' information. A third party creates and manages the information associations. The concept construct (C) is independent of computer language, platform, technology, and data format. In other words, heterogeneous applications based on the Conceptual computing model and single concept construct (C) can interoperate regardless of computer language, platform, technology, and data format.

7. MESSAGING

7.1 Intent

The concept of Messaging allows the interchange of information (Energy) between entities capable of processing information[2]: Turing-complete information machines $(A=(f(m),I))$, part of Conceptual computing model. It improves decoupling, encapsulation, reusability, and scalability by separating entities, message, and communication mechanism. In other words, entities, messages, and messaging mechanism are decoupled and fully independent. Information and messages are represented using the concept construct (C).

7.2 Applicability

The concept of Messaging can be applied to solve a variety of problems in many diverse scenarios [2]. Messages are interchanged all around us. Entities are constantly sending, receiving, and processing messages. Countless processes in nature and the real world rely on messaging: communities, organizations, families, human body processes, social networks, colonies of insects, your banking system, and a collection of local/distributed components working cooperatively.

Human beings for instance: when we watch TV, talk to a friend, talk over the phone, or send an email message. Right now, you are reading this written page which is possible because of messaging. Since computer applications seek to model the real world, it is only natural to design and write applications using a messaging approach. In order to fully understand messaging and its applicability, we need to think in terms of abstractions: information (Energy), messaging, and information machine (see Physical Foundation). Messaging is about transferring or exchanging information (Energy).

Messaging is ubiquitous. In the real world, information (messages) can take many forms all of which can be modeled using computer software: a number, a text/email message, a document, a spoken sentence, a letter, energy (light, sound, electric impulse, analog signal, etc.), biochemical message, and so on.

Components are one essential part of component-based software methodologies. The interchange of information (i.e. messaging) between components is also an important and independent part of a complete and realistic computing/information model. While designing and manufacturing software, we need to think not only in terms of software components but also in terms of the messaging being exchanged between these entities.

7.3 Motivation

Component-based applications consist of a collection of components that need to communicate with each other. As proposed hereafter, this interaction can be accomplished via a messaging approach. Conventional implementations, not based on the concept of Messaging, will present a variety of challenges including:

a) Strong coupling which ties the solution to a specific platform, technology, protocol, multithreading/distributed technology, and/or computer language; specifically, in the context of heterogeneous and distributed applications.

b) Lack of encapsulation usually associated with not relying on the Messaging concept as the communication mechanism between participant components. A 'web' of coupled component interdependencies is created. Versioning of applications and APIs introduce unnecessary complexity. The threading mechanism is usually artificially implemented as a separate object. A single thread may also be artificially associated with multiple objects, which hinders encapsulation.

c) Lack of reusability which usually results from strong coupling, lack of encapsulation, and the inability to provide reusable threading/distributed functionality as part of a framework.

d) Complexities dealing with distributed/SOA technologies based on distributed artifacts such stubs, IDLs, WSDLs, RPCs, descriptors, or similar. Distributed artifacts are also a source of interoperability limitations.

e) Complexity dealing with multithreaded technologies related to thread management, thread synchronization, race conditions, deadlocks, and so forth.

f) Complex quality issues brought about by the previous challenges which get compounded and harder to manage as the number of threads, remote interfaces and/or team members increases.

h) Scalability and interoperability limitations associated with several of the previous challenges.

The challenges and limitations get compounded when additional real-world production aspects are considered such as security, access control, scalability, and fault tolerance. All the aspects outlined above have a negative impact on software cost, overall complexity, maintainability, quality, timelines, and risk.

The following relevant remarks should be carefully considered: "We can note in passing that one of the biggest problems in the development of object-oriented SW architectures, particularly in the last 25 years, has been an enormous over-focus on objects and an under-focus on **messaging** (most so-called object-oriented languages don't *really* use the looser coupling of messaging, but instead use the much *tighter gear meshing of procedure calls* – this hurts scalability and interoperability)." Alan Kay et al.

Tighter gear meshing of procedure calls has also been characterized as "The complex machinery of procedure declarations" while discussing problems associated with traditional APIs [26].

The concept of Messaging helps address the aforementioned shortcomings. Actually, in order to achieve realistic correspondence (accurately mimic reality), messaging needs to be the mechanism of communication between independent components (see Realistic Information Model). The concepts of information machine ($A=(f(m),I)$) and messaging are tightly intertwined. Messaging is the only realistic form of communication between an information machine and its external environment.

Gear meshing of procedure calls (artifact) must never be confused or mischaracterized as real Messaging. The natural concept and the artifact are *different*. Message, messaging mechanism, and communicating entities must be fully independent and decoupled from each other.

Most traditional APIs do not rely on messaging. Since there is no realistic correspondence, it is not an uncommon misconception to think that the technology/application is relying on messaging when *gear meshing of procedure calls* is being employed. Live/Animated components implement the information machine abstraction via software (see Live or Animated Entities). Thus, the following discussion will focus on the messaging being transferred between Live/Animated components.

7.4 Participants

a) **Message Sender**: Live/Animated component that sends the message.

b) **Message Recipient (Receiver):** Live/Animated component that receives the input message and may produce a reply (output message) after processing it. The input message, general in nature, may contain any type of information.

c) **Messenger:** Intermediary that transfers the message from the sender to the recipient. The sender and the recipient do not need to be concerned about how the message is transferred and the transformations performed on the message along the way (communication protocol, message format, encryption/security mechanism, and so forth). Such is the messenger's purpose and responsibility. Similar to the real world, it is often the case that a messenger is not required. The message can be sent directly to the message recipient. All modes of communication are accommodated: synchronous, asynchronous, distributed, streaming, two-way messaging, and so on.

d) **Message:** any piece of information (i.e. data) that needs to be interchanged between sender and recipient. Two messages are usually involved: input message and output message (or reply message). A reply message is optional. Information and messages are represented using the concept construct (C).

7.5 Structure

The concept of Messaging can be implemented using the messaging interface (JtInterface).

Figure 1. Messaging Interface

This interface consists of a single information primitive to process the input message and produce a reply message. It acts as a universal messaging interface that applies to distributed and local components. The Messaging interface is straightforward, yet powerful. The simplicity of this interface can be deceiving.

Actually, the information machine ($A=(f(m),\ I)$) based on the primitive is Turing complete. The interface also applies to all modalities of messaging: synchronous, asynchronous, streaming, distributed messaging, two-way messaging, secure messaging, and combinations of these forms. The interface handles any type of message. It returns a reply (of any type). In Java, the messaging interface can be declared as follows:

public interface JtInterface
   { Object processMessage (Object message); }
Or
public interface JtInterface<Type, Type1>
   { Type1 processMessage (Type msg); }

49

The message receiver needs to implement this interface in order to receive and process incoming messages. Languages that do not use interfaces can simply declare a processMessage() function or method in order to implement Messaging.

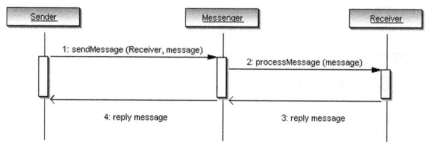

Figure 2. Messaging (synchronous mode)

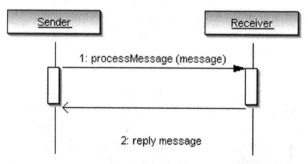

Figure 3. Messaging (synchronous mode without messenger)

7.6 Consequences

Encapsulation: The concept of Messaging improves encapsulation. Each component is a self-contained/independent unit: $A=(f(m),I)$: the only mechanism of communication with other components and applications is via messaging. Messages are also encapsulated entities: they are represented using the concept construct (C).

50

Decoupling: Messaging improves coupling. Again, each component $(A=(f(m),I))$ is a self-contained unit that can perform independently from the rest of the system. The communication mechanism is decoupled from message and component functionality.

Reusability: Messaging improves reusability. Live/Animated components $(A=(f(m),I))$ are similar to the building blocks in a 'Lego' set. Very complex models can be built based on simple pieces that share a common way of interconnecting them (i.e. common interface). The power of the approach is derived from the number of combinations in which these toy pieces can be assembled. Live/Animated Components that rely on messaging can be interchangeably plugged into complex applications and processes.

Live/Animated components can be assembled in a limitless variety of configurations. The user of a component only needs to know the input/output messages that the component handles. Applications are also able to reuse components from other applications at the component level: a single component can be extracted from another application, provided that the Conceptual computing model and associated messaging abstraction are being used.

Live/Animated components do not need to share the same technology or computer language for reusability purposes: they can be reused and communicate via messaging – even when heterogeneous technologies and/or computer languages are being employed. Such characteristic behavior facilitates and fosters reusability.

Scalability: During the review process, it was proposed that the Messaging concept could be applied to improve scalability [2]. Because of tight coupling between client and server, conventional distributed/service technologies based on distributed artifacts (gear meshing of procedure calls) require that client and server application be upgraded at the same time. This is usually not feasible and presents significant scalability limitations for infrastructures running 24/7 and/or expecting to handle a large number of computer nodes.

On the other hand, Messaging does not present this limitation because client component, server component, and communication mechanism are decoupled. Servers can be upgraded one by one without an impact on the client application and the rest of the infrastructure. Once all the servers have been gradually upgraded, clients can be upgraded to take advantage of the new software functionality.

As a consequence, an infrastructure based on Messaging can scale well and handle an arbitrary number of servers and clients 24/7. This application of the Messaging concept assumes that the new software version is backward compatible.

Quality/Testing process: Messaging facilitates testing and debugging efforts. Live/Animated components ($A=(f(m),I)$) are tested as independent units by sending messages to the component and verifying the expected reply messages (black-box testing). Keep in mind that all the components share the same messaging interface. In general, unit testing can be performed via a test harness. No need to include testing code inside the component code which can be time consuming and lead to the unexpected introduction of software defects.

Design process: Messaging helps the design process. The bulk of the design work becomes defining the set of required Live/Animated components and associated input/output messages. There is a tight correspondence between UML design diagrams and the abstractions needed for the implementation. Information and messages are represented using the single concept construct (C).

Several UML diagrams are geared towards messaging (sequence and collaboration) although their implementation does not rely on it. The UML model and the implementation are disconnected when Messaging is not used - in favor of gear meshing of procedure calls. Since Live/Animated components share the same messaging interface, they can also be readily added to BPM/BPEL diagrams and processes.

 As mentioned earlier, Live/Animated components are similar to independent building blocks that can be reused and connected in many different ways. Actually, they can be reused at the component level.

Development process: Since each component that relies on messaging is self-contained, a large team of people can cooperate in the development effort without stepping on each other's work/code. In an ideal situation, responsibility for one component/package can be given to an individual.

The rest of the team only needs to know the concepts (C) and input/output messages that someone else's component is designed to handle. In general, there is no need to change someone else's code. The need for creating, maintaining and merging several versions of the code is also reduced or eliminated (see versioning).

Testing/QA engineers can perform their testing independently via a test harness. As a general rule, there is no need to add testing code to the component itself.

Versioning: Messaging supports backward compatibility. Consider an arbitrary modern human language. After evolving for a long period of time, human languages have become a very efficient, concise, flexible, and versatile mechanism of exchanging information.

New words and terms are being added constantly to the language. Take for instance, the new term 'smartphone'. Some words become archaic and progressively fade away, being replaced by newer ones. A 'new version' of the language, so to speak, is being constantly created to meet changing information requirements. The messages, part of the language, are constantly evolving without having an impact on the mechanism of communication itself (fully decoupled). Messages that use older 'revisions' of the language can still be understood and processed.

The same principles apply to Live/Animated components based on messaging. As a consequence, the need to create, maintain, and merge several versions of the software – which quickly becomes time consuming, difficult, and error-prone – is reduced or eliminated. In other words, a single version of each Live/Animated component needs to be kept. Such single version is able to process new messages as well as older ones (backward compatible). This represents another benefit of relying on messaging instead of tight gear meshing of procedure calls.

Logging and Debugging: Since all the Live/Animated components use the same messaging interface, messages can be logged automatically.

Such logging features reduce the need for print/logging statements inside the code which can be time consuming and error-prone. By taking a look at the messages being interchanged and automatically logged, the user is usually able to quickly track down the message/component that is causing the problem (with a limited amount of extra effort).

Security: Clearly, well-known encryption and authentication mechanisms fit in well with the concept of messaging. Strong security can be provided by the Conceptual framework that implements messaging through the encryption and authentication of the messages being interchanged.

Sender and recipient do not need to be too concerned with how secure messaging is implemented. Strong security is provided by the framework while at the same time simplifying its implementation. If required, custom security mechanisms can also be incorporated: sender and receiver need to agree on and implement the message encryption/authentication mechanism to be shared.

Concurrency and Asynchronous Messaging: Messaging is able to handle the complexities associated with concurrency and asynchronous communication. Components that implement Messaging can execute in a separate/independent thread. This is a natural and realistic representation of the real world: each Live/Animated component is a self-contained unit $(A=(f(m),I))$ and executes independently from the rest of the system.

Messages can be processed asynchronously using the component's own independent thread. The required abstractions are usually implemented in the context of a reusable Conceptual framework. The component itself does not need to add separate logic to handle concurrency which is time consuming, complex, and prone to error.

Fault tolerance: the Turing-complete information machine can readily emulate a state machine. Therefore, it can be extended to provide fault-tolerant capabilities in a very natural fashion by replicating components/messages and coordinating their interaction via consensus algorithms (see Distributed Conceptual Model).

Conceptual paradigm and learning curve: In order to take full advantage of Messaging, people need to think in terms of the concepts when they model, design and build software applications: information (Energy), messaging, and information machine. This may require learning time and training. Although a messaging approach is natural, intuitive, and consistent with the real world, traditional approaches are based on method/procedure invocation (both local and remote).

Keep in mind that messaging, as a concept, has many qualities which are inherited or absorbed by the Conceptual model. Therefore, it is challenging to find drawbacks associated with the concept of messaging which is unexpected within the context of design patterns.

A similar situation occurs when we look at other real-world concepts that may be part of our software model, like Gravity, Energy, and Force. Messaging should be viewed from the standpoint of Concepts when it comes to trade-offs and drawbacks. There are several differences between design patterns and Concepts (see appendix on Related Approaches of Software Reuse).

Overhead: Transferring messages between components introduces a small overhead when compared with traditional method/procedure invocation. This is especially true when a messenger is used. The benefits associated to the proposed abstraction outweigh this performance cost; in particular, the degree of realistic correspondence.

Disciplined approach: the Conceptual model encourages a disciplined approach that may have a small impact on the initial development time of a component. To achieve close realistic correspondence, Messaging should be the only channel of communication between components.

A Live/Animated component $(A=(f(m),I)$ is a self-contained unit that interacts with the other components only via messaging. The additional development time is again outweighed by the benefits introduced by messaging. Moreover, individual components based on messaging can be potentially purchased or extracted from other applications.

7.7 Known uses

Design patterns implementation: Messaging has been used to implement and/or facilitate the reusable implementation of other well-known design patterns like Gang of Four design patterns (GoF), DAO, J2EE Design patterns, MVC, Master-Worker and so forth. Messaging provides a natural, streamlined, and straightforward implementation (see Design Pattern Implementation).

Consider that the concept of messaging is ubiquitous. Therefore, most design patterns need to deal with the exchange of information (i.e. messaging) as part of their implementation. Messaging provides a natural and realistic match for such need.

Component/Conceptual Frameworks: Messaging has been utilized for the implementation of complete component frameworks able to handle, in a *natural* fashion, complex challenges like concurrency, asynchronous communication, native interfaces, distributed component/service communication, interoperability, exception propagation, BPEL/BPM component integration, and so on.

Live/Animated components ($A=(f(m),I)$) that rely on Messaging can be interchangeably plugged into complex framework applications using the "Lego" approach mentioned earlier. Messaging is a fully implementable and reusable concept able to provide the communication framework required for building robust applications.

Distributed component/service model (SOA): Messaging is particularly well suited for the implementation of a complete distributed component/service model (Turing complete). It is able to provide seamless access to distributed components/service regardless of the protocol, technology, and communication mechanism being used. Messaging is able to naturally handle real-world complex considerations including parallelism, security, fault tolerance, interoperability, and distributed component/service communication.

Messages can be transferred via web services, REST, EJBs, HTTP, sockets, SSL or any comparable communication interface. Design patterns implemented using Messaging (adapters, remote proxies and facades) make this possible by hiding the complexities associated with distributed APIs. Messaging solves a whole set of problems dealing with distributed access to components and services. Because of Messaging, sender and recipient do not need to be concerned about the implementation of the messaging mechanism and infrastructure.

Components can be running on multiple computers and operating systems. They can also be implemented using multiple computer languages and technologies. Messaging has been used to implement ESB technologies and frameworks. Once all the building blocks are present (remote proxies, adapters, facades, etc), they can be assembled to create complete ESB solutions.

BPM/BPEL processes and technologies: Messaging has been employed for the implementation of BPEL/BPM technologies, frameworks, and processes. Consider that the information family of concepts is Turing complete. Arbitrary information technologies can be implemented using the Turing-complete Conceptual model. Components that rely on Messaging can also be readily incorporated into BPEL/BPM processes.

Notice that for components to be incorporated interchangeably, they need to share the same interface. The concept of Messaging provides a common and realistic interface. In consequence, a realistic and natural implementation of BPEL/BPM technologies can be achieved: a typical business process consists of a collection of Live/Animated components interchanging information via messaging.

7.8 Implementation

Messaging is about transferring or exchanging information between entities. It is a ubiquitous concept with a straightforward implementation and wide applicability. It is unlikely to find an application or problem area where interchange of information (i.e. messaging) is not present.

Similar to the software model, the implementation of Messaging should also mimic the reality being modeled. There will probably be some implementation differences depending on the specific application. There are many factors to consider based on the type of messaging being implemented and the technology/language in use: messaging delivery characteristics, streaming, messaging reliability, asynchronous messaging, security, and so forth.

The Messaging interface (JtInterface) is mainly a reference software implementation and there are other potential implementations of the messaging abstraction:

public interface JtInterface { Object processMessage (Object message); }

The generic type object is used. This is similar to the implementation of several design patterns (Iterator, for instance).

Advanced object-oriented technologies provide features like Java generics which allow the types to be parameterized:

public interface JtInterface<Type, Type1> { Type1 processMessage (Type msg); }

Notice that arbitrary computer languages or technologies can be used to implement Messaging, including plain old java objects (POJOs):

public Object processMessage (Object message)

Depending on the application, another messaging primitive may be needed:

public Object sendMessage (Object component, Object message);

The sendMessage() primitive sends a message to a local or distributed component. Although Messaging features a straightforward implementation, based on basic primitives, it is able to transparently handle complex real-world scenarios.

7.9 Related Work

Related literature [9] has been published describing messaging patterns in the specific realm of Enterprise Application Integration (EAI) and SOA. This work focuses on the communication between multiple applications.

The Conceptual computing model is distinctively different in terms of Turing-complete mathematical foundation, abstractions, overall simplicity (Occam's razor), single information machine $(A=(f(m),I))$, single information primitive, single concept construct (C), reductionism based on the concept of information (Energy), and degree of realistic correspondence (see appendix on Related Models and Approaches).

The Turing-complete Conceptual model may be confused with message-oriented middleware (MOM) technologies like the Java Messaging Service (JMS). Although MOM *technologies* rely on the *concept* of messaging, they are not the same. MOM is one of the many technologies that utilize messaging. Your e-mail application also relies on messaging.

Mathematical computing *model* and *technology* are two different entities. The *Turing-complete* Conceptual computing model can be applied to arbitrary information/computing technologies. It is not limited to MOM or EAI applications. In general, technologies are more concrete than computing models, and target specific problems or areas of application (see appendix on Related Models and Approaches).

8. CONCEPTUAL INTERFACE (CI)

Software systems should tackle problems at the conceptual level, in order to mimic the mind which is a conceptual engine. As a consequence, the idea of a conceptual interface (CI) should be introduced. In simple terms, a conceptual interface attempts to mimic human communication accomplished via the natural language. Arbitrary sentences (or ideas) in the natural language can be expressed using the concept construct (C).

Human languages constitute examples of conceptual interfaces. A conceptual interface is also a messaging interface. Not every messaging interface is a conceptual interface. In general, graphical user interfaces and human-machine interfaces (elevator buttons, car controls) allow the transference of information via messaging. On the other hand, the messages do not convey concepts like natural languages do. The mind communicates with other components of the body via messaging; however, no conceptual information is exchanged.

The specification of a conceptual interface is in harmony with a software design based on concepts: Conceptual design (CD). In particular, with the conceptualization task which extracts a streamlined set of relevant concepts. From the information standpoint, the following aspects need to be specified as part of an arbitrary conceptual interface (CI):

1) **Concepts/Components**: Specify the entities relevant to the problem in the real world. The entities involved can be divided into two categories: a) Live/Animated entities or components that can process information $(A=(f(m), I))$ and b) Entities that cannot (concept construct (C)).
2) **Messages:** Specify the messages that need to be exchanged in order to achieve the required functionality. A message represents a concept (C) .

There is a straightforward set of operations over information (CRUD) applicable to every conceptual interface.

1) Create (manufacture/write) information
2) Read (retrieve) information
3) Update information
4) Delete (discard) information

The operations above can be translated into four categories of messages. These messages apply to every conceptual interface regardless of the type of information been processed. The shared information concept results in a straightforward set of common messages independent of the type of information.

For convenience purposes other message types may be added. However, equivalent functionality may be accomplished by combining the messages above. A 'Search' message is convenient while looking for information. However, the same results can also be accomplished by repetitive uses of the 'Read' message.

In order to design a conceptual interface, imagine yourself solving the problem at hand with another person instead of a computer. In other words, think about the concepts and messages that need to be shared with another person if you want him/her to perform specific tasks required by an arbitrary application. We can come up with a complete solution for the problem at hand based on a conceptual interface. Human languages already provide the concepts and messages that are required.

For instance, consider a voice-activated mobile application responsible for manipulating documents in several formats (HTML, PDF, etc.). The following are some examples of the messages that you would share:

1) "Please read *page* one of the document"
2) "Update *paragraph* three of page five to read I get the concept"
3) "Update *font* of *page* 3 to Times Romans size 10"

The natural language provides the concepts of document, page, paragraph, sentence, font, header, footer, margin, and so on. It also determines the interrelationships, or information associations that exist between these concepts. For instance, a document (D) is associated to a group of pages:

$D = (P_1, \ldots , P_n)$ where P_i represents a page of the document.

Each page is associated to a group of paragraphs, a header, footer and margins. Each paragraph is associated to a group of sentences, and so forth. These concepts are extracted from reality (verbatim) and represent information to be processed. All of them can be represented using the concept construct (C).

A complete conceptual interface can be implemented, in the form of software, by mimicking the same concepts and messages found in the natural language. Both types of information exchange (between humans and between components) are conceptually isomorphic. Therefore, the same principles and solution can be applied to both scenarios.

A complex problem has been reduced, through conceptualization, to a very manageable set of concepts and messages. The approach can be generalized to arbitrary problems. Obviously, the set of concepts will change depending on the problem at hand. The concepts part of the information family (Conceptual computing model) will be applicable regardless of the real problem being solved. Information (Energy) is a ubiquitous and highly reusable concept. Also ponder that every entity part of physical reality is reducible to the concept of Energy (see Physical Foundation).

In the case of the proposed problem, the same concepts apply regardless of the technology, language, document format, and hardware device being used. Concepts (C) are independent of these considerations. For instance, by operating at the conceptual level, the software application does not need to be overly concerned about the multiple document formats being implemented. A small set of Live/Animated components, with information processing capabilities, are required to implement the solution and manipulate all the concepts (C) involved.

Live/Animated components able to deal with specific formats (HTML, PDF, ASCII, MS Word, XML, etc) will still be required. Their main responsibility is transforming the document information from the specific format to a representation based on the concept construct (C), understandable by the common conceptual interface: Document, Page, Paragraph, Sentence, Font, Header and so forth. Such components serve as adapters.

It is feasible and recommended that the vendor (or creator of the document technology) provide a reusable Live/Animated component or package to deal with their specific format. Such technology could be integrated as part of a heterogeneous solution able to transparently deal with a wide variety of document formats. Consider that the implementation of a document format specification is not a trivial or inexpensive endeavor. A new document format or technology can be transparently integrated without impacting the application (conceptual layer).

9. INFORMATION PROCESS

9.1 Intent

A Process represents a concept. It consists of a collection of independent entities (*Live or Animated*) interacting with each other and interchanging information via *Messaging*: $\{A_1, \ldots, A_n\}$ where $A_i=(f_i(m),I_i)$. This abstraction is founded on the Turing-complete Conceptual computing model and its mathematical foundation: $A=(f(m),I)/C$.

Live or *Animated* entities $(A=(f(m),I))$ are able to process information and exhibit independent behavior (a "life of their own" so to speak). The process abstraction also separates the critical information aspect from how such information is stored, represented, transferred, secured, and processed.

9.2 Applicability and Motivation

The information process abstraction has wide applicability. It can be used to model and solve a variety of problems. Obviously, countless entities in nature and the real world are based on the concept of Process: communities, organizations, families, human body processes, social networks, colonies of insects, your banking system, BPM/BPEL processes, a collection of local/distributed components working cooperatively within the context of a process, and so on.

The aforementioned examples represent a few scenarios that can be modeled using the Process abstraction. All these scenarios share common concepts, challenges, and problems: reliable and secure communication between entities, redundancy, fault-tolerant considerations, process reliability, concurrency, interoperability, scalability, and the need for a realistic/comprehensive model.

A business process (BPM/BPEL) can be modeled as a group of Live/Animated entities working concurrently and communicating via messaging: $\{A_1, \ldots, A_n\}$ where $A_i = (f_i(m), I_i)$.

9.3 Participants

a) **Process components:** Collection of independent entities that participate in the process: $\{A_1, \ldots, A_n\}$ where $A_i=(f_i(m),I_i)$. These entities are modeled as Live or Animated components $(A=(f(m),I))$. They are able to behave and process information (messaging) independently from the rest of the system, through its own processing mechanism.

b) **Messaging:** The interchange of information between Live/Animated components is achieved via the concept of Messaging: sender, receiver, message and messaging mechanism are decoupled, encapsulated, and fully independent.

In the context of a realistic model, messages can take many forms all of which can be modeled using computer software: a number, a text/email message, a spoken sentence, biochemical message, and so on. All forms of messaging are modeled: synchronous, asynchronous, streaming, distributed messaging, two-way messaging, secure messaging, and combinations of these forms.

9.4 Structure

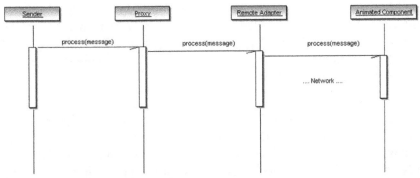

Figure 1. Messaging and distributed Live/Animated component within the context of an information process.

9.5 Collaboration

The information process abstraction and its implementation are based on other abstractions that seek to accurately mimic reality: a) Messaging concept. Sender, receiver, message, and messaging mechanism are decoupled entities, encapsulated, and fully independent. b) Live or Animated components $(A=(f(m),I)$ that interact with each other and interchange information (i.e. *messaging*) within the context of predefined information processes. Animated components rely on messaging as the mechanism of communication with other components and applications.

Live/Animated components can be readily incorporated into distributed BPM/BPEL processes and applications since messaging provides transparent access to distributed components as part of a complete distributed service/component model: distributed components are treated as local ones. Animated/Live entities are able to engage in elaborated patterns of collaboration and dialog with other animated components, in order to exchange information as part of complex processes.

The Process abstractions are capable of modeling all forms of messaging: synchronous, asynchronous, streaming, distributed messaging, two-way messaging, secure messaging, and combinations of these forms. Information itself, encapsulated as a message, can assume many forms as well. In the case of asynchronous communication, Live or Animated components require a queuing mechanism to store incoming messages: *enqueueMessage(message)*.

The Live/Animated component processes incoming messages, one at a time, via its independent mechanism. It relies on the information primitive to process incoming messages. In other words, the Live/Animated component is constantly processing incoming information via its independent mechanism, which mainly waits for incoming messages and processes them by invoking the information primitive (*processMessage(message)*).

Living beings and automated systems are constantly processing and making decisions based on the stream of messaging received through their senses. Messaging is the only channel of *communication* with their external environment. The Process abstractions are able to mimic these behaviors and handle the complexities associated with asynchronous messaging, multithreading, distributed component access, security and so forth.

9.6 Consequences

Encapsulation: Information Process helps improve encapsulation. Process participants are totally encapsulated. Each component $(A= (f(m), I))$, message and concept is a self-contained/independent unit. Again, messaging is the only channel of communication.

Reusability: Information Process helps improve reusability. Most of the functionality required to implement the process abstractions can be reused. A generic implementation can be achieved. The reusable functionality is usually provided by the conceptual framework that implements Messaging.

Information process also improves and encourages reuse because encapsulated components $(A=(f(m),I))$ can be integrated from multiple platforms, computer languages, communication protocols and technologies. In other words, technologies, languages, protocols can be freely mixed and matched within the context of a process.

Obviously, reuse is made easier if the messaging abstraction is being utilized. Processes implemented based on the proposed abstractions can be reused as part of more complicated processes. The proposed abstractions can also be leveraged to provide reusable implementations of design patterns[4,5,2]. For instance, the reusable implementation of Master-Worker is feasible.

Scalability: Processes based on the Conceptual approach are able to transparently scale and handle arbitrary large infrastructures running 24/7. Gradual upgrade of servers and clients is feasible without disrupting the rest of the infrastructure. Once all the servers have been gradually upgraded, client nodes can be upgraded to take advantage of the new software functionality. It is assumed that the new software version is backward compatible.

Distributed Component/Service Model: Process consists of a set of information abstractions required for the specification and implementation of a complete distributed component/service model. Remote Live/Animated components are treated as local ones. Actually, there is no *artificial* difference between local and distributed components. They are both exactly the same component. Stubs, IDLs, RPCs, WSDLs or similar artifacts add complexity and are not required.

The process abstractions provide transparent access to distributed components. As a best practice, it is the responsibility of a conceptual framework to provide the infrastructure required for access to distributed components and SOA services.

Interoperability: The process abstraction can incorporate components and applications that use multiple technologies, languages, platforms, and protocols. As stated earlier, this concept separates the critical information aspect from how such information is stored, represented, transferred, and processed. All these aspects can be altered independently without impacting the actual information.

The information machine $(A=(f(m),I))$ and primitive are independent from a specific computer language, technology and/or protocol. Platforms, languages, technologies and protocols can be freely mixed and matched within the context of a process. For instance, the information remains the same (semantics) regardless of what communication technology or protocol is being used: sockets, .Net, HTTP, RMI, REST, SSL, EJBs, etc.

All these technologies and protocols can be transparently incorporated as part of an integrated information process. As a second example, each encapsulated component $(A=(f(m),I)$, part of an integrated Process, can be seamlessly implemented using a different computer language, technology/platform.

UML/BPM/BPEL diagrams and applications: The abstractions that are part of a process can be readily incorporated into UML/BPM/BPEL diagrams and production quality BPEL/BPM applications. The overall design and UML diagrams are also streamlined making them easier to understand and implement.

68

Fault tolerance considerations: Groups of living beings in nature employ sophisticated fault-tolerant mechanisms as a way of adaptation and survival. The process abstractions, extracted from nature, can be employed to accurately mimic such mechanisms.

Live/Animated entities *(A=(f(m),I)* are Turing complete and can readily emulate state machines. Therefore, they can be extended to provide fault-tolerant capabilities in a very natural fashion by replicating components (or messages/processes) and coordinating their interaction via consensus algorithms [6,16] (see Distributed Conceptual Model).

9.7 Known Uses

UML/BPM/BPEL frameworks and technologies. The Process abstractions have been used for the comprehensive implementation of business process technologies (BPEL/BPM), frameworks, and applications. They can also be readily reused as part of UML/BPM/BPEL diagrams (and processes) in order to design and implement applications with comparable functionality to traditional business process applications.

The proposed abstractions provide a reusable set of components able to deal with process related considerations such as distributed component/service access, concurrency, asynchronous messaging, interoperability, redundancy and scalability. By reusing the process abstractions, improvements can be realized in terms of cost, quality, overall risk, realism, overall reusability, and timelines.

BPM/BPEL processes based on the Conceptual model can invoke local and distributed components seamlessly. Distributed access to Live/Animated components does not require additional artifacts or unnecessary complexity.

Design patterns. The Process abstractions have been used to implement and/or facilitate the implementation (i.e. reusable implementation) of other well-known design patterns like Gang of Four design patterns (GoF) and Master-Worker[2].

Consider that the Process abstractions represent a Turing-complete group and are fully implementable. They can be reused for the implementation of arbitrary computing technologies including design patterns. Actually they can be used for a realistic implementation of design patterns while at the same time improving complexity, reusability, quality, encapsulation, cost, and so on (see Model Evaluation and Metrics).

Distributed component and service model. The process abstractions are well suited for the implementation of a complete distributed component/service model (Turing complete) able to realistically handle complex real-world considerations such as security, redundancy, fault tolerance, concurrency, scalability, and so forth.

The information machine is Turing complete. The Process abstractions also provide a complete information infrastructure able to support and implement, in natural ways, arbitrary technologies including Enterprise Service Bus (ESB). Once a conceptual framework has been implemented (one time), it becomes a matter of reusing its components to implement other technologies. The additional effort required becomes minimal.

9.8 Implementation

As stated earlier, any technology can be used to implement the Conceptual computing model and associated information primitive:

public interface JtInterface { Object processMessage (Object message); }

Advanced object-oriented technologies provide features like Java generics which allow the types to be parameterized:

public interface JtInterface<Type, Type1> { Type1 processMessage (Type msg); }

In particular, BPEL/BPM tools can be extended to implement it. The examples provided use the Jt Framework implementation which extends the BPEL specification to support the Conceptual model and information

70

primitive. The Jt Framework also implements BPEL extensions to manage local and distributed Live/Animated components within the context of BPEL/BPM processes (see BPM/BPEL technologies).

Several authors have proposed extensions to the BPEL specification in order to accommodate specific requirements and make the specification suitable for particular applications [17]. Secure messaging and access control have been implemented by adding suitable components to the Messaging pipeline. These security and access control components are usually provided by the conceptual framework that implements the information/messaging infrastructure (see Conceptual Framework).

9.9 Related Patterns

The reusable implementation of several design patterns may call for concurrency, asynchronous messaging, and distributed capabilities within the context of a process. A comprehensive model and implementation should include the process abstractions to provide realistic functionality (realistic correspondence).

Observer, Master-Worker, Mediator, Model View Controller (MVC) and J2EE Business Delegate are some examples of design patterns that can benefit from using the process abstractions since they accurately mimic real-world processes.

10. GROUP

A group (G) represents a concept. As stated earlier, a concept consists of information about specific aspects of reality. Concepts allow the conceptualization, communication, and processing of information. A group basically represents a collection of entities. Groups serve to organize information (concepts) into more complex structures.

The group abstraction improves reusability, decoupling, encapsulation, interoperability by separating the fundamental information aspect from all other aspects such as how the group is stored, represented, transferred, secured, processed and so forth. Groups are also fully decoupled from the Live/Animated entities ($A=(f(m),I)$) that process them.

Entities (sender/receiver), concepts and processing mechanism are decoupled entities, fully independent Consider that there is clear separation between a concept and the entity that communicates and processes it.

Notice that in many cases, there is not physical connection between the entities in a group. For instance, a group of individuals: there is no physical connection between the individuals themselves. The concept of a group becomes a pure mental abstraction utilized to organize or classify information.

10.1 Applicability and Motivation

The concept of Group is ubiquitous. Consider the variety of real-world scenarios where it can be applied. A *few* examples include:

- A collection of entities is a *group* of entities.

- A list of entities consists of a *group* of entities. Complex structures can be represented as *groups* of entities.

- A document consists of a *group* of pages, which in turn consist of *groups* of paragraphs, composed of *groups* of sentences, and so forth.

- Conceptually, a database is a *group* of interrelated entries. All the information (I) contained in the database can be expressed as a *group* of concepts (C). The same principle applies to a *group* of entries retrieved using an arbitrary database query.

- In general, every time you use the plural form, you are making use of the concept: family members, friends, things, places, hours, messages, and so on.

As a consequence, groups have wide applicability in a variety of scenarios. Consider that a group represents a mathematical concept (set) which pervades modern mathematics (see Set Theory [30]).

10.2 Participants

A group (G) represents a concept and can be expressed using the concept construct (C):

$$G = (C1, C2, \ldots, Cn)$$

Expressed in plain terms, a group is an ordered set of concepts. A concept is defined as a group of information associations:

$$C = (a1, a2, \ldots, an)$$

a_i is an information association of the form (x_i, y_i), meaning that x_i is equal or associated to y_i ($x_i = y_i$). A concept construct (C) can be recursively expressed as:

$$C = ((x1, y1), (x2, y2), \ldots, (xn, yn))$$

- x_i represents a concept as defined by C or a sequence of symbols in the alphabet: $x_i = (b1, , bn)$; $b_i \in \sum$; $i \in [1 .. n]$
- y_i represents a concept as defined by C or a sequence of symbols in the alphabet: $y_i = (b1, , bn)$; $b_i \in \sum$; $i \in [1 .. n]$

A group (G) can be expressed as:

$$G = ((1, C1), (2, C2), \dots , (n, Cn))$$

Each association (x_i, y_i) consists of a concept (C_i) and the position of the concept (i) in the group (i, Ci). For simplicity and readability sake, groups will be expressed implicitly as:

$$G = \{C1, \dots , Cn\}$$

For instance, the result of an arbitrary database query can be expressed as a *group* (G) of concepts. Each individual concept represents a row in the database. Consider a query that returns a group of entries from a database:

$$G = \{C1, C2, \dots , Cn\}$$

$$C1 = \{(name, Danny), (age, 20)\}$$
$$C2 = ((name, Jenny), (age, 19))$$

$$\dots$$

$$Cn = ((name, Paul), (age, 50))$$

10.3 Consequences

Reusability: Concepts (C), and groups (G) in particular, improve reusability. Actually they are highly reusable entities. Groups can be used to convey information in a variety of scenarios. As a consequence, groups can be reused for the implementation of a variety of technologies. Notice that a single abstraction (G) can be reused to represent data structures of arbitrary complexity.

Decoupling: Groups (G) improve decoupling. There is separation between the concept itself (group) and the entity that process it (*A=*

(f(m),I)). Both concerns can be altered independently. Groups also separate the fundamental information aspect from other aspects such as how the group information is stored, represented, transferred, secured, processed and so forth. Groups, like all other concepts, are passive entities that only serve the purpose of conveying information.

Interoperability: Groups help improve interoperability: groups of the form G = {C1, ... , Cn} can be freely interchanged between systems and components regardless of technologies, computer languages, protocols, data representation, and so on. The same principle applies to any arbitrary group (G).

In a sense, concepts are fluid abstractions that can be interchanged between systems, components and applications. An information process, based on Concepts, can incorporate components and applications that use multiple technologies, languages, platforms, protocols, and so forth.

BPM/BPEL/ESB processes: Groups (G) can be readily incorporated into BPM/BPEL/ESB processes because of their interoperability and platform/format agnostic characteristics. Group information can be transparently shared between heterogeneous components and applications.

10.4 Known Uses

Design patterns. Concepts including groups have been used to implement and/or facilitate the implementation (i.e. reusable implementation) of well-known design patterns like Gang of Four design patterns (GoF), DAO, J2EE Design patterns, Master-Worker, and so forth [2].

Consider that many design pattern implementations need to deal with information in the form of groups (G). The concept of group can be applied each time a collection of entities is required. The reusable group abstraction is a suitable match for those situations. By using it, you also avoid coupling, reusability, data representation, and interoperability limitations.

For instance, a DAO implementation often requires that groups of data source entries be returned as part of data queries. Such information may need to be sent to a distributed application based on a different architecture which is readily accomplished by relying on the group concept.

Distributed Component and Service Model. Concepts (including groups) are well suited for the implementation of a complete distributed component/service model (Turing complete) able to handle complex real-world considerations. The group abstraction contributes to achieving such seamless distributed model and implementation because it allows the transparent interchange of information between applications using heterogeneous technologies, data representations, computer languages, and protocols.

BPM/BPEL frameworks and technologies. The group abstraction is part of the conceptual framework required for the implementation of reusable business process technologies (BPEL/BPM), frameworks, and applications. Groups can be readily reused as part of UML/BPM/BPEL diagrams (and processes) in order to design and implement applications with comparable functionality to traditional business process applications.

The group abstraction contributes to the seamless interchange of information between local and distributed components, part of heterogeneous business processes (BPEL/BPM): groups of concepts can be freely exchanged across the board. Groups – and concepts in general – improve coupling, interoperability, and data representation limitations. A group (G) represents a key abstraction part of a communication framework able to support fluid exchange of information between process participants (both local and distributed).

10.5 Implementation

Concepts, including groups, can be implemented using arbitrary computer technologies. The object abstraction (O-O) is implemented via the language compiler or interpreter. Groups can be implemented using similar capabilities. Consider the concepts C1, ... , Cn and the group G:

C1 = ((name, Danny), (age, 20))

C2 = ((name, Jenny), (age,19))

....

Cn= ((name, Paul), (age, 50))

G = {C1, ... ,Cn}

These concepts can be constructed and managed using a hypothetical conceptual computer language as follows:

```
Concept Person1 = new Concept ();
Concept Person2 = new Concept ();
Group G = new Group ();

Person1->name = "Danny";
Person1->age = 20;

Person2->name = "Jenny";
Person2->age = 19;

Person3->name = "Paul";
Person3->age = 50;


G = {Person, Person1};  // Initialize the group

G +=  Person3;          // Add a member to the group
```

The semantics of "->" is similar to "." for O-O objects. It expresses the information association (or attribute). "+" and "-" represent the usual set operations. A conceptual interface (CI) can be defined to manage the group abstraction. The following are the main messages needed:

1) Create information (CREATE).
   1.1) Create group: $G = \{C1, \dots, Cn\}$ where the members C1, ... , Cn are concepts
   1.2) Members can be added to the group: $G + C$
2) Read information (READ).
   2.1) First member of the group: $G\text{->}first$

   2.2) Last member: $G\text{->}last$

   2.3) Next member: $G\text{->}next$

   2.4) Previous member: $G\text{->}previous$

3) Update information (UPDATE). The messages CREATE and REMOVE provide the functionality required to update the group.
4) Remove information (REMOVE).

   4.1) Remove group

   4.2) Remove member from the group: $G - C$

10.6 Related Patterns

The group abstraction (G) is related to the Composite design pattern in terms of functionality. In contrast groups (G) do not have information processing capabilities. The concept, a passive entity, only conveys information. There is complete separation between the group abstraction and the component handling it.

A third party, like a Factory or hypothetical conceptual computer language, is responsible for handling and maintaining the group abstraction. Groups are also handled via a conceptual interface (CI) based on Messaging and a well defined set of information related messages. As a consequence, the group abstraction may be leveraged for the reusable implementation of the Composite design pattern. Groups (G) can also be used for the reusable implementation of design patterns dealing with collections of entities.

11. MEMORY OR INFORMATION REPOSITORY

11.1 Intent

The concept of memory or information repository represents the ability to store persistent information for later retrieval and use. Animated or Live entities $(A=(f(m),I))$ are able to independently process information and usually rely on a memory subcomponent or subsystem to provide information storage capabilities. The Conceptual computing model relies on a single concept construct (C) to store and manage information.

The memory abstraction improves decoupling, encapsulation, and reusability. It also separates the information aspect from other aspects such as representation, storage technology, and computer language. Information (I) is usually stored in the forms of conceptual information: concept construct (C).

11.2 Applicability and Motivation

The memory or information repository abstraction can be applied in several situations. Information processors are able to store and manage persistent information via its memory capabilities. Consider the human memory. It is able to store information in the form of chunks or packets (see Mathematical Model). It also allows individuals to learn new chunks and apply learned ones. Many of their information processing capabilities rely heavily on having a way to store and remember (retrieve) persistent information.

Obviously the same concepts and principles apply to computer systems and software since they are also information processors $(A=(f(m),I))$. Persistent information can be stored using many electronic representations, technologies and APIs including XML, binary files, relational databases, noSQL, object databases, WWW (html), flat files and so on.

An Information Repository may be limited to be used by a single entity. On the other hand, a shared Information Repository is not limited to be accessed by a single Animated/Live entity. Consider the case of a database which is a typical Information Repository. It can handle concurrent and distributed requests coming from a diverse set of components or applications. Thus a shared Information Repository usually needs to handle additional considerations such as transactions, locking, authentication, authorization permissions and so on.

We should consider that information processing (computing) can be achieved without consideration of the specific storage mechanism and/or representation being employed. The same principle applies to software. Systems and applications should be able to operate independently of how the information is being represented and/or stored: storage technology, computer language, data format, and so forth.

Arbitrary information contained in a database, or any other information repository for that matter, can be represented using the concept construct (C). Furthermore, the concept construct (C) is independent of data representation, technology, and computer language. In other words, the construct can be transparently implemented using arbitrary data representations, technologies, and computer language. For instance, consider the XML representation where the concept construct (C) is represented as an XML element.

11.3 Participants

As part of the Conceptual computing model, participants are realistically divided into two main categories: a) entities that can process information (Animated/Live components - $A=(f(m),I)$) and b) Entities that cannot (concepts construct (C)).

a) **Information repository** (Fig. 1). Single Live/Animated component responsible for implementing the abstraction and associated conceptual interface (CI).
b) **Concept construct** (C). All the information (I) contained in the data source can be represented using the concept construct (C).

c) **Data Source Adapter**. Component responsible for interfacing with the data source. It transforms the messages used by the conceptual interface to the appropriate API calls needed to interface with the data source. An independent adapter is needed for each technology, API, and data representation being employed by the application. For instance, the particular application being implemented may need adapters for JDBC, Android, XML, and so on.

11.4 Diagram

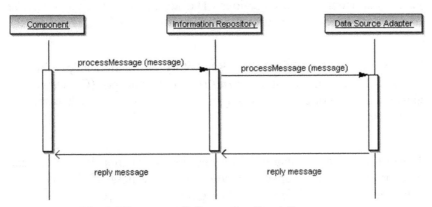

Fig. 1. Memory or Information Repository

11.5 Collaboration

Components and applications interact with the information repository via a conceptual interface (CI), based on the concept construct (C) and four main messages (CRUD):

Create (manufacture) information
Read (retrieve) information
Update information
Delete (discard) information

Messages received by the information repository are forwarded to the preconfigured Data Source Adapter required by the application (Fig. 1). In turn, the Adapter interfaces with the data source using an appropriate API in order to retrieve and maintain the stored information.

For instance, Adapters may be needed for JDBC, Android, relational database APIs, object database APIs, XML, binary representation, flat file, and so on.

11.6 Consequences

Decoupling: The Information Repository abstraction improves decoupling. The component $(A=(f(m),I))$ responsible for its implementation is independent (decoupled). Messaging is the only mechanism of communication between the implemented component and other components and applications. The abstraction also separates the information aspect from how such information is stored and represented.

Encapsulation: The Information Repository abstraction helps improve encapsulation. Component $(A=(f(m),I))$ and concepts (C) are totally encapsulated entities. Messaging is the only mechanism of communication.

Reusability: The information stored by the Information Repository can be expressed as a group of concepts (C) regardless of the type and characteristics of the information being managed: I = {C1, C2, ... ,Cn}. The same straightforward conceptual interface can be reused regardless of technology, language, data representation, and so on.

A reusable implementation of the Information Repository abstraction is feasible and recommended. Such implementation can be reused independently of the specific information being stored. The proposed abstraction also improves reusability because its implementation can be transparently reused as part of heterogeneous and distributed processes.

Because of the complete separation of information (concept construct) and the component processing the information, the memory abstraction improves information reusability. An application can make use of information repositories or data sources intended for other applications.

Using a common conceptual interface facilitates the reuse and sharing of information. The idea of reuse is not limited to computer software and components; it can be extended to information repositories and data sources. A conceptual approach fosters information reuse as well by relying on common interfaces and single concept construct (C).

Interoperability: The Information Repository abstraction facilitates and promotes the integration of heterogeneous processes and technologies. The conceptual interface associated to the Information Repository abstraction can be readily incorporated as part of processes that use multiple technologies, languages, platforms, and data representations. By using a conceptual interface, the information repository can be transparently accessed via a web service (SOA), BPEL/BPM process, and/or distributed interface.

The information stored as part of the Information Repository is independent of computer language, technology, protocol, and/or data representation. In other words, the concept construct (C) can be represented using arbitrary formats and technologies: XML, relational database, non-relational database, object database, flat file, binary representation, and so on. Information, represented via the concept construct (C), can also be transparently transferred in the context of heterogeneous and interoperable applications regardless of protocol, technology, data representation, or computer language – provided that the Conceptual computing model is being leveraged $((A=(f(m),I))/C)$.

11.7 Implementation

Since the Information Repository abstraction is usually implemented as an internal component, the set of software requirements and messages is straightforward. There is no need to be concerned about consideration such as concurrency, security, authentication, authorization, permissions, and so forth. Consider for instance a mobile application running locally and intended for a single user without distributed data access. The aforementioned considerations usually do not apply.

Shared Information Repositories, on the other hand, usually need to handle other key aspects such as transactions, locking, security, connection pools, authentication, authorization, access control, permissions, and so forth. Due to *Turing completeness*, the Conceptual computing model is able to handle such advanced considerations in a natural and comprehensive fashion: an Animated/Live component is capable of computing any computable function or algorithm.

The simplicity of the concept construct (C) can be deceiving. Arbitrary pieces of information can be represented using the concept construct (C). For instance, all the information accrued until the present day, expressed by spoken or written sentences, can be represented using the concept construct (C). The same applies to the information contained in an arbitrary database.

The Information Repository component relies on other Animated/Live components – which server as adapters – to deal with aspects such as technology, API, and data representation. Messages received by the Information Repository component are forwarded to the appropriate adapter. From the standpoint of software, the storage technology, API, and data representation can be independently altered without having any impact on functionality.

In agreement with Biomimetics, it is probably wise to study and mimic the human memory while trying to implement the concept as part of information systems. However, it should be recognized that the human memory represents an Information Repository targeted for a single user. In agreement with reductionism, each neuron can be completely specified using the same concepts leveraged by the Conceptual computing model: information (Energy), messaging, and information machine $(A=(f(m),I))$. A neuron represents an analog information machine or processor.

The human memory consists of a web of interconnected neurons (information processors) cooperating together and working in parallel. Instead of having a single processor responsible for a large chunk of memory (typical computer architecture), human physiology suggests a distinctly unique computing architecture.

Each information machine (neuron) is responsible for a separate partition: $\{A_1, \ldots, A_n\}$ where $A_i = (f(m), I_i)$. A vast amount of information is partitioned over such web of information machines: each information machine ($A_i = (f_i(m), I_i)$) is responsible for a separate partition (I_i). Such distributed and parallel architecture, which can be mimicked, features several distinctive qualities: scalability, parallel processing, performance, and fault tolerance (see Cognitive/AI architecture).

Conceptually, the human memory is analog to the World Wide Web (WWW) which represents a vast information repository made of individual information processors (computer systems). Each processor is responsible for a separate partition of information.

11.8 Known Uses

Design patterns. Concepts including the Information Repository abstraction have been employed for the reusable implementation of well-known design patterns dealing with information persistency; in particular, comparable functionality to Data Access Objects (DAO).

Consider that a large database usually requires a large number of DAO objects and descriptors to represent the stored data. On the other hand, information persistency can be implemented via the memory abstraction. All the information stored can be represented using a single construct: concept construct (C). This eliminates the need for a substantial amount of DAO objects and descriptors.

Component and Conceptual Frameworks. The *Turing-complete* Conceptual computing model is well suited for the implementation of comprehensive component frameworks able to handle, in very natural fashion, complex information challenges like persistency, transactions, locking, connection pools, caching, security, permissions, distributed data access, concurrency, and so on. Data persistency complexities are managed and hidden by the Information Repository abstraction.

Software components and applications do not need to know how information is internally managed in order to successfully retrieve it and use it for processing purposes. Aspects such as technology, computer language, and data representation can be altered independently without having an impact on the information content itself (i.e. semantics) and the processing mechanism.

11.9 Related Patterns

Information Repository is related to the Data Access Object (DAO) pattern. In contrast, Information Repository is based on the Turing-complete Conceptual computing model which is distinctly different and relies on single information machine $(A=(f(m),I))$ and single concept construct (C). The model provides unequivocal separation (decoupling) between information (C) and the entity or component processing it $(A=(f(m),I))$.

DAOs are based on traditional APIs. A conceptual approach eliminates the need for DAO descriptors and objects which ties the solution to a computer language, technology, data representation and/or DAO implementation. A large database may contain a considerable amount of entities and relationships which need to be represented as language-specific objects – and included as part of DAO descriptors and/or configuration files. All these entities can be realistically represented using a single construct (concept construct (C)), without information processing capabilities.

12. INFORMATION FAMILY OF CONCEPTS

"William of Occam opposed the proliferation of entities, but only when carried beyond what is needed --procter necessitatem! ... But computer scientists must also look for *something basic [information/Energy]* which underlies the various models; they are interested not only in individual designs and systems, but also in a *unified theory of their ingredients.*" Robin Milner [29]

"I believe computer science differs little from physics, in this general scientific method, even if not in its experimental criteria. Like many computer scientists, I hope for a broad *informatical* science of phenomena- both manmade and *natural*- to match the rich existing physical science." Robin Milner [29]

The concepts that belong to the information family and associated Turing-complete Conceptual computing model can be classified based on the fundamental information (Energy) aspect as follows:

a) **Live or Animated Entities ($A=(f(m),I)$).** Components or entities able to process information via the information primitive: $f(m)$. They can also interact with other entities as part of real-world processes. Live or Animated entities utilize an independent processing mechanism. They implement, through software, the Information Machine abstraction which makes them Turing complete. A memory subcomponent often provides information persistency capabilities.

b) **Concepts construct (C).** Entity that represents pure information: $C = (a1, a2, \dots , an)$. Information is Energy (see Physical Foundation).

c) **Messaging (M).** Concept that represents the interchange of information between Live or Animated entities. All modalities of messaging are modeled by the Turing-complete Conceptual computing model including synchronous, asynchronous, distributed, and streaming.

The three concepts above represent the Turing-complete Conceptual computing model. They can be organized into more complex entities (aggregates or groups):

d) **Information Process (P).** This abstraction consists of a collection of independent Live or Animated entities interacting with each other and interchanging information via *Messaging*: $\{A_1, \dots , A_n\}$ where $A_i=(f_i(m),I_i)$.

e) **Group (G).** Abstraction that represents a collection of entities: G = $\{C1,C2, \dots ,Cn\}$. The abstraction can be represented using the concept construct (C).

The information family represents a Turing-complete group. Arbitrary computer technologies can be implemented using this family of concepts which includes SOA, ESB, BPEL/BPM and so forth. They also provide a complete information infrastructure required to build reusable components, applications, and frameworks able to deal with arbitrary real-world problems. Physical objects can be represented using the concept construct (C): object attributes are expressed as information associations.

Keep in mind that information (Energy) is a highly reusable concept. It should not come as a surprise that the *information* family is applicable to every technology dealing with information (*information* technologies). According to reductionism, every entity and process part of reality is reducible to the concept of Energy and processing thereof (see Physical Foundation). Based on the Turing-complete Conceptual computing model all *information* technologies are reducible (unified/simplified) to the concepts of information (Energy), messaging, and information machine/processor: $A=(f(m),I)/C$.

The information family can also be classified into two major groups:

a) **Live or Animated Entities** $(A=(f(m),I))$. Entities able to process information (Energy) via the information primitive. In relative terms, there are very few entities able to process information in the real world: living beings, computers, automated systems, machines, and so forth. Notice that the messaging concept represents the one and only *real* mechanism of communication. Animated/Live entities are also known as information machines or A-Machines.

b) **Concepts construct (C).** Entities unable to process information: C = (a1, a2, ... , an). The concept construct represents information (Energy).

There are several other classifications applicable to the information family. In terms of functionality, there are three main areas: Storage, Transference, and Processing.

a) **Information Container (Storage).** Contain or store information: concept construct (C), Groups (G), Information Repository (Memory). These abstractions are related to how information is structured and/or stored.

b) **Information Transference (Messaging).** Associated with the communication and transference of information: Messaging.

c) **Information Processing.** Associated with the processing of information: Live/Animated Entities and Information Process.

There may be other classifications applicable to the information family. In terms of the information structures, there are three levels of ascending complexity in which the information is grouped:

a) **Information Association (a).** Basic building block of information.

b) **Concept construct (C).** Group of information associations. C = (a1,a2, ... ,an)

c) **Group (G).** Collection of concepts some of which may be groups themselves. G = {C1,C2, ... ,Cn}.

Notice that groups can be organized into more complex groups. On the other hand, such structures are still represented using the group abstraction regardless of the level of complexity. Arbitrary data structures can be implemented using the three concepts above. For instance, a tree structure, which can be represented as a group, may consist of several concepts and subgroups. Consider that information is Energy which can be organized into complex entities. For instance, any arbitrary physical message is a collection (or group) of packets of Energy (see Physical Foundation). Structures of any level of complexity can be represented.

13. CONCEPTUAL FRAMEWORK

A Conceptual Framework is designed for the rapid implementation of component-based applications, including Java and Android applications. The framework addresses the following aspects:

A) The framework architecture is based on the Turing-complete Conceptual computing model (mimicked from the mind) which provides simplicity, strong encapsulation, loose coupling, reusability, and scalability. Reusable framework components can be interchangeably plugged into complex heterogeneous applications.

B) The framework relies on a conceptual paradigm which provides a high level of abstraction. It leverages the Conceptual computing model to implement and/or facilitate the reusable implementation of well-known design patterns like Gang of Four (GoF), MVC, DAO, Master-Worker, and J2EE design patterns (see Design Pattern Implementation).

The framework itself is conceived and implemented, from the ground up, based on realistic concepts and design patterns. The framework also facilitates and accelerates the implementation of applications based on the aforementioned abstractions.

All modalities of messaging are accommodated: synchronous, asynchronous, streaming, distributed messaging, two-way messaging, secure messaging, and combinations of these forms.

C) The framework architecture includes a complete distributed component/service model which is able to provide transparent, secure, and fault-tolerant access to distributed components and services (see Distributed Conceptual Model).

The abstractions implemented by the framework (Live/Animated components $(A = (f(m), I))$, messaging, adapter, remote proxy, and facade) make this possible by hiding the complexities associated with distributed APIs and artifacts. Built-in components for message encryption, authentication and logging are provided.

D) The framework, based on the Turing-complete Conceptual computing model, has been leveraged for the implementation of SOA, BPEL, and ESB technologies. Consider that the concept of information is highly reusable. These technologies require the implementation of a complete information infrastructure, which the reusable Conceptual framework already provides.

The framework also provides transparent integration with other technologies via reusable adapters, proxies and the implementation of related design patterns. These technologies include Model View Controller (MVC) implementations, DAO implementations, EJBs, JSP, AJAX, JMS, and XML.

E) The Conceptual framework itself offers high reusability and low overhead (small size footprint). As a consequence, the framework is very lightweight and able to readily run on smartphones under Android. It uses pure Java, therefore other mobile platforms based on Java are also viable. Because of resource constraints, not many other Java frameworks are able to run efficiently on mobile devices.

F) The framework architecture improves and simplifies design/development efforts. There is a tight correspondence between UML design diagrams and the framework messaging-based applications and components needed for the implementation.

The framework provides wizards and automated capabilities for generating framework applications. Framework components can be readily added to BPM/BPEL diagrams and processes. In future versions of the framework, it should be possible for repetitive application modules to be generated directly from the UML design diagrams.

G) The framework architecture facilitates testing and debugging efforts. Live/Animated components $(A=(f(m),I))$ are fully decoupled and encapsulated. They can be tested as independent units by sending messages to the component and verifying the expected reply messages via a test harness. Messages exchanged between components can be automatically logged by the framework which facilitates the debugging process.

13.1 Framework Core Components

Based on the information abstractions part of the Turing-complete computing model, a conceptual framework implements a straightforward and compact group of core Live/Animated components $(A=(f(m),I))$ able to provide support for a comprehensive information infrastructure:

Factory: Live/Animated component that implements the factory method pattern. It is responsible for manufacturing and updating framework components and the concept construct (C). It may also be assigned responsibility for providing reusable Singleton and Prototype functionality: conceptually, a factory should be able to manufacture 'one of a kind' and make copies (i.e. clones) of specific components. The implementation of the factory abstraction should already have all the information (blueprints) required to do so. Such functionality can be reused across the board for all the framework components.

Messenger: Live/Animated component responsible for transferring messages from the sender to the recipient (receiver). All modalities of messaging are supported including asynchronous, distributed, and secure messaging. It delegates responsibility to other framework components for the implementation of security, encryption, authentication, and authorization of the messaging being exchanged.

Logger: Live/Animated component that provides built-in logging capabilities. It handles the information logged by the framework. The framework can be configured or directed to log all the messages interchanged between components which facilitates debugging, testing, and implementation efforts. It can also automatically log all framework operations. Problems can be quickly identified and resolved by checking the messaging being automatically logged.

Registry: component responsible for maintaining the framework registry. It allows framework components to locate other components. This component also implements a naming mechanism to uniquely identify each component being added to the registry.

Live/Animated components are fully encapsulated and decoupled entities; the only realistic mechanism of communication is via inter-component messaging. The registry functionality supports mechanisms for framework components to find and cooperate with each other.

Resource Manager: Live/Animated component responsible for handling the information stored in the properties resource file (or data source) which is used to initialize/configure components when they are first created.

Exception Handler: Live/Animated components can forward detected exceptions to this component for handling. Custom exception handlers are supported and can be incorporated.

Printer: Live/Animated component responsible for printing capabilities. It is able to print detailed information about a component or concept construct (C). The XML format is usually employed since the component or construct (C) being printed may represent a complex hierarchy of entities. A printer component provides additional convenience while building, testing, and debugging applications.

There are several special framework entities that leverage the concept construct (C): Message, Group, Event, Exception, Error, and Warning. Notice that these entities do not require information processing capabilities and are accurately represented using the concept construct (C) which can be readily shared across local and distributed components/applications.

Similar to all the other Live/Animated components, the framework core components can be incorporated as part of BPEL/BPM processes and tools. Distributed access to these local core components may be allowed if necessary.

Think about the significant simplification and reduction in the number of core Live/Animated components required to provide a comprehensive framework implementation as a direct result of using the Conceptual model and associated interfaces (see Model Evaluation and Metrics). Each core component also implements a straightforward conceptual interface which runs seamlessly across the board: from mobile devices all the way up to enterprise servers.

13.2   Conceptual Framework for Android

The Android architecture, like every other computer technology, is about the concept of information. The Conceptual framework and associated Turing-complete computing model have been leveraged to provide comprehensive information infrastructure capabilities for Android.

Most of the functionality implemented by the Conceptual framework runs under the Android platform without any software modifications. The following design principles apply to the Android implementation of the framework:

a) The framework itself is designed and implemented based on a conceptual paradigm. Every framework component implements a conceptual interface (CI) based on single information primitive and a compact set of messages over information.

b) The philosophy behind Java is straightforward: "write once, run everywhere". Obviously, such idea has many benefits in terms of software portability, costs, time frames, quality, and so on. A Conceptual framework is consistent with the Java philosophy.

As mentioned earlier, most of the framework components and associated concepts have been reused to run under the Android platform without any variation. In general, the framework implementation avoids nonstandard Android APIs and configuration files because of incompatibility and portability limitations. They also have a potential impact on overall software complexity, cost, timeframe, and quality.

c) The Conceptual framework based on a Turing-complete computing model offers a high level of reusability. It can be employed to implement arbitrary information technologies. A compact set of framework core components and concepts results in a lightweight implementation (small size footprint) able to accommodate the resource constraints imposed by mobile platforms. Because of resource limitations, not many other Java frameworks are able to run efficiently and seamlessly on mobile platforms.

d) The Conceptual framework offers a complete set of components (Turing-complete) based on pure Java and able run across all Java platforms, including mobile devices.

h) A limited number of framework components need to be specific to the Android platform since their functionality is not provided by the standard Java SDK. The list includes GPS, voice recognition, voice synthesis, device configuration, and GUI components.

To provide Android specific functionality, the Conceptual framework relies on independent Live/Animated components to encapsulate the Android specific functionality via straightforward conceptual interfaces. For instance, there is a framework component that implements a conceptual interface and communicates with the Android GPS API. This reusable component can be employed for the application requirements related to GPS functionality.

If the framework application needs to run on a different platform, Android specific components can be easily replaced. Since a conceptual interface and framework are being used, it is just a matter of substituting the framework component with another component built to support the new platform. No additional software changes are required since both components implement the same conceptual interface.

It is just like taking a part (or electronic component) and replacing it with one from a different manufacturer, designed based on the same specification (conceptual interface). A part built based on a newer and improved design should also seamlessly work, since conceptual interfaces (CI) are designed to be backward compatible.

Traditional APIs, based on 'gear meshing of procedure calls', do not provide this level of versatility, flexibility, and interoperability. Bear in mind that conceptual interfaces are straightforward relying on a single information primitive and a small set of predefined message types.

i) The utilization of a Conceptual framework has practical consequences in terms of Android development, design, debugging and testing. Most of the component development is independent of the platform and can be performed using high-end computers and development environments. This characteristic is a direct result of relying on pure Java and avoiding Android specific APIs and configuration files as much as possible.

Building, debugging and testing applications on the device itself or via the Android emulator can be time consuming and hindered by performance limitations. A limited number of Android specific components need to be developed/tested as separate units avoiding the use of the device and/or Android emulator as much as possible during the development and testing phases.

Several Android APIs are not based on the standard Java SDK. There are several differences to consider:

a) Java Database Connectivity (JDBC) is not supported. However, the Memory or Information Repository abstraction is implemented via an Android Adapter for SQLite. From the standpoint of the application, nothing changes. The same conceptual interface (CI) required to access persistent information still applies.

b) Java GUI APIs are not supported. The conceptual framework provides reusable components based on the Android GUI APIs.

c) The J2EE design patterns implemented by the framework are not supported because Android does not implement the corresponding J2EE APIs.

14. DESIGN PATTERN IMPLEMENTATION (GoF)

The Conceptual computing model has been utilized as the basis for the reusable implementation of well-known design patterns like Gang of Four design patterns (GoF), DAO, MVC, J2EE design patterns, Master-Worker, and so forth [2, 4]. Pattern implementation deals with information interchange, storage, and processing – like every *information technology*.

Consider that the information family of concepts, part of the model, constitutes a Turing-complete group able to provide the infrastructure necessary for the implementation of arbitrary technologies. Pattern implementations can use the ubiquitous information abstractions to achieve a realistic solution, while at the same time improving overall complexity, reusability, encapsulation, cost, timelines, and so on.

Several design patterns will be used to illustrate how this is accomplished. The same concepts apply to the implementation of many others. The Turing-complete Conceptual model also provides a realistic and straightforward implementation. Although synchronous messaging is shown, all forms of messaging are supported.

Design patterns implemented using the Conceptual computing model, can be reused as building blocks. A generic pattern implementation becomes possible. Complex frameworks and applications can be built based on these building blocks which share a simple way of interconnecting them (i.e. common messaging interface). All components involved implement the information machine: $A=(f(m),I)$. Information is represented using the single concept construct (C).

14.1 Proxy

The Conceptual model facilitates the reusable implementation of Proxy. Under the conceptual approach, Proxy is mainly responsible for forwarding information (input message) to the real subject. Notice that all the participants are completely independent (minimum coupling). Encapsulation is improved. Messaging is the only mechanism of communication between participants. Sender, Messenger, Proxy and subject are implemented as Live/Animated components ($A=(f(m),I)$).

98

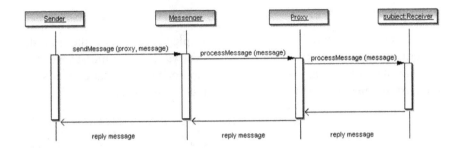

Figure 1. Implementation of a reusable Proxy based on Concepts.

14.2 Adapter

Under messaging and the Conceptual model, the main purpose of Adapter becomes the transformation of information (messages) between message sender and receiver so that these Live/Animated components can be interconnected. For instance, you may need to implement a HTTP Adapter so that your local component can communicate with a remote component via the HTTP protocol. The same principle applies to arbitrary communication technologies and protocols (sockets, web services, REST, RMI, .Net, EJB, etc.). All messages are represented using the concept construct (C).

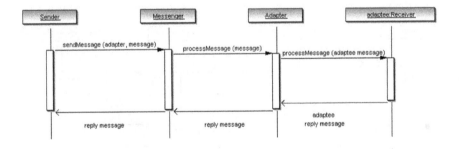

Figure 2. Implementation of Adapter based on Concepts.

14.3 Façade

The Conceptual model facilitates the implementation of the Façade pattern. Façade is mainly responsible for forwarding the message to the appropriate subsystem. In our particular scenario, Façade needs to forward the message to the appropriate Live/Animated component.

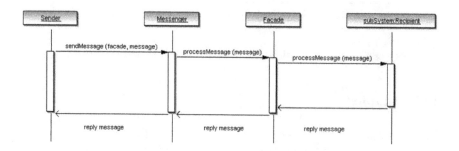

Figure 3. Implementation of Façade based on Concepts.

14.4 Strategy

Under a conceptual approach, Strategy is mainly responsible for forwarding the message to the component that implements the concrete strategy.

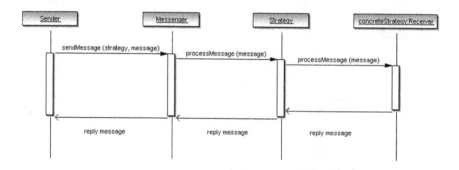

Figure 4. Strategy implementation based on Concepts.

14.5 Bridge

When a conceptual approach is used, Bridge is mainly responsible for forwarding the message to the concrete implementer.

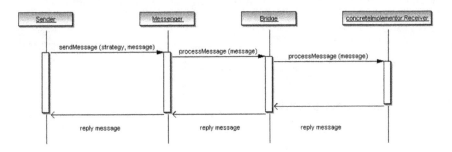

Figure 5. Implementation of Bridge based on Concepts

14.6 Command

The Conceptual approach facilitates the implementation of Command (Figure 6). Under the conceptual approach, Command is responsible for processing the request/message. It may also queue or log requests (RequestLogger).

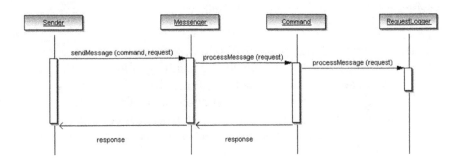

Figure 6. Implementation of Command based on Concepts

14.7 Decorator

When Concepts are used, Decorator is responsible for implementing new functionality. Decorator is also responsible for forwarding messages (related to the existing functionality) to the decorated component.

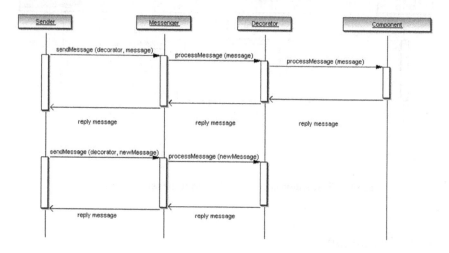

Figure 7. Implementation of Decorator based on Concepts

14.8 Factory

Based on a conceptual approach, a realistic implementation of the Factory pattern serves four main functions:

a) Creation and manipulation of other components and concept constructs (C), which includes the handling of internal attributes. Optionally, a name (component Id) may be assigned during creation which is used for registration via the framework Registry. Registration allows fully independent/decoupled Live/Animated components to find each other in the context of distributed and local processes.

b) Initialization and/or configuration of components when they are first created based on the information stored in the properties resource file (or data source). The Factory implementation relies on the Resource Manager to provide the needed functionality.

c) Singleton Pattern. A realistic implementation of the Factory pattern may also provide Singleton functionality by creating a one-of-a-king component.

d) Prototype Pattern. The Factory implementation may also be responsible for creating copies of a specific component or Concept (clone). It makes sense for the Factory implementation to be able to 'manufacture' clones of a specific component.

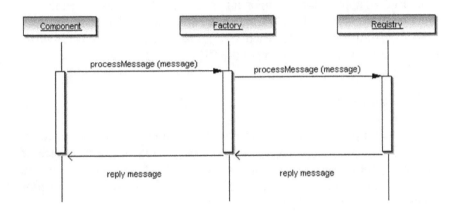

Figure 8. Implementation of the Factory pattern based on Concepts

The following straightforward messages should be part of a conceptual interface for the Factory pattern implementation:

a) **CREATE:** create an instance of the component of the specified class. A name (component Id) may be assigned to the component during creation. The component may also be registered with the framework via the Registry component. The component is initialized via the Resource Manager using the properties resource file or data source.

a.1) **CREATE (SINGLETON):** create a singleton instance of a class. The functionality is implemented via the Registry component which keeps track of Singleton classes.

103

Subsequent attempts to create an instance of the same class will result in the Singleton being returned: no additional instances will be created. Concurrent access to the Registry information is properly controlled by the Registry component.

b) **READ (ATTRIBUTES):** Retrieve the group of attributes and attribute values part of the object. This functionality is mainly required by internal framework components and specialized applications.

c) **REMOVE**: Remove a component from the framework registry.

c.1) **REMOVE (SINGLETON)**: Remove a Singleton instance from the framework registry.

d) **CLONE**: Create a copy of a specific component or concept construct (C). Every application component can be cloned by reusing the functionality provided by the Conceptual framework. The user does not need to re-implement it for each class. The clone functionality can be implemented by using a version of the CREATE message.

14.9 Prototype

A realistic implementation of the Prototype pattern can be provided by the Factory pattern. Factory should be able to 'manufacture' copies of arbitrary application components and concepts (C) by processing the CLONE message (see Factory): Prototype returns a copy of the object or concept when the CLONE message is received.

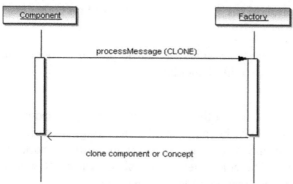

Figure 9. Implementation of Prototype functionality via the Factory pattern

14.10 Model View Controller (MVC)

The information family of concepts can be leveraged to implement the Model-View-Controller (MVC) pattern. Its members provide concurrency and messaging capabilities. In particular, Messaging and Live/Animated components support the required capabilities. All messages are represented using the concept construct (C).

Under a Conceptual model, MVC components are completely encapsulated and decoupled entities. They can be implemented as independent Animated/Live components. All forms of messaging are supported including asynchronous and distributed messaging. MVC components can also run as distributed components on separate computers. This may become useful for specialized distributed applications.

Support for concurrency and asynchronous messaging are particularly useful on Mobile devices where multiple components are usually running concurrently and resource constraints need to be taken into account. The information family of concepts supports a concurrent and distributed implementation of MVC.

Messaging is the only mechanism of communication among MVC components. GUI events are encapsulated as framework messages and sent to the controller for processing. The controller may then interchange messaging with components part of the model. For instance, once a button is pressed, a corresponding event (message) is sent to the controller.

The same mechanism applies to any other event generated by the GUI. Updates to the graphical user interface are performed via messages sent to the GUI by the other components. Conceptual interfaces can be employed for the communication between MVC components; in particular, between the graphical user interface (View) and the other MVC components.

Platform-specific functionality can be encapsulated as a Live/Animated component or group of Live/Animated components. Later on, the component(s) can be readily replaced by a different platform-specific component without having any major impact on the rest of the system. The use of the Conceptual model allows such level of interoperability, encapsulation, and decoupling as part of an MVC implementation.

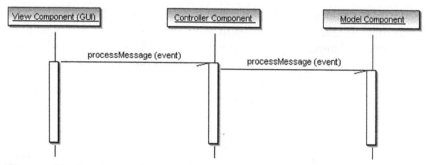

Figure 10. Implementation of MVC based on Concepts. Messages are sent from the GUI in the form of events.

15. J2EE DESIGN PATTERN IMPLEMENTATION

Enterprise Java Beans (EJBs) is one of the technologies that can be used to access distributed components. The next section will illustrate how the Conceptual model is leveraged to implement several J2EE design patterns and provide transparent access to distributed EJB components. The same principles apply to other communication technologies and protocols.

15.1 J2EE Business Delegate

When the Conceptual model is leveraged, Business Delegate is mainly responsible for forwarding the message to the distributed Live/Animate component $(A=(f(m),I))$ via EJBAdapter and J2EESessionFacade. The behavior is very similar to Proxy. Information is represented using the concept construct (C), which includes every message.

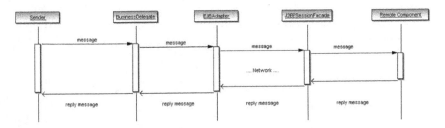

Figure 1. Implementation of J2EE Business Delegate based on Concepts

15.2 J2EE Session Façade

When the Conceptual model is used, Session Façade is mainly responsible for forwarding the message to the appropriate distributed component.

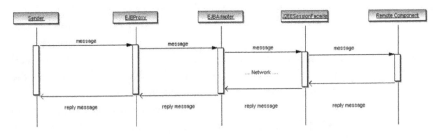

Figure 2. Implementation of J2EE Session Façade based on Concepts

107

The following are the design patterns involved. For clarity sake the messenger component and the intrinsic *processMessage()* method have been removed from the UML diagram (Fig. 2). Every component involved is a Live or Animated component $(A=(f(m),I))$.

1) **Business Delegate**: the message is sent to the distributed component via the business delegate.
2) **EJBAdapter** : adapter responsible for interfacing with the EJB API. It transfers the message to J2EESessionFacade.
3) **J2EESessionFacade**: forward the message to the appropriate distributed component.

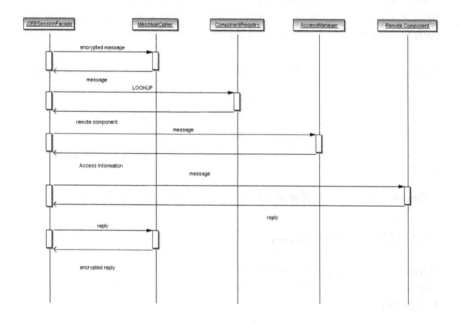

Figure 3. Implementation of J2EE session façade based on Concepts

The J2EE session façade is usually responsible for security as well (messaging authorization and authentication). Notice that under the Conceptual model, this can be made transparent to message sender and receiver. In other words, sender and receiver do not need to be too concerned as to whether or not secure messaging is being used and how it is being implemented.

108

The Conceptual framework should provide the required security mechanisms ("plumbing"). Before the message is forwarded to the Receiver, J2EESessionFacade performs decryption, authorization and/or authentication on it (if required). The following are the Live/Animated components involved (Fig. 3):

MessageCipher: Live/Animated component responsible for decrypting the input message and encrypting the reply message.

Component Registry: allows the system to register and look up components by name.

AccessManager: Live/Animated component responsible for granting/denying access to remote components. It authorizes and authenticates each message received.

15.3 J2EE Service Locator

When the Conceptual model is leveraged, Service Locator is mainly responsible for locating the service (home interface) by interfacing with the JNDI Adapter. JNDIAdapter is a messaging adapter that interfaces with the JNDI API.

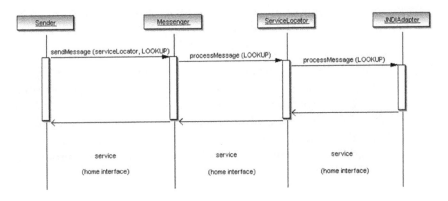

Figure 4. J2EE Service Locator

16. DISTRIBUTED CONCEPTUAL MODEL (DCM)

The Turing-complete Conceptual computing model provides the foundation for a comprehensive distributed component and service infrastructure able to handle complex real-world considerations such as security, redundancy, fault tolerance, parallelism, interoperability, concurrency, and scalability.

Conceptually, communicating with a distributed Animated/Live component $(A=(f(m),I))$ is isomorphic to communicating with a local one since the same concepts are involved. DCM provides transparent access to distributed components regardless of the technology, platform, computer language, data representation, and protocol being used

The issues and limitations associated with traditional distributed and SOA technologies have been studied and documented in the technical literature. In particular, several references deal with complexity [13, 14, 15, 20], interoperability [13, 14, 15, 20], coupling [20] and proprietary limitations [13, 14]. These limitations have a negative impact on software schedule and cost [20, 13].

Let us use a real-world analogy to illustrate the problem and its solution. Consider your phone system, postal service, or email/chat system. You are able to communicate with a friend by simply sending a message to the intended recipient. In the case of the phone system, you are able to communicate with your friend regardless of the technology being used.

For instance, you may be using a land line while your friend is using wireless, internet or satellite technology. All these technologies are able to interoperate in a seamless fashion (from a user's perspective) . You can communicate with a friend across the room or thousands of miles away. You and your friend do not need to be overly concerned as to how your conversation is transmitted: technologies, communication protocols, security mechanisms, etc.

The service provider is responsible for putting together the infrastructure or *framework* to make it possible. Such framework consists of interconnected *components* to transmit voice, video and/or text to the receiver. For instance, the framework will probably include bridges and *adapters* to transport information and transform it into the appropriate signal or message format.

A similar principle applies to the postal service and the internet service. You are able to send a message or letter regardless of the technology used to transport the message. For instance, your letter may be carried via air, ground, or ship.

The communication between distributed components should be accomplished in a similar fashion. All these systems share the same concepts; messaging in particular. There is no *real* reason for the aforementioned complexities and shortcoming.

DCM provides the building blocks required to overcome the aforementioned issues and limitations. Obviously, if true realistic correspondence [30] is to be achieved, *all* the relevant concepts must be mimicked as part of a comprehensive solution: model, design, and implementation.

Messaging is about transferring or exchanging information. As a concept, messaging is straightforward, effective, efficient, versatile, robust, scalable, interoperable, etc. Messaging can also be made reliable, secure (authenticated and/or encrypted), redundant, and fault-tolerant. Just consider the amount of vital information exchanged every single moment in the realm of human communication. All these qualities become part of DCM and its implementation.

DCM and design patterns can be combined to implement distributed access. Due to Turing-completeness, DCM can be leveraged to implement arbitrary distributed technologies including SOA, REST, ESB, Master-Worker [2, 5]. A process, based on DCM, can transparently incorporate distributed components ($A = (f(m), I)$) and applications that use heterogeneous technologies, languages, platforms, and protocols: for instance, web services, EJBs, RMI, HTTP, REST, Sockets, SSL or any other comparable distributed technology. DCM and the design patterns being employed make it possible by hiding the complexities associated with distributed APIs.

The following UML diagram illustrates how distributed access is accomplished. In the real world, you can communicate with a friend across the room or thousands of miles away via a phone conversation. You and your friend do not need to be overly concerned as to how the telephone conversation is transmitted. It is transparent to you. The phone company provides the messaging framework to make it possible. By mimicking such behavior, DCM is able to provide transparent communication between local and distributed components.

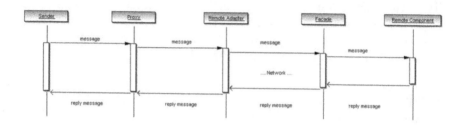

Figure 1. Access to distributed components and services based on DCM

The following are the DCM components and design patterns involved (Fig. 1). For clarity sake the messenger component and the intrinsic information primitive (*processMessage(Message)*) have been removed from the UML diagram.

1) **Proxy**: the message is sent to the remote component via a reusable proxy applicable to arbitrary remote components.
2) **Remote Adapter**: adapter responsible for interfacing with the remote API.
3) **Façade**: forward the message to the appropriate remote component. It usually provides security capabilities as well.

All the Animated/Live components involved implement the information machine abstractions $(A = (f(m), I))$ and communicate via messaging.

16.1 Security, Naming and Access Control

DCM can deal with security challenges in a straightforward manner. It provides end-to-end security, non-repudiation and message-level security (as opposed to transport level security). It can also be used for selective encryption so that only sensitive portions of the message are encrypted. Well-known security mechanisms fit well with the Conceptual model.

On the other hand, messaging is not limited to a specific message format (XML, SOAP, binary, etc.). Any message format can be accommodated including proprietary and custom message formats. Bear in mind that the information machine is Turing complete. Therefore, any arbitrary distributed computing model or technology can be implemented based on the information abstractions and single primitive.

Most of the security aspects can be made transparent to message sender and receiver (Fig. 2 and 3). For instance, sender and receiver do not need to be overly concerned as to whether or not security is being used and how it is being implemented. DCM provides the required information infrastructure ("plumbing") – including security components and mechanisms.

Using our real-world analogy, in general you and your friend do not need to be overly concerned about how the service provider is encrypting your conversation because of privacy and/or security considerations. The DCM implementation can also rely on declarative security which avoids the need for error-prone security coding.

Finally, custom security mechanisms can be readily accommodated based on specific requirements. For instance, the sender may decide to use a mutually agreed security mechanism (encryption and/or authentication) without relying on the built-in security facilities provided by the DCM implementation.

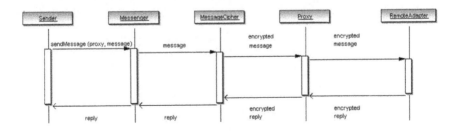

Figure 2. Secure messaging (client side)

Going back to the proposed analogy, the communication framework maintained by the service provider will require some sort of *registry* (phone book) so that participants can locate each other. Each entity will have associated a phone number or *ID*.

A straightforward naming mechanism is all that is required. The postal service, your internet service provider, and email implementation also use straightforward naming schemes. In the case of distributed Live/Animated components, they can be readily located based on component name, class, and URL.

Other service providers take advantage of the communication framework and use custom *authentication/authorization* mechanisms. Your banking institution, for instance, makes use of the phone system and has *Access Control* mechanisms for authorization and authentication purposes. We are required to provide some piece(s) of information to authenticate our identity before being granted access to an account.

Similar mechanisms can be readily mimicked by DCM. All these situations share the same concepts: conceptually isomorphic. The analogies presented should help illustrate the ideas involved based on a healthy dose of intuition.

DCM, based on the Turing-complete information machine, is able to implement arbitrary security schemes. For example, access to distributed components and SOA services can be granted depending on several factors: a) role of the sender a) type of access granted to the sender based on its role b) type of message being exchanged c) name or class of the receiver.

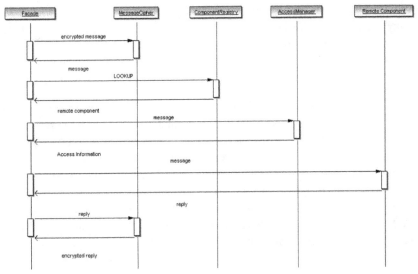

Figure 3. Secure access to distributed components based on DCM (server side)

The additional components required for the implementation of DCM and associated communication framework mimic the functionality outlined above (Fig. 3). The Façade component is usually responsible for implementing security (messaging authorization and authentication) by invoking relevant DCM components. Before the message is forwarded to the receiver, Facade performs decryption, authorization, and authentication on it.

The following are the Animated/Live components involved:

MessageCipher: Animated/Live component responsible for decrypting the input message and encrypting the reply message. This component can be configured to use a specific encryption scheme.

Component Registry: allows the system to register and look up components by ID.

AccessManager: responsible for granting/denying access to remote components. It authorizes and authenticates each message received. If the access manager is unable to authenticate the message, it never reaches the receiver.

Live/Animated entities (information machines/processors) and messaging are ubiquitous in daily life. Distributed applications represent just another example. Information is constantly exchanged between participant entities as part of predefined processes. It should become obvious the ubiquity of the proposed concepts as part of distributed processes and the faithful correspondence [30] between DCM and reality. Also, notice the accurate correspondence (i.e. realistic) between DCM and proven/robust distributed frameworks of communication that make modern life possible for most communities at a massive scale.

16.2 Performance, Scalability, and other considerations

DCM is straightforward yet versatile and robust. It is able to handle complex issues associated with distributed applications. The model is fully compatible with common scalability and availability mechanisms: clustering, load balancing, failover, caching, etc.

DCM plays an important role in supporting the aforementioned mechanisms. For instance, distributed applications/components $(A = (f(m), I))$ based DCM can readily run on a cluster of computers to improve performance, reliability, and availability.

DCM helps improve interoperability. It provides the flexibility of transparently combining heterogeneous platforms, protocols, data representations, languages, and technologies. Concepts separate the critical information aspect from how such information is stored, represented, transferred, and processed. All these aspects can be altered independently without impacting the actual information.

DCM is technology agnostic: computer language, platform, protocol, data representation and so on. The concept construct of the form $C = ((x1, y1), \ldots, (xn, yn))$ can be freely interchanged between systems and components. Arbitrary technologies, implemented based on DCM, can be readily incorporated as part of an integrated information process:

116

sockets, .Net, HTTP, RMI, REST, SSL, EJBs, and so forth. They can be mixed and matched depending on specific system requirements.

Because of tight coupling between client and server, conventional distributed/service technologies based on distributed artifacts require that client and server application be upgraded at the same time [2]. This is usually not feasible and presents significant scalability limitations for infrastructures running 24/7 and/or expecting to accommodate a large number of computer nodes.

On the other hand, DCM does not present such limitation because client, server and communication mechanism are fully decoupled. Servers can be upgraded one by one without an impact on the client application and the rest of the infrastructure.

Once all the servers have been gradually upgraded, clients can be upgraded to take advantage of the new software functionality. As a consequence, an infrastructure based DCM can scale well and handle an arbitrary number of servers and clients 24/7. It is assumed that the new software version is backward compatible in terms of the messaging being exchanged.

In terms of garbage collection, a straightforward garbage collection mechanism can be employed to support the implementation of DCM. A leasing approach, for instance. Keep in mind that few extra overhead components need to be maintained when using DCM. The mechanism implemented can also take advantage of the garbage collection mechanism provided by the computer language at hand.

16.3 Fault-tolerant capabilities

The abstractions part of the Conceptual computing model can be readily replicated to provide a fault-tolerant information infrastructure. The Turing-complete information machine $(A=(f(m),I))$, usually implemented by a Live/Animated component, can implement arbitrary models including state machines.

Therefore, DCM can provide fault-tolerant capabilities in a very natural fashion by replicating Animated/Live components (information machines) and coordinating their interaction via consensus algorithms [6, 16]. No redundant abstractions, primitives, or APIs are required for implementation.

Using a real-world analogy, consider the scenario where a critical task is given to a group of team members by the team leader. Redundancy is provided so fault tolerance can be achieved: the critical task can get completed even if some of team members fail to complete their share.

The leader will interchange messages with the members via phone, internet, or face-to-face conversations to assess progress and deal with failures. Once the task is completed by a quorum of team members, the leader will be able to compare the preliminary results and arrive to final results based on consensus.

DCM can be utilized to implement fault-tolerant capabilities. The replicated *state machine approach* is a general method for implementing fault-tolerant systems. An information machine $(A=(f(m),I))$ can emulate any arbitrary state machine. The following fault-tolerant aspects apply within the context of DCM:

Redundancy: It is possible to use several replicas of the component (information machine) to achieve fault tolerance. Input messages are sent to all the component replicas. Each component replica is running on a separate host. Instead of replicating a monolithic system, Live/Animated components $(A=(f(m), I))$ are replicated.

In other words, fault tolerance can be modeled and implemented at the component level in a straightforward fashion. Message redundancy and process redundancy are also possible. Actually, under DCM, redundancy can be realistically provided for every level of organization: information association, message, information machine, and information process.

Consensus: The output coming from a *quorum* of Live/Animated replicas $(A= (f(m), I))$ can be compared to detect failures or achieve consensus. The leader component (part of the client application) is responsible for checking progress on a regular basis and gathering/comparing the outputs.

Auditing and failure detection: Non-faulty component replicas will always have the same component information and produce the same outputs.

Replica-group reconfiguration: This is done in case of a new replica Animated/Live component *(A= (f(m), I))* being added to the group or in case of a component malfunction. In the latter scenario, the faulty component needs to be removed from the replica group.

Component State Transfer: Before a new component replica *(A= (f(m), I))* is added to the group, the component information (I) must be the same. It can be readily copied from a non-faulty component replica.

Checkpoints: Component information (I) is saved so that the input messages processed up to a point can be discarded.

DCM takes a holistic and realistic approach based on information and the Turing-complete information machine. It views fault tolerance from the information perspective. DCM supports redundancy of information at all levels.

Think about an organization or group of individuals working cooperatively. In order for the group to accomplish its goals, redundant processes are put in place to monitor vital areas. The group also relies on multiple individuals to accomplish key processes - redundancy at the individual level.

As part of such processes, individuals are constantly engaged in multiple dialogs, possibly redundant, where vital information is exchanged via messaging. Furthermore, sentences and information associations can be made redundant. Individuals also rely on redundant information repositories and/or experts to find information and accomplish their common goals.

DCM can mimic all these scenarios as related to arbitrary processes. As mentioned earlier, it is also geared towards the implementation of fault tolerance at the component level (Live/Animated component) as opposed to the system level. Live/Animated components $(A= (f(m), I))$ are by nature ready to be replicated as part of fault-tolerant systems without any required changes to the component itself. No additional abstractions, primitives, or APIs are required for implementation.

Consider the realistic correspondence between DCM and the reality it seeks to represent, specifically when it comes to mimicking fault tolerance aspects. Every aspect, including fault tolerance, should be viewed from the information perspective – the fundamental concept.

As a best practice, it is recommended that a reusable framework implements DCM and the underlying conceptual computing model (see Conceptual Framework). Although a framework is not strictly required for implementation, it is strongly encouraged because of multiple considerations including reliability, reusability, fault-tolerant capabilities, quality, implementation cost, and security. All the components required by the information infrastructure and DCM are implemented by the reusable conceptual framework.

In summary, DCM is able to *naturally* manage complex real-world challenges and requirements: security, interoperability, fault tolerance, parallelism, concurrency, scalability, and reliability. All relevant concepts are mimicked by DCM and the underlying Turing-complete computing model.

17. INFORMATION MACHINE AND TURING COMPLETENESS

This section discusses the Conceptual mathematical model and demonstrates its Turing-completeness. A Turing machine is specified as a 7-tuple $M = (Q, \Gamma, b, \Sigma, \delta, q_0, F)$. Given an arbitrary Turing machine, let us demonstrate that an equivalent information A-machine can be built based on the information primitive $f(m)$.

The machine tape can be implemented as an array, vector, or any other comparable data structure. It is part of the information (I) stored in the machine's memory (subcomponent). The machine's transition table, current state, initial state, and set of final states are also part of (I).

```
// Pseudocode implementation based on the information primitive (f(m)).
// The message (m) consists of a single symbol.

void processInformation (symbol) {
    Transition transition;   // Consists of next state, symbol to be written,
                             // and tape movement ('L' or 'R')

    // Transition table being replicated.
    transition = transitionTable[currentState, symbol];

    updateTape(transition.symbol);     // Update the machine tape

    moveHead (transition.movement); // Move the head

    currentState = transition.nextState ; // Part of the information stored in the
                                          // machine's memory
}
```

For any arbitrary Turing machine, an equivalent information machine (A) can be built, which demonstrates that $A = (f(m), I)$ is Turing complete. As a consequence, and based on the Church-Turing thesis, any computable function or algorithm can be computed by using the information machine (A).

f: $\Sigma^* \rightarrow \Sigma^*$ is a generalization of *processInformation(symbol)* applicable to messages (information chunks) of finite length (Σ^*), as opposed to a single symbol. Live/Animated components represent a software implementation of the Turing-complete information machine (A-machine). In other words, Live/Animated components based on the information primitive can be used to implement any arbitrary computer technology, protocol, and language.

There is a second approach that can be employed to demonstrate Turing completeness. Let us demonstrate that the information primitive *f* can be utilized to implement the same functionality implemented by a Turing complete language or process technology. Let us consider an arbitrary process, function, or procedure (*p*) written in an arbitrary Turing complete language (or process technology like BPEL): *output = p (x1,x2,... ,xk); x1, x2, ... ,xk* are the parameters processed by the function, procedure, or process. *Output* is optional since procedures do not return a value.

A Live/Animated component (*A= (f(m), I)*) can be implemented to provide equivalent functionality regardless of the complexity associated to the procedure, function, or process. Notice that *f(m)* is a generalization of any arbitrary function or procedure (*p*). Within the context of the Conceptual model, instead of using parameters (*x1, x2, ... ,xk*), the information is passed to *f* as a fully decoupled *message*(m) with attributes *x1,x2,....., xk*. In consequence, the realistic information primitive expressed by *f(m)*, can be utilized to implement any arbitrary functionality (or algorithm) provided by a Turing-complete language or process technology.

Based on the earlier discussion, it should also be fairly obvious that Live/Animated components (*A=(f(m), I)*) and associated information primitive can be leveraged to compute any arbitrary mathematical function expressed as *(y1, y2, ...,yn) = f (x1, x2, ...,xm)*. An Animated/Live component is equivalent to a Turing machine (or computer) in terms of processing power. It is necessary to emphasize the fundamental and ubiquitous aspect: *information (Energy)*.

It can also be demonstrated that Boole's Conceptual Machine (*A=(β(m),I)*) is also Turing complete. The machine relies on its memory subcomponent for storage and retrieval of conceptual information (I).

The scope of the information primitive $\beta(m)$ has been substantially simplified (i.e. narrowed) to the implementation of logical processing as specified by Boole's algebra of logic: logical operations (AND, OR, NOT, Boolean equality, and so forth) applied to information represented using the concept construct (C).

Basic flow of control is also required to execute procedures (P). Set theory and operations represent a Boolean algebra. The machine is able to understand/produce sentences (S) and execute procedures (P) in the language (L). Implementing Boole's machine is straightforward – mirrors the mathematical formulation.

For convenience and versatility sake, the machine can also execute procedures (P) that use a syntax similar to the one employed by traditional computer languages. Also for convenience, advanced flow of control is recommended (while, for, and so forth). For any arbitrary Turing machine (M= $(Q,\Gamma,b,\Sigma,\delta,q_0, F)$), a procedure (P) can be built to simulate it which proves Turing completeness.

```
// Procedure (P) that implements a Turing Machine.
// It is written using a conceptual language targeted to be
// run by a Boole's Conceptual machine, A = (β(m), I).

Procedure simulateTuringMachine {

Concept TM;              // Turing Machine
Concept Transition;      // Consists of next state, symbol to be written,
                         // and tape movement ('L' or 'R')
Concept stateTransitions; // Transitions associated to a specific state

// This specific procedure implements logical negation (bitwise)
// A procedure (P) can be written, for the conceptual machine, to
// emulate any arbitrary Turing machine – simply by changing
// the TM initialization section to match M= (Q,Γ,b,Σ ,δ,q0, F)
```

```
// Initialize the Turing Machine (TM)
TM->initialState = TM->currentState = "q0";
TM->finalStates = {"q1"};

// Initialize Transition Table

// State q0 (transitions)
Transition->operation = "W"; Transition->newSymbol = '1';Transition->movement = 'R'; Transition->newState = "q1";
TM->transitionTable->q0->0 = Transition;

Transition->operation = "W";Transition->newSymbol = '0';Transition->movement = 'R'; Transition->newState = "q1";
TM->transitionTable->q0->1 = Transition

...

while (!(TM->currentState ∈ TM->finalStates))  {

  TM->symbol = readTape ( );
  // Retrieve transitions associated to the current state

    stateTransitions = TM->transitionTable[TM->currentState];
    Transition = stateTransition [TM->symbol];   // Retrieve transition for symbol

    updateTape(Transition->symbol);            // Update the machine tape
    moveHead (Transition->movement);         // Move the head
    TM->currentState = Transition->nextState ;
  }
}
```

A variable or index (j) can be utilized to access concept associations. If the value of j is x_i ($i \in [1 .. n]$), $C[j]$ retrieves the value of $C\text{->}x_i$.

Boole's Conceptual Machine mimics the mind and features cognitive abilities including learning and logical reasoning (see Cognitive/AI architecture). In consequence of the previous demonstration, a full-blown computer can be implemented based solely on the three natural concepts part of the mind's conceptual paradigm: $A=(\beta(m),I)$.

18. BPM/BPEL TECHNOLOGIES

The Turing-complete Conceptual computing model and associated framework can be leveraged to model arbitrary business processes in a realistic and accurate fashion. They can be reused for the comprehensive implementation of business process technologies (BPEL/BPM), frameworks, and applications.

The information process abstractions can also be readily incorporated into UML/BPM/BPEL diagrams in order to design and implement applications with comparable functionality to traditional business process applications. There is a direct correspondence between the proposed abstractions and specific modeling diagrams and tools.

A business process (BPM/BPEL) can be modeled as a group of Live/Animated entities working concurrently and communicating via messaging: $\{A_1, \ldots, A_n\}$ where $A_i = (f_i(m), I_i)$. Information is represented using the concept construct (C). No additional abstractions, primitives, or APIs are necessary.

Because of the simplicity of the Turing-complete Conceptual model, a straightforward information primitive needs to be implemented: *processMessage (message)*. Any BPEL/BPM technology can be utilized and/or extended to implement the information primitive required. For convenience, the examples that follow use the BPEL implementation provided by the Jt conceptual framework [10].

The BPEL diagrams have been produced using the Eclipse BPEL designer. By using these tools and frameworks, complete production quality applications can be generated with comparable capabilities to the ones provided by traditional business process technologies.

The following straightforward process (Fig 1.) sends a message ("hi") to a local component (HelloWorld). Notice the compact syntax. The information primitive (*processMessage()*) is not included but assumed implicitly:

reply = component(message);

This is equivalent to *reply= component.processMessage (message);*

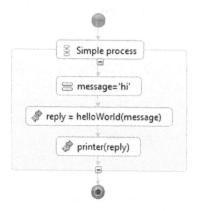

Fig 1. Simple example of the information process (synchronous messaging)

The following BPEL syntax represents the component invocation (using the Jt BPEL extensions):

```
<bpel:invoke   component="helloWorld"
   inputVariable="message"
   outputVariable="reply">
</bpel:invoke>
```

The component helloWorld has been defined as a class instance:

```
<bpel:variable
   name="helloWorld"
   type="java:Jt.examples.HelloWorld">
</bpel:variable>
```

As part of a process, all modalities of messaging are supported: synchronous, asynchronous, streaming, distributed messaging, two-way messaging, authenticated, encrypted, and combinations of these forms. For instance, asynchronous messaging requires the attribute *synchronous="false"* as part of the component invocation.

The following process invokes a web service (Fig. 2). A synchronous message is sent to a distributed component/service via its local framework Proxy. The reply message is printed. The same can be accomplished by using the *messenger* abstraction instead of a Proxy (not demonstrated here). If an exception is detected during the service invocation, the process prints it. The distributed service/component invocation is described by following process diagram:

proxy.processMessage (message);

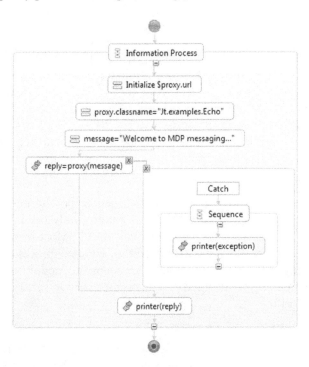

Fig 2. Distributed component/service invocation using the information process abstraction

127

The following BPEL code represents the distributed service/component invocation. The Proxy instance needs to be initialized beforehand with the name and address associated to the distributed component/service. Exception handling is also demonstrated.

```
<bpel:invoke component="proxy" inputVariable="message"
    outputVariable="reply" exception="exception">
  <bpel:catch faultMessageType="java:java.lang.Exception">
    <bpel:sequence>
      <bpel:invoke component="printer"
                   inputVariable="exception">
      </bpel:invoke>
    </bpel:sequence>
  </bpel:catch>
</bpel:invoke>
```

18.1 Master-Worker Pattern

This section illustrates a reusable implementation of the well-known Master-Worker pattern, based on the Turing-complete Conceptual model The pattern is also known as divide-and-conquer. Using the realistic model, a business process can be conceptualized as a group or *team (T)* of Live/Animated entities working concurrently: $T = \{A_1, \dots , A_n\}$ where $A_i=(f_i(m),I_i)$. Tasks are assigned to a team of members to complete. Team members can be local or distributed components providing services.

All modalities of messaging are supported: asynchronous, synchronous, distributed, two-way, secure, etc. The user of this pattern, only needs to provide the logic associated with the member (task itself). Most of the complexities associated with the development of distributed processes are handled by using the *Turing-complete* Conceptual model and associated abstractions: distributed communication, security, concurrency, and so forth .

The following section of the process (Leader) assigns tasks to the team members by sending an asynchronous message (task) to the member (Fig. 3). A task table (taskTable) is maintained to keep track of the task assignments and the corresponding team member assigned to each particular task.

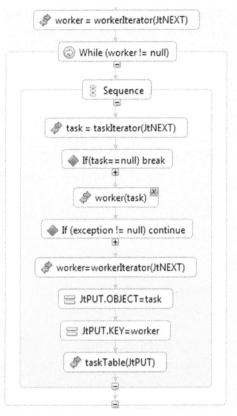

Fig 3. Task assignments within the process (via asynchronous messaging).

The following section of the process (Leader) checks on progress, on a regular basis via synchronous messaging (Fig. 4). Notice that progress notifications, sent to the *team leader* via asynchronous messaging, are also feasible. Once the task is completed, the task results are retrieved; the member is removed from the work-in-progress list (worker) and added to the list of available members.

In case a member is unable to complete a specific task, the task is reassigned to another available member. This straightforward example can be modified to provide sophisticated redundancy and fault-tolerant capabilities, like the ones required by any modern business process (see Distributed Conceptual Model).

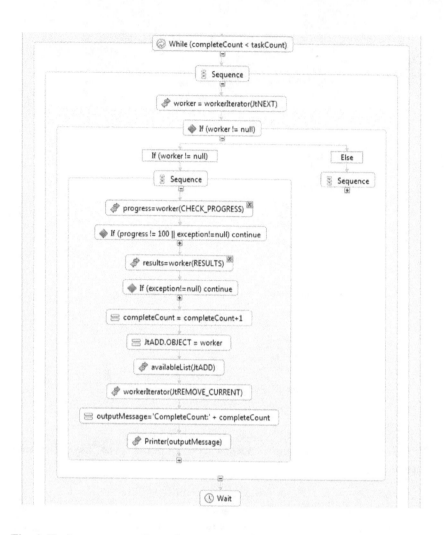

Fig. 4. Task progress and results tracking via synchronous messaging.

Keep in mind that the Conceptual model consists of the complete set of abstractions (Turing complete) required to model arbitrarily complex information processes. For instance, a hierarchy consisting of layers the supervision can be added, in order to monitor and supervise the work.

Each layer consists of *Live/Animated* components acting as *team leaders, supervisors,* or *managers* and interchanging information with other participants (via messaging) in order to make process decisions.

Additional redundancy and fault-tolerant characteristics can be achieved by assigning the same task to a *team* of members (T) instead of individuals. Once the task is completed by a quorum of team members, the *team leader* will be able to compare the preliminary results and arrive to final results based on consensus.

19. MODEL EVALUATION AND METRICS

The Conceptual approach can be evaluated based on the following aspects which are a direct result of its mathematical foundation.

Simplicity. This aspect can be measured using the number of primitives and abstractions required by the mathematical model. The Conceptual model requires a single information primitive and one language construct (Concept). The complexity metric measured by Weighted Methods Per Class (WMC) is one [37],[38]: only one method (information primitive) is required. The method level complexity [40] can be measured as well: one input parameter (message).

Now consider the simplification in terms of the measurable number of classes (NC) required for implementation: in reality most entities can be represented as pure information (Concept), unable to process information. NC represents a system level measurement of complexity [40]. It is related to the number of key classes (NKC) [41].

As indicated earlier, complexity can be measured by calculating the number of abstractions required for implementation (NC/NKC). All redundant abstractions and primitives add complexities (WMC & NC) and are ultimately unnecessary.

The concepts part of the model (information/Energy, messaging, information machine) constitute a small, but Turing complete, set of realistic abstractions able to implement arbitrary technologies and applications – in particular, a comprehensive distributed information infrastructure. Picture the application represented as a graph $G = (V, E)$ where V represents the component classes and E represents the inter-dependencies between such classes. Under the Conceptual approach, the order of the graph (cardinality $(V) = NC$) is reduced by mimicking the reality being represented.

The number of key classes required for the reference implementation of a conceptual framework can be quantified:

a) Main framework classes (2): Live/Animated Component ($A=(f(m),I)$), and concept construct (C).

b) Additional core classes (5): Factory, Messenger, Component Registry, Logger, and Exception Handler. Support classes include Resource Manager, Printer, and XML Adapter.

c) Distributed Infrastructure classes (5): Façade, Message Cipher, Access Manager, Proxy, and Adapter (see Distributed Component and Service Model – UML diagrams).

A total of 12 key classes (NKC = 12) are required to implement the Conceptual framework and the associated distributed component/service model. A Proxy and Adapter (NKC+=2) need to be implemented in order to plug a new technology into the distributed information infrastructure provided by the Conceptual framework. Adapters and Proxies for widely used technologies are already provided.

The concept of inheritance is not part of the mathematical model which is conceived from the information standpoint. Consider the *real* meaning of the concept within nature. As a consequence, the Depth of the Inheritance Tree metric is zero (DIT=0). The Number of Children is also zero (NOC=0). On the other hand, class inheritance is readily accommodated in the few cases when it becomes beneficial for implementation. In such cases, inheritance is kept to a minimum (shallow): DIT<=2 and NOC<=2.

Completeness. Turing-completeness has been demonstrated via formal proof (see Information Machine and Turing Completeness). Again, the concepts part of the model constitute a compact, but complete (Turing complete), set of abstractions able to implement arbitrary technologies and applications.

Efficiency. This aspect can be quantified by determining the number of abstractions and primitives that are part of the model and associated implementation. The Conceptual model leaves no room for unnecessary redundancy or inefficiencies: single information machine, one information primitive and single language construct (concept).

The Conceptual model relies on a streamlined set of information abstractions, perhaps optimal – in agreement with Occam's razor. As discussed previously, the number of class components (NC) is reduced since most entities represent concepts (C) unable to process information. Consider the implementation size, measured in key components part of the reference implementation: NKC=12. Efficiency can also be measured based on application footprint (see size and application footprint).

Efficient message-level security can be transparently built in as part of the distributed model and framework – in lieu of transport level security, which is computationally more expensive. In general, keep in mind that nature and natural processes are highly efficient. By mimicking natural concepts, the Conceptual model and its implementation 'absorb' nature's qualities including efficiency. Obviously, this is consistent with the motivations behind Biomimetics.

Effectivety. This aspect can be evaluated qualitatively based on the number of real-world problems solved by the Conceptual computing model. Also, consider Turing-completeness which allows for the implementation of arbitrary information technologies. Again, nature is very effective in solving information related challenges – a quality that is readily absorbed by the distributed model. Alan Kay's comments should be carefully considered during the evaluation.

The Conceptual model has produced tangible and measurable results: several production quality applications and a reference implementation of the model (Conceptual framework) have been built, which demonstrates its viability and wide applicability [10],[2],[4],[5]. A variety of technologies have been designed and implemented by levering the Conceptual model, including SOA, REST, ESB, Master-Worker, and BPEL.

Size and application footprint. A compact set of concepts and single information primitive result in a streamlined implementation. The size of the Conceptual framework can be accurately measured in terms of key classes (NKC=12) and file size.

The current reference implementation of the framework takes about 512K which is very small (lightweight) when compared against

134

traditional frameworks with similar functionally. The Conceptual framework provides a comprehensive distributed information infrastructure [2],[4],[5]. In the realm of technology, smaller is often better and more efficient.

The Conceptual framework is able to comfortably run on mobile devices where resource constraints are prevalent and need to be taken into careful consideration. Small application footprint are a direct consequence of other aspects including simplicity, straightforward mathematical model, reusability, and the compact/complete set of concepts part of the information family.

Requiring a streamlined set of components, as part of the design/implementation, is also a contributor because most entities are realistically represented as concepts (pure information). This aspect is also related to the aspect of efficiency discussed earlier and can be evaluated quantitatively: 512K lightweight footprint.

Coupling and Encapsulation. By relying on messaging, encapsulation and coupling are improved: the only realistic mechanism of communication between fully encapsulated components ($A=(f(m),I)$) is via messaging. The number of interdependencies between components can be measured by counting the number of procedure calls required between components.

The Conceptual model does not present the web of coupled interdependencies required by traditional technologies/APIs based on "gear meshing of procedure calls". Picture the application represented as a graph $G = (V,E)$ where V represents the components and E represents the interdependencies between such components. Under the Conceptual approach, the size of the graph (cardinality (E)) is reduced.

Coupling between object classes (CBO) is a related complexity metric [37]. A Live/Animated component ($A=(f(m),I)$) is fully encapsulated and decoupled (CBO=0): messaging is the only realistic mechanism of communication between components. A messenger subcomponent is responsible for providing the messaging functionality, when necessary.

Calls to built-in classes provided by the computer language are not taken into account since they remain the same regardless of the approach being employed to implement the component. They can also be refactored to leverage messaging and mimic the real world (CBO=0).

Due to complete component encapsulation, some complex Live/Animated components may grow to be large in terms of methods and lines of code. Such scenario can be mitigated by splitting the code and creating support subcomponents. Access to support subcomponents is always accomplished through the main component of the hierarchy (key component). From the system perspective, and for all practical purposes, the main component and its supporting components are viewed as a unit – single component.

Reusability. Based on empirical studies, it is widely accepted that encapsulation and decoupling (CBO) improve reusability [37], [39]. Therefore, by improving CBO metrics, the Conceptual model is bound to enhance reusability. The measured CBO value is below the recommended limit (CBO<=5) [39].

The abstractions part of the Turing-complete Conceptual model need to be implemented once. Usually they are implemented as part of a Conceptual framework. After the initial implementation, the framework can be reused over and over again for the implementation of arbitrary technologies and applications. The same cannot be said about models and technologies based on artificial abstractions like distributed artifacts and multithreading which hinder reusability in multiple ways [2],[4],[5].

Live/Animated components that rely on the information primitive and messaging can be readily reused regardless of technology, computer language, platform, protocol and so on. Because of their encapsulation and decoupling properties, they can be reused at the component level: a single Live/Animated component $(A=(f(m),I))$ can be extracted from another library/application and reused.

The web of dependencies produced by gear meshing of procedure calls is effectively eliminated. Live/Animated components can also be readily exposed as distributed components/services within SOA implementations. Additionally, they can also be readily reused via native interfaces.

Scalability and Interoperability. As documented in detail and expressed by Alan Kay, the lack of messaging imposes scalability and interoperability limitations. Most technologies based on distributed artifacts present such limitations which have a negative impact on the overall quality.

Scalability is usually measured in terms of the number of computer nodes that can be accommodated. A distributed infrastructure based on the Conceptual computing model can scale well and handle an arbitrary number of computers (servers and clients) 24/7 – without imposing limitations.

As discussed earlier, the Conceptual model is platform, technology, language, and protocol agnostic. Consider a distributed application implemented based on a specific technology. Interoperability can be measured based on the number of technologies that can interoperate with the given technology.

For instance, a technology based on gear meshing of procedure calls like Java RMI can only readily interoperate with a client implemented using Java RMI: limited interoperability. A similar situation applies to .NET and EJB. On the other hand, an Animated/Live component ($A=(f(m),I)$) can interoperate with an application/component implemented using any arbitrary language and communication technology/protocol: in other words, full interoperability is provided by the Conceptual model in a natural fashion.

An adapter is required for each technology to be supported. Think about the adapters that allow you to transparently connect your computer to the internet infrastructure regardless of the technology/protocol being used: Wireless, TCP/IP, modem adapter, cable adapter, and so forth.

Realitic Correspondence (realism). Realistic correspondence is a key aspect in science and technology (Correspondence Theory of Truth [30]); specifically, in the realm of scientific models and their evaluation. The Conceptual model accurately mimics the conceptual mind and associated natural concepts: information (Energy), messaging, and processing of information. Furthermore, the model is in correspondence with or supported by leading research and theories related to the mind (see Cognitive/AI architecture and Related Theories, Studies, and Research).

To attain true correspondence there must be one-to-one correspondence between the implemented abstractions and the concepts extracted from reality. In agreement with Occam's razor, artificial abstractions and primitives often lead to unnecessary redundancies, complexities, and inefficiencies. Consider that as consequence of correspondence with natural reality, the model absorbs nature's qualities which can be evaluated and often measured in quantitative terms.

The absence of the messaging concept would be an example. Artifacts are in direct conflict with natural concepts and Biomimetics principles. Tight gear meshing of procedure calls (artifact) must never be confused or mischaracterized as real messaging. The natural concept and the artifact are *different*. Clearly, the *artifact* lacks realistic correspondence. Careful attention should be paid to whether or not the real entity is able to process information. From a realistic perspective, concepts (C) are passive entities unable to process information.

Quality. There are several metrics that can be applied to measure quality, including the number and severity of the software defects detected. Providing and analyzing detailed empirical data is outside the scope of the current effort.

On the other hand, and based on empirical studies, there are well-known interdependencies between quality and the complexity metrics presented above: WMC, CBO, DIT, and NOC [37], [38]. They are below the recommended limits [39][41]: WMC <= 25, CBO <= 5, DIT<=5, and NOC<=5. As a consequence, quality can be improved by leveraging the Conceptual model. It is also well-known that improvements in reusability result in better quality measurements.

Another area would be the elimination of multithreading artifacts which results in better quality by overcoming the complex problems presented earlier [2],[4],[5]. Lack of scalability and interoperability should arguably be viewed as measurable quality issues (defects) that are overcome by leveraging the Conceptual model. In any case, they represent limitations to be overcome and should be part of a complete model evaluation.

Maintainability. Based on an empirical study, maintainability is improved by enhancing complexity metrics [42], [37]: WMC, CBO, DIT and NOC. This aspect is related to software quality, risk, and overall timeframe/cost.

Cost and Timeframe. All the aspects described above have an impact on cost and timeframes which can be accurately measured during project implementation. Given a system consisting of n classes (NC), cost and time can be calculated:

$$\text{Total Cost} = \sum \text{Cost}(\text{component}_i); \ i \in [1.. n]$$

$$\text{Total Time} = \sum \text{Time}(\text{component}_i); \ i \in [1.. n]$$

The function Cost() measures the design, implementation, testing, debugging, and maintenance costs associated to a specific component. Time() measures the amount of time required.

The interdependency between reusability and cost/timeframe is direct and well known. For instance, by reusing a Conceptual framework there is a significant improvement in terms of cost and timeframes because it needs to be implemented once – if it is not already available. The cost/timeframe of such implementation is also improved due to the streamlined amount of realistic concepts to be implemented (NKC = 12). The simplicity and quality aspects discussed earlier also have a direct impact on cost/timeframe.

Backus provided the following criteria for classifying models of computing [26]. Such classification is a useful tool that can also be applied to evaluate the Conceptual computing model.

139

Mathematical Foundations: "Is there an elegant and concise mathematical description of the model? Is it useful in proving helpful facts about the behavior of the model? Or is the model so complex that its description is bulky and of little mathematical use?"

Absolutely: $A=(f(m),I)\&C$. A very concise and straightforward mathematical foundation that clearly expresses all the concepts associated with the model and their interrelationships.

History sensitivity. "Does the model include a notion of storage, so that one program can save information that can affect the behavior of a later program? That is, is the model history sensitive?"

Yes, it is history sensitive. Information (Energy) is the model's fundamental concept. A straightforward set of operations over information are part of the model, including retrieve (read), store (write) update, and logical processing. System behavior is impacted by the information already known by the machine.

Clarity and conceptual usefulness of programs. "Are programs of the model clear expressions of a process or computation? Do they embody concepts that help us to formulate and reason about processes?"

Absolutely: The conceptual approach is based on a foundation of natural concepts extracted and mimicked from reality (realistic correspondence): information (Energy), messaging, and information machine. There is a one-to-one correspondence between reality and the concepts part of the model. As a consequence, the implementation is clear and conceptually useful.

Type of semantics. "Does a program successively transform states (which are not programs) until a terminal state is reached (state-transition semantics)? Are states simple or complex? Or can a "program" be successively reduced to simpler "programs" to yield a final "normal form program," which is the result (reduction semantics)?"

140

No states, natural semantics of concepts (information/Energy, messaging, information machine).

Based on his criteria, Backus characterizes three classes of models for computing. He underscores that the classification is "crude and debatable": The Conceptual approach can also be categorized and evaluated using his criteria.

"Simple operational models. Examples: Turing machines, various automata. Foundations: concise and useful. History sensitivity: have storage, are history sensitive. Semantics: state transition with very simple states. Program clarity: programs unclear and conceptually not helpful."

"Applicative models. Examples: Church's lambda calculus, Curry's system of combinators, pure Lisp, functional programming. Foundations: concise and useful. History sensitivity: no storage, not history sensitive. Semantics: reduction semantics, no states. Program clarity: programs can be clear and conceptually useful."

Conventional programming languages. "Foundations: *complex, bulky, not useful.* History sensitivity: have storage, are history sensitive. Semantics: state transition with complex states. Program clarity: programs can be moderately clear, *are not very useful conceptually.* "

Conceptual model. Based on Biomimetics, natural concepts, and the conceptual framework mimicked from the mind. Foundations: very concise and useful $(A =(f(m),I))$. History sensitive: *realistically* mimics the conceptual mind; history sensitive, concept constructs (C) can be stored and retrieved (as part of I). Information (Energy) is the model's fundamental concept. System behavior is impacted by the information already known (I). Semantics: no states, natural semantics of concepts. Program clarity: programs can be very clear based on realistic concepts, are useful conceptually. The model operates at a high level of abstraction relying on straightforward/streamlined set of concepts and associated operations over information: information (Energy), messaging, and information machine. In agreement with reductionism, realism, and

Occam's razor, computing is reduced (unified/simplified) to these concepts, part of the Turing-complete model.

Although the classification criteria was proposed by Backus a while ago. It is still relevant in the context of computing models and languages. Several of the same issues apply today including lack of "conceptual usefulness", "complex/bulky" mathematical foundation, the "complex machinery of procedure declarations", and "tighter gear meshing of procedure calls".

As expected, nature's approach excels in multiple areas proposed by Backus – naturally; in particular, in the areas of conceptual usefulness and mathematical foundations. This demonstrates in tangible terms the qualities 'absorbed' by an approach that attempts to mimic nature's information model and concepts – which is consistent with Biomimetics and Occam's razor. Nature's conceptual mind exhibits a unique paradigm of computing: conceptual paradigm.

20. COGNITIVE/AI ARCHITECTURE

The Conceptual computing model can be leveraged as the basis for proposing a cognitive architecture: Model for Information Navigation and Decision-making. Such architecture consist of a single Turing-complete module responsible for implementing the Boole's conceptual machine $(A=(\beta(m),I))$. As a unified architecture, the cognitive architecture being proposed is also a UTC candidate [32].

The Turing-complete mathematical Conceptual model relies exclusively on the concepts of information (Energy) and processing thereof, expressed by a compact set of operations: storage (write), retrieval (read), and logical processing. *Logical* Processing of information is performed according to Boole's algebra of logic ("Laws of Thought").

The following discussion will focus on the mind's conceptual cognitive abilities. The Conceptual computing model and cognitive architecture are consistent with or supported by leading scientific theories/research including psychological theories (see appendix on Related Theories, Studies, and Research).

According to psychological associationism, intelligent behavior is the result of associative learning (see Behaviorism [30]). Associations allow the mind to acquire knowledge about the "causal structure" of the world. An association represents the pairing between a perceptual experience (message/energy) and the information (thoughts/memories) already contained in the mind which is mimicked by the conceptual mathematical model (see Mathematical Model). In psychology, an association refers to the connection between conceptual entities.

20.1 Participants

Boole's Logical Engine (Boole's LE): module's single main component responsible for logical processing of information: implementation of the conceptual deductive approach founded on Boole's algebra of logic defined by the single β-function (see Conceptual deductive approach). It implements the conceptual machine abstraction $(A=(\beta(m),I))$ and provides inference capabilities. The engine relies on the memory subcomponent for the storage and retrieval of conceptual information and knowledge (K).

The scope of the information primitive *(f(m))* has been substantially simplified (i.e. narrowed) to the implementation of logical processing as specified by Boolean algebra *(β(m))*: logical operations (AND, OR, NOT, Boolean equality, and so forth) applied to information represented using the concept construct (C). Basic flow of control is also required to execute procedures (P). The concept construct (C) represents the single entity required for representing conceptual information: Procedures (P) and Sentences (S). The operation performed by the *β*-function will depend on the type of incoming message (m) received and processed. There are several types of message.

a) Write operation. When the message (m) is received, the *β*-function *((β(m))* updates the conceptual information stored (learned) by the machine (K):
a.1) Sentence (S). The *β*-function stores the sentence (S): $K = K \cup S$
a.2) Procedure (P). The *β*-function stores the procedure (P): $K = K \cup P$

b) Read operation. Information previously stored or inferred can be retrieved from the machine: sentences (S), associations (a), and procedures (P).

c) Logical deduction. The *β*-function is also able to make logical inferences based on the incoming message (m) and the information stored (see Conceptual deductive approach). The machine information is updated with the inferences $S_1, S_2, \dots, S_n$ derived: $K = K \cup \{S_1, S_2, \dots, S_n\}$ where $S_1, S_2, \dots, S_n$ are inferred sentences (S).

d) Procedure execution. Based on the basic operations above, the *β*-function is able to sequentially execute a procedure (P), previously stored by the machine.

Memory subcomponent: The Conceptual machine's memory subcomponent is responsible for storing and retrieving conceptual and non-conceptual information (I/K). The Boole's logical engine is constantly interacting with its environment thorough messaging: chunks of information/Energy received. These packets or chunks of information are stored ('recorded') by the memory subcomponent (I).

Acquiring new knowledge (i.e. learning) is tightly intertwined with the concepts of storing and retrieving information via the memory subcomponent. Conceptually, in agreement with psychological

144

associationism, the information stored inside the mind can be viewed as a web of information, similar to the world wide web (WWW). A WWW page contains links (i.e. references) to other pages, videos, images, and sounds.

Multiples forms of information can be linked together, on the page, to provide a comprehensive/integrated view. The information on the WWW can be navigated through the links (associations). *Keep in mind that this WWW metaphor is used for illustration purposes.* It elucidates *similarities* between the WWW and the conceptual mind. Both scenarios are conceptually isomorphic dealing with the same concepts: information (Energy), messaging, and information processing.

According to the Conceptual computing model, the information stored in the mind (I) is organized in a similar way based on the single concept of information (Energy). Multiple forms of information (Energy) are accommodated: sounds, images, smells, flavors, and tactile sensations. Each message received (information chunk) may consist of one or more references to information (chunks) already learned.

For instance, when you hear or read the sentence (S): "Mary married George Boole". The message (m) is stored as an information chunk inside the memory. It also contains associations to other information (Energy) chunks previously stored (*part of I*): Mary (person's name), married (verb/action) and George Boole (person's name, mathematician, etc.).

The Boole's LE is responsible for navigating the web of information, through algebraic operations in order to gather and combine meaning. Algebra comes from the Arabic, meaning reunion of broken parts which fits the required combination of information (chunks). The principle of compositionality also applies (Frege's Principle) [30]: the meaning of a complex expression [concept] is determined by the meanings of its constituent expressions [concepts] and the rules used to combine them.

The mathematical model does not make distinction between short term and long term memory. All memories are stored in a single 'bucket' of Information (I), as part of the mathematical model. It is not clear from current cognitive research how the mechanism is realistically implemented within the mind.

20.2 Cognitive Abilities

"Thought was still wholly intangible and ineffable until modern formal logic interpreted it as the manipulation of formal tokens."
  Allen Newel and Herbert Simon [25]

The logical engine and subcomponent just described provide the conceptual machine with its cognitive abilities.

Memory: the memory subcomponent is able to store and retrieve conceptual and non-conceptual information (I/K) based on a compact set of operations: retrieval (read) and storage (write/record).

Logical Reasoning: the Boole's LE provides the system with reasoning capabilities by implementing the conceptual deductive approach (β-function) which has been demonstrated via formal proof (see Conceptual deductive approach). The approach is based on well-known forward/backward chaining methods of reasoning, employed by AI systems and founded on Boole's algebra of logic [1, 22]. It basically consists of navigating the web of conceptual knowledge (K) to retrieve information and/or make new inferences based on concepts/associations already learned.

Learning: the module is constantly interacting and learning from the environment via messaging. The module can readily learn (or be taught) new concepts (C) in the form of sentences (S) and procedures (P), which are stored in memory, based on information associations with concepts already mastered. Learning literally means acquiring new information or knowledge.

In the case of conceptual information, the 'web' of knowledge (K) is augmented by adding new information in the form of concepts and/or associations. Procedures (P) to perform tasks are concepts as well. Learning may also occur by levering the Boole's LE and inferring new facts or conclusions from the information already known. The graph (K) is navigated to retrieve known concepts, reason, and/or perform learned tasks (procedures). Obviously, memory and logical reasoning are crucial in supporting the module's learning abilities.

146

Like the human mind, the innate potential of Boole's conceptual machine is vast in terms of how much the machine is able to learn and the problems it can tackle. The innate abilities of communication with its environment, learning, and reasoning provide the machine with such potential. On the other hand, there is another side to this coin, as clearly expressed by the two-tuple formulation $(A=(\beta(m),I))$:the machine's effective computing power (i.e. 'reasoning power') is also determined by how much knowledge is mastered by it (I/K).

The Conceptual computing model and cognitive architecture are consistent with Turing's paradox/views on learning machines as well (see appendix on Related Theories, Studies, and Research). The main focus is on the mind's *conceptual* cognitive abilities: Boole's Conceptual machine $(A=(\beta(m),I))$. Other cognitive abilities like motor skills, emotions, and pattern/image recognition are beyond the current scope.

Problem solving: Problem solving usually consists of using specific methods/procedures, in an orderly manner, for finding solutions to problems. Procedures (P), defined based on sentences (S) in the language (L), can be learned and executed to solve problems or perform tasks. For instance, a procedure (P) may be able to sort a collection of numbers or perform arithmetic operations between two numbers.

The human mind learns procedures to solve problems based on concepts (information) already mastered. A procedure can be learned by several means including written and verbal communication. Take for example a cooking recipe which represents a concept: a procedure (P) that defines a written sequence of steps to be followed by the mind.

Language/Symbol manipulation: The Conceptual cognitive architecture is able to mimic the conceptual mind in terms of language/symbol manipulation. A separate section describes this capability in more detail (see A Natural Language of Concepts).

Verbal/written human communication is achieved through sentences which are represented using the concept construct (C). From a physical perspective, sentences (S) and procedures (P) represent aggregates of Energy (information).

The language (L) is a concept that can be represented using the concept construct (C): L = {(symbol$_1$, Definition (symbol$_1$)), ... , (symbol$_n$, Definition (symbol$_n$))}. Symbols in the language (L) and their meaning (logical definitions) are learned by the architecture.

In agreement with PSSH [25], the Turing-complete Conceptual architecture/model is able to manipulate symbol structures (Sentences (S) expressed via the concept construct (C)) using *logical* transformations according to well-defined inference and grammatical rules.

Cognitivism advocates the separation between model (theory) and implementation [61]: the mathematical foundation is fairly independent from the physical representation (logical mind vs. physical brain). It is similar to the independence between logical and physical representation exhibited by relational database systems (RDBMS) and computer languages. The Conceptual model relies on the concept construct (C) for the logical (mathematical) representation that is mapped onto the physical representation (physical engram).

20.3 Physical symbol system hypothesis (PSSH)

The physical symbol system hypothesis has been very influential in the realm of AI and cognitive architectures [61]. It represents a law of *qualitative* structure [25]:

"A physical symbol system has the necessary and sufficient means for general intelligent action."

The heuristic search hypothesis represents a related law of qualitative structure [25]:

"The solutions to problems are represented as symbol structures. A physical symbol system exercises its intelligence in problem solving by search – that is, by generating and progressively modifying symbol structures until it produces a solution structure."

The Conceptual computing model/architecture is in harmony with PSSH. The Turing-complete Conceptual architecture represents a physical symbol system; therefore, according to the PSSH, capable of *general intelligent action* [25]. Human beings and computers are examples of physical symbol systems. *PSSH does not represent a mathematical*

148

model. It relies on qualitative "generalizations" and structures "rather than mathematical"[25].

PSSH generalizations primary rest on empirical evidence and *further formalization is left for future efforts* [25]. In contrast, the Turing-complete Conceptual computing model provides a precise mathematical foundation/formalization, relying exclusively on Boole's algebra of logic.

In agreement with PSSH, the Conceptual architecture/model relies on logical transformations (algebra of logic) in order to generate potential solution structures. Specifically, in terms of language/symbol manipulation and problem solving abilities. All symbol structures are represented using the concept construct (C).

20.4 Combinatorial Challenge

Consider the large amount of information (I) that the human mind is able to learn and manipulate. This presents a combinatorial/scalability challenge associated with the vast amount of information leveraged by the architecture. The challenge is very common in the context of Cognitive/AI architectures and PSSH [61, 25, 56]. Heuristics and parallelism are required in order to search/combine relevant information quickly and efficiently.

Several heuristic search algorithms have been proposed including depth-first search, bi-directional search, and A* algorithm (see Heuristic Search [56]). Suitable heuristic/search algorithms and parallelism can be applied in conjunction with the Conceptual architecture in order to prevent and/or manage combinatorial explosion.

Notice that the challenge is primarily engineering/implementation related. From a *theoretical* perspective, the amount of information managed by the architecture ($I = (IC_1, \ldots, IC_n)$) can grow arbitrarily: the mathematical value (n) can be arbitrarily large. From a practical/implementation perspective, such vast amount of information will present performance and storage challenges unless a suitable engineering implementation is devised.

Again, consider the aforementioned separation between the logical/mathematical model (theory) and the physical implementation, consistent with cognitivism: the same mathematical model $(A=(\beta(m),I)/C)$ can have multiple suitable engineering implementations.

In agreement with reductionism, each neuron can be completely specified using the same concepts leveraged by the Conceptual computing model: information (Energy), messaging, and information machine $(A=(f(m),I))$. A neuron represents an analog information machine or information processor. The brain consists of a web of interconnected neurons (information processors) cooperating together and working in parallel. Implementation connectionists assert that the brain neural network implements a symbolic processor $(A=(\beta(m),I))$ at a higher and more abstract level. Their research is aimed at figuring out how symbolic processing can be accomplished on a foundation of a neural network [30].

The WWW metaphor can be used to visualize the challenge and its potential implementation/engineering solution: vast amounts of information dispersedly located are stored on the WWW which comprises of a web of computers (information processors) working in parallel. Conceptually, similar to a web of neurons $(A=(f(m),I))$ storing information and working in parallel. Both problems are isomorphic dealing with *information* dispersedly located on multiple information processors.

To be displayed, a single page may require the computation, retrieval, and combination of pieces of information (chunks) from multiple machines on the WWW. The client computer is responsible for requesting, receiving, combining, and displaying information partitioned over multiple WWW computers working in parallel. Information partitioning and parallelism are able to provide a suitable engineering implementation: multiple information processors working in parallel and cooperating through messaging (interchange of information).

Influential cognitive approaches have shown disaffection with sequential (serial) processing in favor of parallel, real-time, and distributed architectures [61, 56]. The Conceptual computing model is a suitable fit for the realistic implementation of a scalable, parallel, real-time, and distributed architecture in a natural fashion. The Conceptual computing architecture is able to scale and handle a vast distributed web of Turing-complete information machines working in parallel and communication via messaging: $\{A_1, \dots, A_n\}$ where $A_i = (f_i(m), I_i)$. A vast amount of information part of $A=(\beta(m),I)$ is partitioned over such web of information machines: each information machine $(A_i = (f_i(m), I_i))$ is responsible for a separate data partition (I_i).

In agreement with implementation connectionists, such web of interconnected information machines $(\{A_1, \dots, A_n\})$ implements a symbolic processor at a higher level [30]: $A=(\beta(m),I)$. The model is also consistent with empirical research regarding engrams and the encoding of memories on specific web of neurons (see Physical Foundation). A scalable and efficient distributed architecture – capable of managing the combinatorial challenge – is achieved through straightforward parallelism and information partitioning.

20.5 Frame Problem

The original frame problem is related to the challenge of representing a changing world [56, 30]. In its narrow technical form, how is it possible to write logical formulae that describe the effects of actions without having to write a large number of accompanying formulae that describe non-effects of those actions? It should be stated that the frame problem, in its narrower technical form, is largely solved (see Frame Problem [56, 30]). Reiter's approach to the frame problem is based on classical logic (monotonic) [56, 30].

The Conceptual cognitive architecture also remains within classical logic, which avoids the need for additional formalisms. Reiter uses database theory as a relevant analogy. The evolution of a database is determined by *explicit* transactions whose purpose is to update the database information. Conceptually, the mind and a database are isomorphic: both are information repositories based on straightforward information operations.

The Conceptual cognitive architecture addresses the frame problem by mimicking the logical mind. Our mind is constantly learning from the environment (changing world) through perception: in the form of incoming pieces of information (Energy).

In consequence, the information (I) contained in our mind is constantly and explicitly being updated based on the environment; for instance, when we hear a new fact in the form of a sentence (S). Additional changes are the result of reasoning: pieces of information being inferred. Thus, changes to the information stored by the Conceptual architecture (I) are explicit: either learned (perceived) from the environment or logically inferred. The architecture is also able to deal with uncertainty in a way that mimics human reasoning and language (see A Natural Language of Concepts).

In agreement with the reductionism, every aspect of cognition and physical reality including the frame problem, must be studied from the perspective of the universal concept of Energy and its laws/Logos (see Physical Foundation). Physical actions and their effects (cause and effect) are reducible to the concept of Energy and its laws (Logos). Notice that all physical objects and beings are reducible to the concept of Energy. The same applies to all physical processes and actions.

Causes and effects (of Energy) can be explicitly expressed in the form of sentences (S) in the natural language; for instance, pushing an object causes it to move (due to transference of Energy). Actions are stated explicitly during communication and their effects logically inferred. There is the implicit assumption that everything else remains unchanged (see Frame Problem [56, 30]). For instance, pushing an object (cause/action) changes its position (effect). It is implicitly assumed that the action does not affect its many non-relevant characteristics (color, size, shape, etc.).

Causal determinism asserts that every event is necessitated by antecedent events and conditions together with the laws of nature/physics (see Causal determinism [30]). Thus, Energy behaves in a deterministic fashion (in agreement with causal determinism). The concepts of cause, effect, conditions, state, event, and even universe are all reducible to the physical concept of Energy and its laws.

"We ought to regard the present state of the universe as the effect of its antecedent state and as the cause of the state that is to follow." Laplace

152

In order to process each incoming message, relevant information contained in memory needs to be identified in order to reason and solve problems. Consider that mind contains a vast amount of information. Only the information relevant to the incoming message needs to be taken into account during processing. In terms of conceptual information (symbolic), the subset K' part of K needs to be considered.

In agreement with PSSH, the Conceptual architecture is able to manipulate symbol structures (Sentences (S) expressed via the concept construct (C)) and solve problems using logical transformations over relevant information. Heuristic search is also a critical aspect in the context of PSSH and the Conceptual architecture (Heuristic Search Hypothesis [25]). Consider that in order to process each message learned (perceived), the vast information stored in memory (I) needs to be searched to identify what is relevant. Furthermore, multiple lines (paths) of logical reasoning based on relevant information may be followed during processing.

In the context of PSSH and AI, such plausible paths are part of the search tree which needs to be traversed while searching [25]. Several suitable heuristic search algorithms have been proposed including depth-first search, bi-directional search, and A* algorithm (see Heuristic Search [56]). The frame problem is related to the combinatorial problem which the Conceptual architecture addresses (see Combinatorial Challenge). The aforementioned heuristic search algorithms also help manage combinatorial explosion.

The scientific challenge of understanding the mind's cognitive function has been compared to the Apollo challenge in terms of difficulty and potential impacts for society [18]. As an example of the frame problem, consider the following question/problem and think about how the mind would solve it (process it).The Conceptual architecture can explain and mimic the mind's behavior.

Who was the first man to walk on the Moon?

In order to process the question, the following pieces of information are relevant. All of them are part of the conceptual information contained in our memory (expressed by K, part of the Conceptual architecture).

- Grammatical rules

- Logical definitions for each symbol part of the question (man, Moon, walk, and so forth).

For our example, it is assumed that our mind contains a vast amount of information/knowledge – and specifically, comprehensive knowledge about space exploration. Based on the question and relevant information, we can logically infer that we are looking for the name of a man: first man to walk on the moon. Obviously, the word *who* refers to a person. Additionally, there are several sentence (S) part of K that are relevant (among many others):

S1: Apollo 11 was the first NASA mission to land on the Moon.

S2 Apollo 11 was manned by Neil Armstrong, Buzz Aldrin, and Michael Collins.

Based on the additional relevant pieces of information, we can logically infer that one of the members of the Apollo 11 crew was the first man to walk on the Moon which significantly narrows the search to three possibilities. As a next step, the information relevant to these three individuals needs to be searched.

The following relevant piece of information (biographical fact) further narrows the search to a single man and resolves the question.

S3: Neil Armstrong was an American astronaut and the first person to walk on the Moon.

Based on this line of logical reasoning (path of reasoning), the answer can be inferred: Neil Armstrong.

A different line of logical reasoning (path of reasoning) can be followed based on other pieces of relevant information:

S4: Persons that travel to the Moon are called astronauts

154

Based on the relevant information, we can logically infer that an astronaut was the first person to walk on the Moon, which significantly narrows our search. There is a limited number of astronauts. Once again, as a next step, biographical information relevant to each astronaut needs to be searched. S3 can be found again which solves the question. The answer can be logically inferred: Neil Armstrong

Obviously, there is a large number of other sentences that are not relevant during processing (part of K). A number of them may even include some of the words, part of the question. All such sentences need to be discarded or excluded, as irrelevant. For instance,

- Many people like to look at the Moon
- The Moon has a round shape
- People often enjoy walking under the Moon

For each astronaut, there are also many biographical facts that are not relevant and need to be discarded. As a second example, the Yale shooting problem will be presented. The situation is described by the following sentence:

S1: A loaded gun was fired at Fred

In order to process the sentence, relevant information (part of K) has to be taken into account which again includes: grammatical rules and word definitions. Additionally, there are several sentence (S) part of K that are relevant (among many others):

S2: If a gun is fired at a person then s/he may be wounded

S3: If a person is wounded then s/he may die

S4: If a loaded gun is fired then it will contain one less bullet

S5: A loaded gun has one or more bullets

The following sentences (S) that can be logically inferred based on classical logical (monotonic):

- Fred may have died or been wounded.
- The gun has one less bullet and it may be still loaded.

Later, we may learn additional pieces of information (sentences/facts stated explicitly). For instance,

S6: The gun had only one bullet left when it was fired

If so, we can logically deduct:

- The gun was not longer loaded after firing.

Later, we may also explicitly learn additional facts. For instance,

S7: Fred didn't die nor was wounded by the bullet.

The latter piece of information represents a certain fact which deals with the uncertainty found earlier (S2 and S3). Notice that a potential logical reply to S1 would be trying to get additional information (knowledge) to deal with uncertainty:

Q: Was Fred wounded or kill?

Notice that the fact (S7) does not contradict the earlier inference expressing uncertainty: Fred may have died or been wounded. However, such inference must be discarded (not longer valid) given the new fact (S7). The previous examples illustrate how the Conceptual architecture is able to handle uncertainty by mimicking the logical mind and human communication (For additional information, see A Natural Language of Concepts). Again, the Conceptual approach is based on classical logic (monotonic).

The Conceptual architecture mainly focuses on high-level cognitive abilities (symbolic processing). However, it should be *briefly* mentioned that the unified Conceptual architecture and associated computing model are able to readily accommodate all forms of information (Energy) – both symbolic and non-symbolic: images, sounds, smells, and so forth. Based on the WWW metaphor symbolic and non-symbolic information may be linked together (see Cognitive/AI Architecture). In a similar fashion, our brain is capable of associating the symbol/word *astronaut* with the appropriate non-symbolic entity(s): for instance, the image of an astronaut in a space suit.

Keep in mind that both symbolic and non-symbolic information represent forms of Energy. For instance, you may remember watching Neil Armstrong leaving the Apollo lunar module (Eagle) and stepping on the Moon for the first time. This is probably a memorable event not easy to forget. Such relevant piece of information (non-symbolic) would be relevant to answer the question/problem posed earlier. The symbols *astronaut* or *Apollo11* may trigger the recollection of the event stored in memory. It represents a line of reasoning in which symbolic and non-symbolic cognitive abilities (and information) are combined as part of a unified architecture. The Conceptual cognitive architecture is able to explain and mimic such unified abilities.

20.6 Conceptual Deductive Approach

Think about a mobile application required to communicate with the user and provide personal assistant capabilities: voice activated calls, directions, reservations, weather reports, traffic alerts, trivia, and so on.

In order to improve service, increase efficiency and reduce delays, modern computer systems are being required to provide advanced communication and cognitive/AI capabilities. Examples are everywhere these days: banking system, car systems, reservation systems, and so on. The Conceptual computing model and associated cognitive architecture are ideal when dealing deal with such computer communication challenges.

Consider the question who was Mr. Jefferson's wife? It is a vague question, on purpose. As you can see, there is no enough information (i.e. information associations) to precisely define what is being asked. Additional information (context) needs to be given so that your mind is able to make the right associations. For instance, the following: the question is referring to Mr. Thomas Jefferson, principal author of the U.S. Declaration of Independence.

You may not know the answer to the question, which is fine, because it helps illustrate how the mind processes information associations. The same principles apply to any other questions for which you do not know the answer. It is also relevant to applications like the mobile app being discussed. To answer the proposed question, you will need to find sources of information related to the subject. In particular, you may need to use the internet and read Mr. Jefferson's biography.

From the question itself, several associations can be derived that will help resolve the proposed problem. Specifically, the question is asking for the identity of his wife (X). From the question you can deduct the following information associations (using logical transformations):

X is a Person

X is a Woman

X represents Mrs. Jefferson (unknown piece of information). You can find the solution by reading his biography and looking for people related to Mr. Jefferson. At some point during the search, you should find a sentence like: "... Jefferson married Martha ...". This sentence gives enough information to answer the question. However, there is one additional information association that needs to be made in order to arrive to the answer. Since Mr. Jefferson married Martha, they became husband and wife.

The proposed problem can be specified using the conceptual construct (C) and notation. C represents Mr. Jefferson:

C = ((name, Mr. Jefferson), (wife, X), (principal author, Declaration of Independence))

X= ((Person, true) , (Woman, true))

After reading the sentence S = ((Mr. Jefferson), (married), (Martha)) the following associations can be drawn. If two people (X, Y) get married, it can be logically deducted that Y becomes the wife of X and X becomes the husband of Y. Using the conceptual notation:

158

$((X), (marries), (Y)) \rightarrow (X\text{->wife} = Y)$ and $(Y\text{->husband} = X)$

The same associations can be found by retrieving the definition of 'wife' from the dictionary. Therefore, the answer is found: Martha

Martha $= X =$ ((Person, true), (Woman, true))

If there is a logical answer to the question, the mind will find it, provided that the question contains enough information (i.e. information associations). As a later section demonstrates, the deductive approach based on information associations can be generalized and applied to arbitrary information domains.

For the specific mobile virtual assistant, consider the following question: Can I make a flight reservation to Hawaii for next Tuesday? For this specific question, the mobile assistant will need to handle the concept of reservation and its associations in order to proceed: city of departure, city of destination, time, date, airline, ticket class, etc.

The concept of reservation (R) can be expressed as follows:
$R =$ ((passenger, me), (city of departure, my home city), (city of destination, Hawaii), (airline, X), (date, next Tuesday), (ticket class, X_1))

As shown, the question itself will contain some of the required associations. Some other associations can be implicit (city of departure, passenger). The application needs to inquire about the unknown associations before searching for potential flights.

The application may need to handle other concepts and associations. For instance, the user may use concepts like 'next Monday', Today, Tomorrow, and so forth while communicating information about a specific task. A realistic implementation should be able to handle these concepts.

A more advanced system should be able to handle concepts like: "same flight as last time", "tickets for the whole family", and so on. The mind is able to handle all these concepts and associations. A computer system, based on a conceptual approach, can do it too.

Many concepts and associations may already be known by the mobile application, based on previous interactions, like personal information, family members, previous itineraries, preferences, and so forth. Such personal information can be conveniently and securely stored by the mobile device.

The conceptual deductive process described earlier can be generalized. The question itself provides a group of concepts and related information associations. Other relevant concepts and associations may already be known (knowledge acquired previously). The whole group of concepts (I) can be expressed as:

$C1 = ((x11, y11), \dots , (x1n, y1n))$
$C2 = ((x21, y21), \dots , (x2n, y2n))$
$\dots$

$X = Cn = ((xn1, yn1), \dots , (xnn, \ ynn))$

In order to resolve the unknown association Ci->xij = X, additional information associations are required. New associations (xi, yi) and concepts (C) can be logically deducted from the existing associations or gathered from the new information being acquired (learned). Such information can be searched for, read, and/or requested from the user. It comes in the form of sentences expressed using the conceptual notation, S= ((x1, y1) ... (xn, yn)).

The process can be repeated until an answer is found or until the information sources and clues are exhausted. Notice that C1, , Cn can be represented as a graph, where the nodes represent concepts (C1, , Cn). The edges represent information associations. By using concepts and information associations, a computer system can realistically mirror the procedure described above and find in deterministic ways the solution to proposed questions – based on logical transformations.

160

I hope you had the chance to browse through Mr. Jefferson's biography. You may have come across his ideas and writings. In any case, I would like to leave you with enlightened concepts, grasped by a timeless and inspired mind, which define the idea of America (i.e. creed):

"We hold these truths to be self-evident, that all people are created equal, that they are endowed by their Creator with certain unalienable Rights, that among these are Life, Liberty and the pursuit of Happiness."

Note: Mr. Jefferson would not mind the minor edition.

20.6.1 Mathematical Demonstration

In order to demonstrate the conceptual deductive approach, a graph representation can be used. $C_1, , C_n$ can be represented as the nodes of the graph. Associations of the form (x_i, y_j) represent the edges of the graph. The answer to the question is represented by one of the edges: C_i->$x_{ij} = X$

It is necessary to prove that the conceptual approach can find the correct answer (X) based on known information (provided and acquired): $I = \{C_1, \dots, C_n\}$

There are three possible cases that need to be proved:

a) X does not exist according the information known: $I = \{C_1, \dots, C_n\}$. Therefore no such association exists. The correct answer is found: no such association exists.

b) Explicit information association. The association is made explicit as part of $\{C_1, \dots, C_n\}$. In other words, C_i->$x_{ij} = C_k$ is part of $\{C_1, \dots, C_n\}$. Therefore the correct answer is found: $X = C_k$.

c) Logical deduction. The association can be logically deducted from known information $\{C_1, \dots, C_n\}$. To prove this case, the pertinent inference rules $\{P_{e,1}, \dots, P_{e,n}\}$ need to be looked at.

Consider the predicate P that represents the association between C and X:

$$P (C, X) = (Ci\text{->}xij = X)$$

And all the rules related to the creation of the information association (edge) between C and X:

$$Pe,1 \rightarrow P (C, X)$$
$$Pe,2 \rightarrow P (C, X)$$
$$.....$$
$$Pe,n \rightarrow P (C, X)$$

The cause and effect principle applies. If there is an association between C and X (predicate P), at least one predecessor predicate (Pe,k) needs to be true for the association to exist. In other words, for $P(C,X)$ to be true, at least one predecessor predicate (Pe,k) needs to be true so that $P(C,X)$ can be logically deducted.

If the predicate Pe,k is true, we prove $P(C,X)$: Ci->xij=X. To directly prove Pe, k, explicit information needs to exist (step b). If Pe,k is part of $\{C1, ...,Cn\}$, Pe,k is true. Therefore the answer is found. If Pe,k cannot be proved using $\{C1, ..., Cn\}$, logical deduction (step c) needs to attempted to prove Pe,k.

The process is repeated until finding explicit information to prove Pe,k or until the inference rules are exhausted. In which case, the correct answer cannot be found using logical deduction and known information $I = \{C1, ..., Cn\}$. In summary, for each predicate P there is a group of predecessor predicates (Pe,k) that needs to be checked (zero or more):

$$Pe,1 \text{ v } Pe,2 ....v Pe,n \rightarrow P (C,X) \text{ where } n>=0$$

It has been demonstrated that for all the possible scenarios, the correct answer is found, either explicitly or by logical deduction. The process is also able to offer a detailed and rational explanation (i.e. logical) of how the answer was derived based on information associations.

Consider the example provided. According to the demonstration, there are three possible scenarios:

a) X does not exist. If the sentence S = (Mr. Jefferson did not have a wife) is part of {C1, ... ,Cn}. The current answer is found: no such association exists.

b) Explicit association. If, for instance, the sentence S = (Martha was Mr. Jefferson's wife) is part of {C1, ..., Cn}. The correct answer is found: X = C->wife = Mrs. Martha Jefferson

c) Logical deduction. While applying logical deduction to find a wife association (C->wife=X) the pertinent inference rules need to be checked:

X married Y → X->wife = Y ^ Y->husband=X

The predicates involved are P: Y became the wife of X, and Pe,1(X,Y): X married Y. The information provided {C1, ... , Cn} is checked looking for explicit information to prove Pe,1 (X married Y). If such association is explicitly found S= ((Mr. Jefferson) (married) (Martha)), the correct answer can be given.

In other words, Pe,1 (X,Y) is true, therefore P is true by logical deduction. Otherwise the answer cannot be logically deducted since the inference rules have been exhausted. Unless, there are additional inference rules like the one associated with the concept of 'Honeymoon':

X went on a Honeymoon with Y → X married Y →
X->wife=Y ^ Y->husband=X

If so, such inference rule (deeper level) needs to be checked against known information (step c).

If incomplete information is provided, the deductive process is unable to produce comprehensive results. Consider the sentence S = (Our friend, Mr. Jefferson, married this year). It does not give enough information to determine a specific answer (name).

Obviously, in terms of implementation considerations, it is necessary to provide the system with a complete set of conceptual information (I) and inference rules, in order to expect comprehensive answers.

Notice that known information $I = \{C1, \ldots, Cn\}$ can be *massaged* (or preprocessed) to avoid deep levels of inference as a way of producing better performance. Inference rules may not have to be given explicitly.

An advanced AI/cognitive system may be able to generate inference rules automatically based on the meaning or definition of the concepts involved. For example, the inference rules above can be automatically derived from the definitions (meaning) of 'wife', 'husband', 'married' and 'honeymoon'.

There is another way in which the conceptual deductive process can be demonstrated. Let us assume that the correct answer is $Y \neq X$. The answer given (X) is incorrect:

$P(C,Y)$ is true. $Ci\text{-}>xij=Y$, where $Y \neq X$

If there is an explicit association, the answer Y needs to be consistent with known information $\{C1, \ldots, Cn\}$. However, this would be a contradiction: Y would have been the answer given, by applying the conceptual process, not X. Therefore, inference had to be used in order to derive the answer Y:

$Pe,1 \text{ v } Pe,2 \ldots.\text{v } Pe,n \rightarrow P(C,Y)$

Based on the assumption, ~P(C,X) is true. Therefore, the following can be inferred:

~P(C,X) → ~(Pe,1 v Pe,2 ....v Pe,n)

~P(C,X) → ~Pe,1 ^ ~Pe,2 ....^ ~Pe,n

This represents a contradiction because X was given as the correct answer: at least one predicate Pe,k had to be true. Therefore Y = X, the correct answer.

20.7 Conceptual Abductive Approach (rules of probable cause and effect)

"Probability is expectation founded upon partial knowledge. A perfect acquaintance with all the circumstances affecting the occurrence of an event would change expectation into certainty, and leave neither room nor demand for a theory of probabilities." George Boole

A rich set of inferences can be derived from the information stored by the Conceptual machine either via deductive reasoning or adductive reasoning. In the latter case, the goal is finding one or more reasons (causes) to explain the effect. There may be several plausible reasons (hypothesis) for a given effect that need to be considered. In deductive thinking, we go from the causes to the effect. In abductive reasoning the process is reversed. Abductive reasoning is a form of *logical inference.*

Psychologists and philosophers tend to agree that abduction is used in everyday reasoning (see abduction [30]). The term abduction was coined by Charles Sander Peirce (see Peirce on Abduction [30]): "abduction is the process of forming explanatory hypotheses." Consider the following examples taken from common sense knowledge:

a) if a person cries then s/he may be sad

b) if a person cries s/he may have something stuck in her/his eye

c) if the grass is wet it may have rained

d) if the grass is wet the sprinkler may have been on

All the sentences (S) above can be represented using NATURAL and the concept construct (see Language Examples). Many of them follow a cause and effect structure: if S then S' where S and S' represent probable cause and effect respectively (see May – Abductive Reasoning).

In general, the following rules or principles of probable cause and effect can be stated.

a) If probable cause is true, then the effect may be true.
b) If effect is true, then the probable cause may be true.

(cause$\rightarrow$P(effect)>0)$\equiv$(effect$\rightarrow$P(cause)>0), cause and effect are sentences (S).

It can also be expressed with the same semantics, as follows,

P(effect|cause)>0$\equiv$P(cause|effect)>0 where cause and effect are sentences (S).

Multiple causes can potentially be associated with a particular effect. The rules apply for each probable cause associated to a given effect. A web consisting of interconnected probable causes and their corresponding effects can be readily created to represent common sense facts and make inferences.

In terms of depth, several levels of inference are possible. For instance, if a mother cries there are several probable causes. The computer is able to reason. Potential lines of reasoning, based on the relevant context above, may be: a) she may be sad because her daughter went missing, or b) she may be sad because her daughter got sick.

The probable causes can be ordered in terms of potential likelihood. *If available,* numerical values may be used as well for ordering and probability comparison. The first potential choice is used because it is the most probable logical cause (reason): if a person cries then s/he is probably sad. On the other hand, the computer is able to 'reason' and recognize several probable causes – using multiple levels of inference. This example also elucidates how the machine is able to judge probabilities, and choose the most probable cause.

A large number of common sense facts can be represented and inferences made based on the rules above, which are similar to Polya's patterns [63]. A key difference is that the logical implication (cause → effect) is not a premise. Instead, (cause → P (effect) > 0) is used: the cause *may* bring forth the effect. On the other hand, the mathematical demonstration is very similar relying on Bayes' theorem (see Mathematical Demonstration). The approach also emphasizes the intimate and realistic relationship between cause and effect (i.e. causality).

"... We know that in the realm of natural science, the absolute connexion between the initial and final elements of a problem, exhibited in the mathematical form, fitly symbolizes that physical necessity which binds together effect and cause." George Boole [1].

Consider the following common sense examples:

a) P (fire | smoke) > 0 ≡ P (smoke | fire) > 0

If there is smoke, it may have been caused by a fire

b) P (being sick | symptom) > 0 ≡ P (symptom | being sick) > 0

c) P (burglary | house alarm) > 0 ≡ P (house alarm | burglary) > 0

d) P (distraction | car accident) > 0 ≡ P (car accident | distraction) > 0

d) P (smoking | cancer) > 0 ≡ P (cancer | smoking) > 0

For instance, a distraction can be texting while driving. A *possible* cause (hypothesis) is discarded if/when a new piece of information (S) is received that invalidates it: (~cause). This is consistent with human reasoning in which new evidence (information) invalidates or corroborates hypotheses made earlier about probable causes. In abductive thinking, we deal with probable hypotheses that may or may not be true.

167

Notice that in the context of the Conceptual approach and the natural language, no numbers (probability values) are typically required for knowledge representation or reasoning. Determining exact probability values is a challenging task [60, 63] which the Conceptual abductive approach avoids. On the other hand, numeric values to express probability can be used in conjunction with the approach (when available).

It should be stated that the principles of probable cause and effect are particularly applicable when there is a 'physical connection' between cause and effect (physical necessity). It is also assumed that a cause always precedes its effect(s).

The previous statement and Boole's remarks are in agreement with causal determinism which is the idea that every event is necessitated by antecedent events and conditions together with the laws of nature/physics (see Causal determinism [30]).

"We ought to regard the present state of the universe as the effect of its antecedent state and as the cause of the state that is to follow." Laplace

We must also think about reductionism and Energy, since nature is reducible to the concept Energy and its laws (Logos). In physical reality, the concepts of cause, effect, condition, state, and event are all reducible to the physical concept of Energy and its laws (see Physical Foundation). Such reduction brings forth theoretical simplicity and unification.

20.7.1 Mathematical Demonstration

A probabilistic function is a function P: L → R where L represents a proposition language. A and B are sentences in the language L.

- If A is false, then $P(A) = 0$
- If A is true, then $P(A) = 1$
- $P(\sim A) = 1 - P(A)$

The conditional probability of A given B is defined as follows:

$P(A|B) = P(A \wedge B)/P(B) = P(B|A) * P(A) / P(B)$ where $P(B) > 0$

The following rules or principles of probable cause and effect can be stated using logic and probabilities. Cause and effect are sentences (S) in the language L.

cause → P (effect) > 0 ≡ effect → P (cause) > 0

With the following semantics:

a) If probable cause is true, then the effect may be true.

b) If effect is true, then the probable cause may be true.

The rules should seem intuitive and can also be expressed using the Bayesian formalism:

$P(\text{effect}|\text{cause}) > 0 \equiv P(\text{cause}|\text{effect}) > 0$ where $P(\text{cause}) > 0$ and $P(\text{effect}) > 0$

The mathematical demonstration is straightforward using Bayes' theorem:

$P(\text{effect} | \text{cause}) = P(\text{cause} | \text{effect}) * P(\text{effect}) / P(\text{cause})$

$P(\text{cause} | \text{effect}) = P(\text{effect} | \text{cause}) * P(\text{cause}) / P(\text{effect})$

Since P (cause | effect) > 0, P (cause) > 0, and P (effect) > 0, we infer that P (effect | cause) > 0. By assuming P (effect | cause) > 0, it can also be derived that P (cause | effect) > 0. Actually, P (effect | cause) is directly proportional to P (cause | effect) and vice versa.

The demonstration can be generalized to multiple probable causes for a given effect: $\text{cause}_1, \text{cause}_2, ..., \text{cause}_n$

$P(\text{effect}|\text{cause}_i) > 0 \equiv P(\text{cause}_i|\text{effect}) > 0$ where $P(\text{cause}_i) > 0$ and $P(\text{effect}) > 0$

169

The previous demonstration is very similar to the one used for Polya's pattern: "The verification of a consequence renders a conjecture more credible". A key difference is that the logical implication (cause → effect) is not a premise. Instead, (cause → P (effect) > 0) is used: the cause may bring forth the effect.

Polya's pattern can be expressed in mathematical terms,

$$((cause → effect) \& effect) → (P(cause | effect) > P(cause))$$

Assuming P(cause) > 0 and P (effect) > 0

- P (cause | effect) = P (effect | cause) * P (cause) / P (effect)

- P (effect | cause) = 1, since (cause → effect)

- P (cause | effect) = P (cause) / P (effect)

Since P (effect) <= 1, we obtain

$$P(cause | effect) >= P (cause)$$

20.8 A Natural Language of Concepts

This section represents work/research in progress. As part of the conceptual computing model and cognitive architecture, a language (NATURAL) can be proposed able to mimic human communication capabilities. Let us think about such a language using a conceptual design methodology (CD), which calls for the specification of concepts required for the solution.

In order to identify the relevant concepts associated to the problem, consider the analogy in which you talk to a friend to accomplish a

170

specific task or procedure. The first concept that comes to mind is the concept of procedure. A procedure (P) is defined as the sequence of steps (S1, S2, ,Sn) required to accomplish a specific task. It can be expressed using the conceptual notation:

$P = (S_1, S_2, \ldots, S_n)$ where $S_1, S_2, \ldots, S_n$ represent the steps/sentences to be executed.

Each step/sentence (S_i) is also a concept. It comes in the form of sentences in the natural language (L) and can be represented using the conceptual form (C): $S_i = (a_1, a_2, \ldots, a_m)$

For example, the following straightforward procedure can be expressed using the conceptual form described above:

if today is my wife's birthday, please notify me

or

Please notify me on my wife's birthday

In order to perform the task, your friend will need to know the meaning of the following concepts and associations: Today, wife, wife's birthday, notify, me. Let us safely assume that your friend knows all or most of them. Any piece of information that is not known can be requested as part of a dialog. For instance: When is your wife's birthday?

The process just described can be generalized to handle any arbitrary procedure. The procedure is executed sequentially, one step at a time as described above. As usual, bear in mind that concepts are highly reusable entities and can be applied to diverse scenarios. The concept of procedure (P) is not an exception. In summary, the definition of the proposed language consists of the following main concepts:

a) **Natural Language**: concept construct (C) that consists of a set of words (i.e. symbols) and their associated definitions. L = {((symbol1), Definition (symbol1)), … , ((symboln), Definition (symboln))}.
b) **Procedure**: $P = (S_1, S_2, \ldots, Sn)$

c) **Step/Sentence**: $S = (a_1, a_2, \ldots , am)$ where $a1, a2, \ldots , a_m$ are information associations that reference other concepts part of the hypothetical language.

Since the steps are expressed using the natural language (L), there will be many other concepts, taken from reality, that need to be considered. The context of the conversation is one important concept to take into consideration. Words like 'this' and 'it' will have specific meaning depending on the context.

The example above will require concepts like today, wife and birthday. New concepts can be incrementally added to the language based on their information domains and the intended application. For instance, a restricted information domain can deal with time related concepts (*when*): 'next Tuesday', 'tomorrow', 'today', and so forth.

Another information domain can deal with location related concepts (*where*): 'Hawaii', 'Orlando', 'Seattle', 'home' 'in', 'on', 'above', 'near', 'at the window', and so forth. Yet another information domain may deal with concepts related to people (*who*): 'friends', 'family', 'wife', 'daughter', 'son', 'me' and so on.

As demonstrated, a conceptual approach can be utilized to ask an intelligent person to perform a specific task or procedure. There is no real reason why the natural language cannot be mimicked using the proposed approach.

Conceptually, there is no difference between human and person-machine communication. The same concepts and principles apply to both scenarios including information, messaging, dialog, and the other concepts found in reality. Both situations are conceptually equivalent or isomorphic.

Actually, we must say that computer systems *need* to bridge the 'communication gap' and be improved by mimicking human languages. Such technology should have an impact on many other technologies including human-machine interfaces, IVR systems, robotics, information retrieval systems based on web technologies, database interfaces, and so on. Machine learning based on concepts should also be included.

At this point, you may be wondering how the computer is supposed to execute the given procedure. In reality, it should mimic your friend's thinking patterns in regards to how the conceptual information is processed. Based on the proposed approach, Information (I) can be represented as a group of concepts: I = {C1, C2, ... ,Cn}. Suppose that the given procedure should be executed on your mobile phone.

At some point in time, before running the procedure, you need to communicate the following pieces of information (associations):

My name is George Boole.

My wife is Mrs. Mary Boole.

Her birthday is on July 11.

Using the conceptual notation (C):

C1 = ((name, George Boole), (wife, C2))

C2 = ((name, Mary Boole), (birthday, July 11))

All the representations are semantically equivalent. On the other hand, the concepts and information associations may be easier to visualize using the syntax employed by the proposed conceptual language:

C1-> name = George Boole

C1->wife = C2

C2->name = Mary Boole

C2->birthday = July 11

if (today == C2->birthday) then notify C1;   //if today is my wife's birthday please notify me)

Again, the mobile device may not have enough information and request additional items: George, what is Mrs. Boole's birthday? Based on the concepts and information associations above, the mobile device will be able to execute the procedure, one step at a time.

The example should also illustrate the algebraic and logical properties of the process which can be visualized as an algebra of concepts (or meaning): concepts are substituted by semantically equivalent concepts (same meaning) – manipulated based on logical transformations.

$X = 1$

$Y = X$

Therefore, $Y = 1$

Concepts and information associations are logically manipulated instead of numbers and letters. In the end, all of them are symbols. George Boole gives us insight into the matter based on his remarkable conclusions [1,22]:

"The truth that the ultimate laws of thought are mathematical in their form, viewed in connexion with the fact of the possibility of error, establishes a ground for some remarkable conclusions. If we directed our attention to the scientific truth alone, we might be led to infer an almost exact parallelism between the intellectual operations and the movements of external nature.

Suppose any one conversant with physical science, but unaccustomed to reflect upon the nature of his own faculties, to have been informed, that it had been proved, that the laws of those faculties were mathematical; it is probable that after the first feelings of incredulity had subsided, the impression would arise, that the order of thought must, therefore, be as necessary as that of the material universe. We know that in the realm of natural science, the absolute connexion between the initial and final elements of a problem, exhibited in the mathematical form, fitly symbolizes that physical necessity which binds together effect and cause."

Boole is specifically referring to logical thinking, mathematically modeled by what is known today as Boolean algebraic logic or Boolean logic.

Natural languages are dynamic and versatile entities changing constantly by adding new words and concepts (symbols). They do not consist of a fixed number of constructs which should also call our attention. A procedure is a concept, pure information: a fact that has some interesting consequences.

174

The human mind learns procedures to perform new tasks based on concepts already mastered. A procedure can be learned by several means including written and verbal communication. The proposed language mirrors and shares the same abilities. Information (data) becomes the 'program' so to speak. Take for example a cooking recipe which is a concept. On the other hand, it also represents a procedure (program) that defines a written sequence of steps to be followed *by* the mind.

Obviously, natural languages have many advantages. Consider the concepts of expressiveness, conciseness, richness, efficiency, simplicity, and realism. In the abstract, obviously the proposed language mirrors and absorbs these *natural* qualities. It can take just a few concepts to communicate elaborate ideas. A significant amount of information can be communicated with one concise message:

Please make reservations to Hawaii for the whole family departing next Thursday on Pacific airlines. Don't forget to make arrangements for Copernicus (family pet).

Try to emulate the exchange using other forms of communication or interface and the difference should become evident. Concepts and information associations make it possible. No wonder, given the fact that human communication has evolved to become the ultimate mechanism of interchanging information. Although no small task, the main implementation challenges become the faithful (realistic) imitation of the existing human communication model based on concepts. A divide-and-conquer engineering approach ensures steady improvements over time.

Since a Conceptual computing model and language are being discussed, it probably makes sense for a new computer to host it: Heuristic, Algebraic, and Logical Computer or Holistic, Algebraic, and Logical Computer. Information expressed as a group of concepts: $I=\{C1,C2, \dots , Cn\}$; n measures the number of known concepts (n = cardinality (K)).

An early version of the implemented system should be able to handle 100 concepts or so, in several domains: Time (when), Location (where), national airlines, job titles. Such a system should be able to answer relatively straightforward and useful (common) queries in the natural language:

a) Can you please find all the Pacific flights for Hawaii that depart next week?

b) Retrieve all the papers that have been published in the last ten years on Artificial Intelligent.

c) Please find all the teaching positions that opened this week in Florida.

A relatively small number of information domains and concepts are involved. It is assumed that the system also has access to databases or web interfaces hosting the requested information. Once an information domain is implemented, it can be reused for arbitrary applications based on the proposed language.

The mind is able to reuse the same concepts across daily activities. As shown above, the straightforward domains of time and location can be applied to diverse applications: Mobile reservations, information retrieval, and other applications dealing with these information domains.

For instance, an initial version of the language targeted to mobile devices (NATURAL100) should provide enough capabilities to control most of the phone functionality: weather, news, calls, calendar, trivia, electronic reader (eReader), SMS messaging, GPS, directions, CallerID, voice activated (IVR) features, speech synthesis, safe driving, and so on. All personal information can be safely stored by the device: family members, address, preferences, payment information, passwords, health information, primary physician, and so forth.

As an example of a custom application, a healthcare professional would be able to instruct a device or smartphone using the proposed language and appropriate information domains (who, where, when, etc.):

  a) Please remind Mr. Smith to take his medicine every four hours. Make an appointment for him to see the doctor on the 22nd and remind him.

b) In case of an emergency call his family, his doctor, and paramedics. If requested, give his location and health history to the paramedics.

Several preexisting procedures would be required: remind, call, make an appointment, etc. The proposed system can describe in detail, using the natural language, a specific procedure and/or the logical deduction based on the known conceptual information. The proposed system can 'learn' new concepts based on the definition of the ones already mastered, much the same as your friend is able to learn new information and make new associations. For instance, it can learn the meaning of Tomorrow and Hawaii, by making new associations based on information already known:

Tomorrow is the day after today (Time domain)
Hawaii is an island in the United States (Location domain)

If the above is what the series 100 can do, we can only imagine what the series 10,000 will do, after its conceptual information bank has been increased couple of orders of magnitude. The proposed language can scale to accommodate multiple domains and a large bank of concepts.

The aspect of ambiguity becomes a bigger issue as the number of information domains and concepts increases. Hypothetically, the series 10,000 should be able to 'learn' autonomously by reading and associating new concepts to the large bank of known ones. Similar to what the minds does when learning a new word or idea based on its definition, which provides associations to known concepts.

For the engineering and practical perspectives, the challenges are somewhat similar to the computer graphics arena. The early systems were able to display a small amount of objects using a limited level of realism. After a few years of progress, the level of realism achieved is significant, based on additional processing power and improved realistic techniques. The analogy can be applied to the proposed language based on its conceptual capabilities and an incremental divide-and-conquer strategy applied to the universe of concepts.

An increase in 'conceptual understanding' should result in better and more realistic human-computer communication, over time: a system able to master a substantial amount of concepts associated to the reality surrounding the application domain; and able to follow learned procedures using logical deductions based on acquired knowledge.

The mind is able to handle a substantial amount of conceptual information as the basis of highly intelligent behavior. On the other hand, regardless of how far the language is able to evolve, it should represent a substantial improvement when compared with traditional approaches of computer-human communication not based on a conceptual paradigm mimicked from the mind.

20.8.1 Primary/Elementary Concepts

There are three primary/elementary concepts taken from physics (see Physical Foundation).

Energy/Mass: all entities in physical reality are part of this category including all living beings and unanimated objects. Every physical action represents transference or transformation of Energy.
Time: category related to Time (When): now, today, tomorrow, next week, Monday, etc.
Space: category related to Space (Where): in, on, above, near, at the window, etc.

Per previous remarks, the concepts of time and space represent abstract entities (mental constructs) that only exists within the mind (see Physical Foundation). We can comfortably work with three (3) *primary/elementary concepts* to mirror the way with think, without excessively upsetting natural conceptual parsimony, so to speak. The primary/elementary concepts above are consistent with linguistic reductionism which states that everything can be described in a language with a limited number of core concepts, and combinations of those concepts.

Intuitively, you can think of the primary/elementary concepts like primary colors. Any other color can be created by combining them which ensures completeness. Conversely, an arbitrary color can be understood by separating the primary colors involved in its composition; in agreement with Frege's principle of compositionality. Ideas of *physical reality* can be expressed by appropriately combining these primary/elementary concepts according to the grammatical/semantic rules of the language. For instance, consider a typical sentence that combines the primary concepts: "I travelled to Orlando last Monday".

20.8.2 Mathematical Universe

"There is in my opinion no important theoretical difference between natural languages and the artificial languages of logicians; indeed, I consider it possible to comprehend the syntax and semantics of both kinds of languages within a single *natural* and *mathematically* precise theory" Richard Montague

Human languages and fundamental areas of the language of mathematics, seek to express the *same physical* reality. They are part of the same concept: language. They are also ruled by equivalent principles of logic, meaning, and truth. Although the symbols are different, equivalent mathematical (i.e. logical) rules and concepts apply.

"We know that in the realm of natural science, the absolute connexion between the initial and final elements of a problem, exhibited in the mathematical form, fitly symbolizes that physical necessity which binds together effect and cause."

George Boole [1]

In the context of a 'Mathematical Universe', ruled by natural laws that can be precisely expressed in the language of mathematics, this should be expected [31]. Consider the mathematical nature of the concepts being described as part of the proposed Turing-complete Conceptual model: concept construct (C), Language (L), Procedure (P), Sentence (S), Knowledge (K), and logical processing of information $(\beta(m))$.

The main challenge is finding appropriate ways of mapping meaning (i.e. semantics) to mathematical concepts. The information domains of Time (when) and Space (where) are relatively straightforward to implement because of size and their mathematical nature.

In other words, concepts associated with Time and Space can be readily expressed using the language of mathematics. These information categories are also highly reusable across application domains.

20.8.3 Natural Classification of Information

I KEEP six honest serving-men

(They taught me all I knew);

Their names are What and Why and When

And How and Where and Who.

…

Rudyard Kipling

While implementing a natural language, it makes sense to mimic human communication by classifying concepts within the following categories or information domains: based on the interrogative pronouns (Who, What), Associated With, When, Where, Why, and How. These words part of the natural language allows us to gather *information* about all aspects of reality. A 'natural' classification, if you will. As expected, information is at the center of it.

The natural classification is also related to the 5 W's (Who, What, When, Where, and Why) whose answers are fundamental in the process of information gathering. They are often utilized in the context of journalism, education, police investigations, and research as a way of finding the complete story about a subject matter – originally, rooted in the method proposed by the Greek Hermagoras of dividing a topic into its 'seven circumstances'.

It should be emphasized, that the classification pursues a strong foundation on mathematics and physics to match the *mathematical (logical)* essence of known nature and its physical laws. Several categories and associated concepts are tightly related or reducible to the primary concepts discussed earlier (Energy, Time, and Space). For instance, arbitrary physical objects and beings are reducible to the concept of Energy. Physical processes are also reducible to the concept of Energy and governed by its laws (Logos).

180

Based on a natural classification, concepts can be classified as follows according to the type of information (i.e. conceptual information) being conveyed:

Who (People/Animals). Concepts related with individuals and their interrelationships: 'me', 'wife', 'aunt', 'my doctor', 'my supervisor', 'my friends', and so forth. Animals are informally included as part of this category since they are often intelligent beings referenced using names or personal pronouns.

What. Concepts related to physical objects (i.e. concrete) and actions in the real world: ticket, airplane, travel. This category also includes abstract entities like reservation, bank account, and so on.

When (Time). Concepts related with Time: Today, Tomorrow, 'Next week', 'Next Tuesday at 9:am', and so on.

Where (Space). Concepts related to Space: Orlando, Hawaii, Florida, Distance, Up, Down, and so on.

How (P/Es). Sequence of steps that describe how to accomplish a procedure (P) or how something happened: (S1, S2, ... , Sn) where S_i is a sentence in the natural language expressed using the Concept construct (C). In the latter scenario, each sentence (S) represents an Event (E) in the past.

Why (Cause/Effect). Logical relationships between cause and effect. For instance, she is my aunt *because* she is the sister of my father (or mother): $(C->father->sister = Y) \lor (C->mother->sister = Y) \equiv (C->aunt = Y)$. Logical relationships can be derived directly from the definition of the concept in the natural language (L).

Associated With (Relation): Information associations that represent relationships between Concepts. They are expressed using the arrow (C1->association = C2). For instance, the relationship of ownership.

In general, Concept attributes or properties are represented using information associations (C->associations). Relations are also expressed using information associations. Notice the highly associative nature of the Conceptual model which mimics our thinking patterns. Plural forms are expressed using the concept of a group (mathematical sets).

The above classification captures main elements of other modern and traditional Ontological categories proposed earlier by several authors including Aristotle, Kant, and Reinhardt Grossman [30]. On the other hand, it leverages the Conceptual mathematical model based on algebra of logic and the concept construct (C). It also leverages the 'natural' mechanism of classification provided by the language itself based on common sense and the interrogative forms of gathering information.

The use of who, what, when, where, why, associated with, and how should not create confusion around the concept category being considered. There are several ways in which a question can be asked: How far is Hawaii? or What is the distance to Hawaii ? However, the concept involved is distance which belongs to a specific category or information domain: Space (where). The main aspect to look at is the concept itself (i.e. conceptual perspective).

The natural classification is also a top-level classification that will probably need to be refined based on the target application domain. Each information domain can be subdivided further. For an engineering perspective, the natural classification limits the number of high-level information domains that need to be implemented to seven (7), which is a very manageable number. In relative terms, there are few 'natural' domains or categories of information.

As aforementioned, the categories of Time (when), Space (where) and People (who) are relatively straightforward to implement because their straightforward 'mathematical nature'. An arbitrary sentence (S) consists of words that represent concepts in one or more of the above categories of information. For instance, the sentence "I travelled to Orlando last Monday" can be expressed as follows:

S = (("who", "I"), ("what", "travelled"), ("where", "Orlando"), ("when", "last Monday))

The previous sentence (S) also represents an Event (E) which combines several top-level information domains (categories) and describes something that happened previously: an aggregate concept.

Once the conceptual machine $(A=(\beta(m),I))$ processes a sentence like the previous one, it can readily answer questions: Who? What? Where? and When? Logical inferences can also be made based on the information provided. The approach can be generalized to arbitrary information domains (see Conceptual deductive approach).

20.8.4 Ambiguity, Context, and other challenges

The proposed conceptual language works well for information domains of limited scope. The information domain (D) is restricted to a set of concepts which makes it more manageable:

$D = \{C1, \dots ,Cj\}$ where C1, ...,Cj are concepts within the specified information domain (D)

For example, the concepts of 'Airline', 'Departure city', 'Ticket', 'Next Monday' have very specific meaning within the context of a reservation application. The degree the ambiguity the application has to deal with is therefore limited. The context of the communication is also very specific.

On the other hand, the more concepts a system is able to handle, the more complex it becomes. A rich and expressive language allows the same idea to be expressed in many different ways. Versatility comes at a cost in terms of system implementation. There are many ways to express "Thomas married Martha". For instance:

A) Thomas married Martha

B) Thomas and Martha got married

C) Thomas wed Martha

D) Thomas and Martha were joined in marriage

The system may need to limit the number of ways in which the information is communicated. Obviously the more flexibility the system provides, in terms of acceptable concepts and sentences, the more realistic the system becomes.

The general challenge can be specified as follows. Two concepts (C1 = C2) are said to be equivalent if they have the same meaning: semantically equivalent. A, B, C above are equivalent concepts. The computer system needs to be able to process all these sentences and make the associations of equivalence.

Definition (C) = Definition (C1) → C = C1

Sentences need to be 'normalized'. Under the current discussion, it means transforming their structure so they can be readily compared. For example, B, C and D can be normalized as A because they have the same meaning: semantically equivalent.

Consider another example. The request "I'd like to make a reservation" is ambiguous. In order to prevent ambiguity, the application must request information about the type of reservation being requested. Such piece of information clearly indentifies the subject being discussed and the information domain to be used.

In general, a concept (C) may have several meanings based on the context (Ctx) which is a concept that needs to be taken into account. The context can be formally represented using the concept construct (C): Ctx =((x1, y1), ... , (xn, yn)). In particular, the context will contain an information association related to the *subject* or *topic* being discussed.

The definition of a specific concept may be dependent on the context being used. In other words, the same concept may have associated several meanings depending on a specific information context.

C = Definition (C, Ctx)

A highly interactive application, like a mobile application, may request additional information in order to avoid ambiguity: What type of reservation would you like to make? After hearing the question, who is Mr. Jefferson's wife? , the first thing that comes through your mind probably is: Who is Mr. Jefferson? Who is he referring to? The answer to this question clearly identifies the subject of the discussion and deals with ambiguity.

We could be speaking about Mr. Jefferson in several contexts including friends, co-workers, and so forth. The meaning of the name will depend on the specific context. Once the context is identified, the ambiguity is resolved. Notice that for systems restricted to specific information domains, the meaning of each concept is usually well-defined. There is a unique definition for each concept being employed.

Other applications may not be as interactive and require autonomous or semi-autonomous processing of information. Such applications need to deal with ambiguity in different ways.

Obviously, the mind can process what-if scenarios. The Conceptual architecture can mimic such behavior. Since one or more concepts may have several meanings, depending on the specific context, the application needs to apply heuristic approaches and work with several what-if scenarios concurrently. Such scenarios need to be created and exhaustibly evaluated in order to cope with ambiguity during autonomous or semi-autonomous processing. The approach is in close correspondence with PSSH [25]: the Conceptual architecture exercises its intelligence in problem solving by *logically* generating and modifying symbol structures until it produces a solution structure.

20.8.5 Language Examples

NATURAL building blocks (symbols) are defined using the natural language: like entries/symbols in a typical dictionary, which is highly user friendly, and exhibits *realistic correspondence* with human languages.

The following examples briefly illustrate how to map natural language categories (grammatical categories) into its *internal* mathematical representation based on the concept construct (C), algebra of logic, set theory, and probabilities.

20.8.5.1 Information Associations (*Is*, the magic word)

The word 'is' allows us to define information associations. For instance, the following sentences can be expressed using algebraic notation:

The color of the house is red: House->color = 'red'

The pet's name is Copernicus: Pet->name='Copernicus'

My name is George Boole: Self->name = 'George Boole' (self represents me)

Information associations express relations between entities in the real world represented by the concept construct (C). The examples can be generalized as: C->association = value.

20.8.5.2 Possessive forms

The possessive form can also be expressed using information associations (C->association):

Boole's wife is Mary Boole: Boole->wife = 'Mary Boole'

The possession preposition 'of' is similar:

The sister of my father: self->father->sister

20.8.5.3 Group (plural forms)

Group is a key concept. It is ubiquitous within the context of natural languages via the plural form: Women, Men, Cities, Family, Friends, Contacts, Uncles, Aunts, and so forth. It can be modeled using mathematical sets. Set theory and associated operations represent a Boolean algebra.

Consider the following examples and their associated mathematical representation. Membership in a group is often expressed using *is a*. In several natural languages, the plural form (Group) is created by adding the letter s.

George Boole is a Man: George Boole ϵ Men

Orlando is a City: Orlando ϵ Cities

Hawaii is an Island: Hawaii ϵ Islands

Semantically, all the members of a group usually share similar characteristics. There are logical inferences that can be made from the fact of an individual being part of a group. For example, all men have a father or have had a father.

A group can also be defined by enumerating its constituent elements. For instance, the immediate family is the *group* of people related by blood:

family = {spouse, children, parents, aunts, cousins, grandparents, nephews, nieces}

20.8.5.4 Logical definitions

The natural language is an entity that grows 'organically' to accommodate arbitrary aspects of reality allowing the mind to increase its knowledge and ability to cope with its environment. So does its implementation (L). The magic word ('is') is also used to define other words part of the natural language: L = {((symbol1), Definition (symbol1)), ... , ((symboln), Definition (symboln))}. Each symbol is associated to its definition which consists of other symbols in the language:

Definition (Aunt) = (sister, of, one's, father, or, mother)

The definition of Aunt can be expressed in mathematical terms using the conceptual notation:

$$(C\text{->}father\text{->}sister = Y) \lor (C\text{->}mother\text{->}sister = Y) \equiv (C\text{->}aunt = Y)$$

The idea can be generalized to every member of a family including uncle, cousin, and so on. Let's try to define the concept of Tomorrow:

Definition (Tomorrow) = (day, after, today).

It can be expressed in mathematical terms as follows. Tomorrow *is a* day. Days represent an ordered group: Days= {d1, d2, ..., dn}:

$$(Today = d_i) \equiv (Tomorrow = d_{i+1})$$

The same principle can be generalized to every concept part of the information domain of Time (when): yesterday, next week, next Tuesday, next month, and so forth.

20.8.5.5 Aggregates or Composites

New aggregate concepts can be created by combining primary/elementary concepts. For instance, an Event: "I travelled to Orlando last Monday", S = ((Who, "I"), (Action, "travelled"), (Where, "Orlando"), (When, "last Monday))

The concept of reservation is very similar. Frege's principle of compositionality applies[30, 57]. Aggregates represent abstract entities. Keep in mind that Time and Space are abstract entities.

20.8.5.6 Grammatical rules

A grammatical rule, part of the language, is a concept and can be expressed using the concept construct (C). For instance,

1) Gr = ((Who), (Action), (Where), (When))
2) Gr1 = ((Who), (Action), (Where))
3) Gr2 = ((Who), (Action), (When))

A large number of sentences in the English language can be generated using these basic grammatical rules. For example, the following sentences can be generated using the rules above and NATURAL building blocks (concepts):(Who, "Mother"), (Action, ("cries", Past)) (Where, ("at the window")), ((When), yesterday). Notice that the action consists of a 2-tuple: verb and tense.

Mother cried at the window

Mother cried at the window yesterday

Mother cried

The representation above is used because it corresponds with a conceptual approach/notation, based on the three primary/elementary concepts and the concept construct (C). On the other hand, NATURAL building blocks are consistent with traditional phrases and grammatical categories.

Phrases:
a) Noun phrases (NP)
b) Prepositional phrases (PP)
c) Verb phrases (VP)
d) Adjective phrases (AP)

Parts of speech (grammatical categories) including:
a) Nouns (plural, singular)
b) Pronouns (nominal pronouns, interrogative pronouns)
c) Adjectives (comparative, superlative)
d) Articles
e) Quantifier (all, many, some, etc.)
f) Verbs (present tense, infinitive, past, progressive, irregular, modals, phrasal verbs)
g) Adverbs
h) Prepositions

For versatility and user convenience, the NATURAL implementation (API) should generate all potential variations of the sentence: present, future, past, progressive, past perfect, modal, interrogative(s), negative, and so forth. It mainly entails rearranging the building blocks using grammatical rules (Logos). Obviously, all these sentences are applicable while accurately mimicking human communication. For instance,

Mother will cry at the window

Mother did not cry at the window

Mother may cry

Mother is crying at the window

Who cried at the window?

When did Mother cry?

Where did Mother cry?

Why did Mother cry at the window?

The NATURAL API should also generate sentence variations with the same or similar semantic meaning. For instance,

190

Mother wept at the window

Mother cried near the window

Mother cried by the window

By the same token, the NATURAL API needs to implement functionality to normalize sentences and determine if they are semantically similar or equivalent.

20.8.5.7 May – Abductive reasoning

The auxiliary verb *may* expresses probability or possibility. The symbol can be mathematically modeled using abductive reasoning (see Conceptual Abductive Approach). This type of reasoning can be leveraged for making rich inferences. By adding *may* to the sentence (S), the semantics is changed: from factual to probable. Given the sentence (S), P(S) represents the probability of S.

According to Polya's patterns of plausible inference which he formalized using probability theory [63]:"The verification of a consequence renders a conjecture more credible".

S → S' & S' makes S more credible: $P(S \mid S') >= P(S)$

For instance, consider the following sentences.

S = (it rained last night)

S' = (The grass is wet)

If S' is true, S becomes more credible (probable). Thus, S may be true: $P(S) > 0$. We can derive that it may have rained last night. Since we are talking about probabilities, there is no contradiction if later on it is determined that the sprinkler was on and it didn't rain. The probabilities of rolling a dice do not contradict the fact that after rolling it, only one outcome is true.

Intuitively, it is similar to working with multiple hypotheses. Each hypothesis is probable (may be true) until you find evidence (facts) to prove it or disprove it. However, a cause (S) being *probable* (P(S)>0) does not make it true. ~S may be true with probability $1 - P(S)$.

The following sentences can be represented using 'may'. In general, if we have a probable cause (S) for a given effect (S'), then:

$$S \rightarrow P(S') > 0 \equiv S' \rightarrow P(S) > 0$$

With the following semantics:
a) If effect (S') is true, then the potential cause (S) may be true.
b) If potential cause (S) is true, then the effect (S') may be true.

These rules of probable cause and effect are similar to Polya's pattern above. However, there are differences as well (see Conceptual Abductive Approach). Consider the following examples:

if daughter goes missing her parents may become sad
if parents are sad their daughter may have gone missing

if daughter gets sick her parents may become sad
if parents are sad their daughter may have gotten sick

if a person is sad then s/he person may cry
if a person cries then s/he may be sad

All these sentences (S) can be represented using NATURAL and the 'may' symbol. The following sentences/ideas are semantically equivalent:

the person may be sad
it is possible that the person is sad
there is chance that the person is sad

there is a probability that the person is sad

it may be true that the person is sad

All of them can be normalized to the first sentence.

20.8.5.8 Probably and Quantifiers (most, few, and all)

Similar to *may* (auxiliary verb), the adverb *probably* expresses probability and can be represented via the corresponding mathematical formalism. A similar idea applies to the quantifiers most, few, and all, which can be utilized for making inferences about individuals of the group. Consider the following sentences:

a) S = (the bird can fly)

b) S'= (the bird can probably fly).

The word (symbol) is added to the second sentence to express that the probability (P(S)) is high. In mathematical notation:

$P(Fly\ (x)) = HIGH$, where the predicate Fly (x) represents x can fly.

In general, members of a group have multiple common characteristics and inferences can be made about all or most of the members:

a) Most birds can fly

b) All people are created equal (self evident)

By being a member of the group, it can be inferred that the general statement is also true for most or all of the members: the bird can probably fly.

Given a predicate Q that is true for most of the members of a group (G). Let's designate G' to be the group of members for which the predicate is true (most of G). The probability of the predicate (Q(x)) being true for a member (x) of a group (G) can be calculated:

$P(Q(x))$ = cardinality (G')/cardinality (G) = HIGH where x ϵ G

Semantically, if the predicate Q(x) is true for most of the members of a group (G), it is probably true for a given member (y):

Most x Q(x) $\rightarrow$ P (Q(y)) = HIGH where x ϵ G and y ϵ G

The quantifier Most has similar semantics to the universal $\forall$ and existential $\exists$ (see Generalized Quantifiers [30]). The following inference rules can be demonstrated using a similar mathematical proof.

a) Some x Q(x) $\rightarrow$ P (Q(y)) > 0, where x ϵ G and y ϵ G
   Some people can sing well

b) Few x Q(x) $\rightarrow$ P (Q(y)) = LOW, where x ϵ G and y ϵ G
   Few spiders are harmful to people

c) $\forall$ x Q(x) $\rightarrow$ P (Q(y)) = 1, where x ϵ G and y ϵ G
   All people are mortal

d) $\sim\exists$ x Q(x) $\rightarrow$ P(Q(y)) = 0, where x ϵ G and y ϵ G
   No man can fly.

e) if (x ϵ Birds) $\rightarrow$ P (Fly (x)) > .9
   More than 90% of all birds can fly

Notice that in the natural language, no numbers (probability values) are required to 'reason' and make the type of inferences presented above. Determining exact probability values is a challenging task [60, 63] which the Conceptual approach avoids by providing a realistic representation and mimicking human communication (may). On the other hand, numeric values to express probability may be used if/when they are available.

20.8.5.9 Coreference ambiguity

The Conceptual approach can be utilized to resolve coreference ambiguity. Pronouns and other references must be associated to the right entities. This is done by performing logical inferences, which include matching gender and cardinality. The concept construct (C), based on associations of information, can readily represent such interrelationships.

For instance, consider the following sentences (S):

a) A mother cried at the window.

b) She was sad because her daughter went missing.

The second sentence references the first sentence. A match can be logically inferred between the pronoun 'she' and 'a mother' in terms of cardinality and gender.

20.9 Implementation Considerations

Cognitivism asserts the separation between the model and its implementation (logical mind vs. physical brain) [61]. Thus, multiple valid implementations (i.e. realizations) of the same Turing-complete mathematical model are feasible. As a specific example, a Turing machine represents a mathematical model that can have multiple realizations.

Viable implementations of the model and its associated concepts should realistically mimic the physical world. For instance, consider the variety of instances of the concept of messaging found in the real world.

One straightforward software implementation of the Turing-complete Conceptual machine *(A=(β(m),I))* is via an encapsulated object or component (Live/Animated component) consisting of a single method with a single parameter (message). The following *simplified* pseudocode snippet elucidates the operation of the machine at a high level (see Participants).

```
public Class LogicalEngine {

  /**
   * Process messages
   */

  private Object processMessage (Object msg) { // Process messages received by the Logical Engine

      String operation = retrieveOperation (msg);   // Identify the operation to be performed

      if (operation == READ) return (readMemory (msg));   // Retrieve (read) information

      if (operation == WRITE) return (writeMemory (msg));  // Store/write information to memory

      if (operation == INFER)  return (infer (msg));                   // Perform logical inferences

      if (operation == EXECUTE) return (executeProcedure (msg)); // Execute stored procedure (P)
  }
}
```

The Logical Engine (LE) seeks to mimic or simulate the behavior of the logical mind through software based on a straightforward set of operations over information (Energy): read (retrieve), store (write), and logical processing based on Boole's algebra of logic. The Logical Engine (LE) is constantly interacting and learning from its environment through messaging. Sentences (S) and procedures (P) can be learned by the machine: added to the machine's memory (I). Procedures (P) previously stored can be recollected (read) and sequentially executed.

The LE is also able to make logical inferences based on the incoming message (m) and the information previously learned (stored as part of the machine's memory). The LE that implements the Conceptual machine *(A=(β(m),I))* is Turing complete and has equivalent power to a modern computer: capable of computing any computable function or algorithm.

Arbitrary facts, in the form of sentences (S), can be learned (WRITE operation). For instance, "Mary married Mr. Boole". Symbols in the

196

language (L) can also be learned. For instance, the logical definition of the symbol married: if a man marries a woman then she becomes his wife and he becomes her husband. From the information provided (fact and definition), we can logically reason that Mary became Boole's wife. By relying on the Conceptual deductive approach, the Conceptual machine $(A=(\beta(m),I))$ and associated implementation (LE) can mimic such behavior (INFER operation).

"Thought was still wholly intangible and ineffable until modern formal logic interpreted it as the manipulation of formal tokens."
   - Allen Newel and Herbert Simon [25]

In agreement with PSSH, the Turing-complete Conceptual machine is able to manipulate symbol structures (Sentences (S) expressed via the concept construct (C)) using logical transformations according to well-defined inference rules. The example can be generalized to any arbitrary fact and symbol part of the natural language. Arbitrary sentences in the language can be represented using the concept construct (C). A separate section presents multiple examples (see A Natural Language of Concepts and Mathematical Universe).

"There is in my opinion no important theoretical difference between natural languages and the artificial languages of logicians; indeed, I consider it possible to comprehend the syntax and semantics of both kinds of languages within a single *natural* and *mathematically* precise theory"   Richard Montague

As a second example, the machine can mimic how the mind learns and executes procedures (P) in the natural language to perform arithmetic calculations (base 10). First, we learn (memorize) the arithmetic rules in the form of sentences (WRITE operation): 1+1=2, 1+2=3 ... 9+9=18. Based on the acquired knowledge (set of sentences (S)) we can perform arithmetic operations (EXECUTE operation): add 1+1. Using similar principles, the machine can mimic how we learn, remember, and execute a procedure (P) to perform arithmetic operations on numbers with multiple digits.

The Conceptual machine/architecture is able to handle a vast amount of information. Consider all the facts (sentences) and symbol/word definitions that you store in your memory and leverage for logical reasoning. Also consider all the procedures that you are able to remember in order to perform tasks.

For an engineering perspective, the LE can potentially be implemented based on a single processor. However, such implementation would face multiple challenges in terms of scalability and performance.

The scalability and performance challenges were discussed earlier (see Combinatorial Challenge). By mimicking a neural network of information processors the challenge can be addressed. The Conceptual computing architecture is able to scale and handle a vast distributed web of Turing-complete information machines working in parallel and communication via messaging: $(\{A_1, \dots, A_n\}$ where $A_i=(f(m),I_i))$. A vast amount of information (I), part of $A=(\beta(m),I)$, is partitioned over such web of information machines/processors: each information machine $(A_i=(f(m),I_i))$ is responsible for a separate data partition (I_i).

Implementation considerations have been presented in a cursory fashion, based on high-level pseudocode, which requires further elaboration to be performed during the implementation phase of the architecture. The main focus has been on theoretical aspects (logical mind) which are independent from implementation ones.

20.10 Preliminary Evaluation of the Conceptual Architecture

The Conceptual architecture can be characterized as a UTC candidate. Key cognitive abilities are modeled and/or explained in a unified fashion. The UTC evaluation criteria is relevant and will be applied to the Conceptual architecture [32]:

1) Behave as an (almost) arbitrary function of the environment [Turing completeness]
2) Operate in real time
3) Exhibit rational, (i.e., effective adaptive behavior)
4) Use vast amounts of knowledge about the environment
5) Behave robustly in the face of error, the unexpected, and the unknown
6) Integrate diverse knowledge
7) Use (natural) language
8) Exhibit self-awareness and a sense of self
9) Learn from its environment
10) Acquire capabilities through development

11) Arise through evolution

12) Be realizable within the brain as a physical system [realistic correspondence].

A brief evaluation of the Conceptual cognitive architecture based on UTC's criteria illustrates multiple qualities:

a) Turing completeness: Boole's Conceptual machine is Turing complete (see Information machine and Turing completeness).

b) Real time operation: Theoretically, capable of operating in real time through the implementation of parallelism and data partitioning over a large amount of information processors/machines (see Combinatorial Challenge).

c) Rational behavior: capable of logical reasoning capabilities by implementing the conceptual deductive approach based on Boole's algebra of logic (see Cognitive Abilities).

d) Vast amounts of knowledge: The architecture is able to leverage a vast amount of knowledge (I) by leveraging straightforward parallelism and information partitioning: the vast amount of information managed by the architecture is partitioned over a web of information machines $(A=(f(m),I_i))$ working in parallel (see Combinatorial Challenge).

e) Learning from its environment: The Conceptual machine is constantly interacting with its environment and learning through messaging which mimics the mind's behavior. The machine can readily learn (or be taught) new concepts (C) in the form of sentences (S) and procedures (P), which are stored in memory.

f) Integration of diverse knowledge: All knowledge stored by the mind is reducible to the concept of information (Energy). According to the Conceptual model, our knowledge can be represented as a set of chunks of information (Energy): $I = (IC1, \ldots ,ICn)$, where $IC1, \ldots ,ICn$ are information chunks (or packets). Each message received and processed by the mind represents an information chunk, part of what we know/learn.

Diverse forms of information (Energy) are accommodated by the model in correspondence with the WWW metaphor: sound, image, smells, flavors, and tactile sensations (see Cognitive Abilities).

199

g) Use (natural) language: The architecture is able to mimic the conceptual mind in terms of language/symbol manipulation. In agreement with PSSH [25], the Turing-complete Conceptual architecture/model is able to manipulate symbol structures (Sentences (S)) using 'logical' transformations according to well-defined inference and grammatical rules (see Cognitive Abilities).

h) Realizable within the brain as a physical system [Realistic correspondence]: The proposed architecture has been conceived by accurately mimicking the conceptual mind and associated natural concepts. The approach is in correspondence with or supported by well-known theories and scientific research about the conceptual mind (see appendix on Related Cognitive/AI Models).

Simplicity (Occam's razor): Like realistic correspondence, theoretical simplicity (Occam's razor) is another fundamental aspect in the realm of science and scientific models; specifically, in the context of mathematical models of computing [26].

Conceptually, the logical mind is an entity of beautiful and mathematical simplicity, which single function is *logical* processing of information, in correspondence with the Turing-complete computing model: $(A=(\beta(m),I))$. In agreement with reductionism, the Conceptual architecture and model are based on straightforward concepts mimicked from nature: information (Energy), messaging, and information machine/processor.

Furthermore, the model is based on a straightforward set of operations. Our *conceptual* cognitive abilities can be explained or mimicked based on straightforward set of operations over information (Energy): store (write), retrieve (read), and logical processing mathematically modeled by Boole's algebra of logic.

Mathematical foundation: According to George Boole's remarkable assertions, the laws of thought are mathematical in their form [1]. Thus, our approach has a strong mathematical motivation/foundation. The Conceptual cognitive architecture mimicked from the logical mind, is an entity of mathematical *simplicity*; responsible for a single function: logical processing of information $(A=(\beta(m),I))$.

200

"Thought was still wholly intangible and ineffable until modern formal logic interpreted it as the manipulation of formal tokens."
  - Allen Newel and Herbert Simon [25]

The main source of validation (i.e. evidence) is its formal demonstration of Turing completeness. Due to Turing completeness, the Conceptual machine $(A=(\beta(m),I))$ is equivalent to a Turing machine or a modern computer in terms of processing power: capable of computing any computable function or algorithm.

Physical Symbol System Hypothesis (PSSH): The physical symbol system hypothesis (PSSH) has been very influential in the realm of cognitive architectures [61]. The Conceptual architecture is in correspondence with PSSH. The Turing-complete Conceptual architecture represents a physical symbol system; therefore, according to PSSH, capable of *general intelligent action* [25].

PSSH is in close correspondence with the Conceptual cognitive architecture from a theoretical perspective. Furthermore, the Conceptual architecture/model provides a precise Turing-complete mathematical foundation/formalization for PSSH: $A=(\beta(m),I)$. PSSH primary rests on empirical evidence and *further formalization is left for future efforts* [25].

Model's explanatory capabilities: cognitive architectures, and scientific models in general, are also evaluated by their explanatory capabilities (see Models in Science [30]). It should be fairly evident that the Conceptual architecture/model is able to naturally explain key cognitive abilities in a unified and realistic fashion – in agreement with UTC, PSSH, and other widely accepted research/theories about the mind (see Cognitive Abilities).

"Theory, modeling and statistics play at least four key roles in our effort to understand brain dynamics and function.
...
Finally, formal theory seeks to infer general principles of brain function that unify large bodies of experimental observations, models, and simulation outcomes. The brain computes stably and reliably despite its construction from billions of elements that are both noisy, and constantly adapting and re-calibrating. Elucidation of the general principles underlying this remarkable ability will have a profound impact on neuroscience, as well as on engineering and computer science."   Brain 2025 Report [18]

Biological/Neurological imitation and interaction based learning:
These key aspects exhibited by the Conceptual cognitive architecture
have been identified for their potential in advancing the state of the art in
the realm of cognitive architectures [61, 62].

The architecture mimics the neural network of information processors to
achieve a parallel and highly scalable infrastructure; theoretically, able to
manage vast amounts of information in real time. Learning is achieved
through interaction with the environment as opposed to programming or
programmer-based representations/languages. This aspect is related to
the UTC criteria (learn from its environment).

Scalability and Performance (parallel vs. serial architecture): these
aspects are closely related the UTC criteria: real time operation and
ability to handle a vast amount of knowledge. Carefully consider the
differences between von Neumann models (serial processing) and the
associative nature (parallel) of the Conceptual architecture being
proposed [56, 61, 26].

Backus coined the term "von Neumann bottleneck" referring to the
limitations (including performance limitations) [26]. *Theoretically*, the
Conceptual cognitive architecture is able to overcome such limitations,
operating in real time, by leveraging parallelism and information
partitioning of a vast amount of data. Influential cognitive approaches
have shown disaffection with sequential (serial) processing in favor of
parallel, real-time, and distributed architectures [56, 61].

In summary and as expected, the Conceptual approach demonstrates its
outstanding qualities in many areas part of the preliminary evaluation
above – naturally. This preliminary evaluation demonstrates such
qualities in a tangible fashion. The conceptual mind exhibits a unique
computing paradigm that is realistically mimicked by the proposed
architecture: conceptual paradigm. It should be stated that at the present
time there is a lack of standard benchmarks and problem domains to
evaluate the various cognitive architectures at the system level [62].

21. BACK TO THE FUTURE

In regards to the question "Can Machines Think?" It seems that George Boole helped answer it far ahead of his time. Over 150 years ago, to be more precise. Consider his conclusion:

    A) "The laws of thought are mathematical".

In other words, thinking is a mathematical process. In particular, he was referring to *logical* thinking based on his mathematical proofs and findings: what is known today as Boolean Logic or Boolean Algebraic Logic.

    B) On the other hand, computers are mathematical machines. Based on the Church-Turing thesis, any computable function or algorithm can be computed.

By combining the premises A and B, the following conclusion is deducted:

Computers can think logically.

As a consequence, and from pragmatic scientific and engineering perspectives, computers can realistically mimic the logical thinking (i.e. reasoning) mechanisms utilized by the mind to process information. Mathematical models based on Boolean algebra are able to accurately mimic logical thinking.

Consider that the concept of "logical thinking" (reasoning), which is unambiguous, precisely describes what it is, and its logical nature. It would be contradictory otherwise. If you look at reasoning from a conceptual standpoint, it literally means "to form conclusions, judgments, or inferences from facts or premises"; in other words, *logical* processing of information. Facts and premises are part of the knowledge already acquired.

"Thought was still wholly intangible and ineffable until modern formal logic interpreted it as the manipulation of formal tokens."
  Allen Newel and Herbert Simon [25]

The Turing-complete Conceptual cognitive/AI architecture and deductive approach are based on Boole's algebraic logic. As discussed previously, the architecture can scale to 'understand' reality and make decisions based on a large bank of conceptual information via logical and algebraic manipulation.

The title of Boole's seminal book (The Laws of Thought …) and his conclusions are unequivocal. A number of other authors, in many fields, have put forth results and theories consistent or founded upon his work [23, 25, 28, 30, 34]: seminal "ground for remarkable conclusions" that shed light on the inner secrets of the logical mind, the pinnacle in terms of information processing $(A=(\beta(m),I))$. As faith led him to believe, God's greatest creation!

22. IN THE BEGINNING WAS THE LOGOS ...

Major portions of this chapter differ sharply from the rest of the book, in the sense that they are speculative in nature. They are mainly aimed to stimulate thought and imagination about the potential futuristic applications of the conceptual paradigm. An open mind is needed in order to enter here – so to speak. However, some scientific facts are included.

Based on reductionist hypothesis, which is widely accepted by most scientists, all science can be reduced to physics (see Physical Foundation). On the other hand, physics can be reduced to the universal concept of Energy and its physical laws. Everything in the universe and reality represents a form of Energy.

Conceptually, Nature *is* simple. Nature is one. Nature is Energy! – the universal concept. Paraphrasing Galileo, Mother Nature is simple and does not multiply a thing; that she makes use of the universal concept of Energy, and its laws (Logos), for producing all her effects. Such effects include all physical phenomena: gravity, electromagnetism, nuclear interactions, and so forth.

Packets of Energy are combined to create more complex forms of Energy. Every object part of physical reality represents a composite form (i.e. aggregate) of Energy. Every process or action is reducible to transformation of Energy according to its laws (Logos). Consider Lego building blocks as an analogy. Like atoms, DNA molecules, and living cells, Lego building blocks can be *combined* to create a great diversity of complex structures.

"There are not more than [seven] musical notes, yet the combinations of these [seven] give rise to more melodies than can ever be heard. " Sun Tzu

Complexity comes as a result of *combining* a large number of straightforward Lego components (combinatorics): simplicity at the component level and complexity at the structure (group) level – naturally. Structures of arbitrary complexity can be built and/or understood using such straightforward components and rules. The idea is also consistent with the Principle of Compositionality (Frege's Principle) [30]: the meaning of a complex expression is determined by the meanings of its constituent expressions and the rules used to combine them.

In agreement with the Conceptual model, it is theoretically feasible to add, replace, or remove memories via an engram or memory machine. After all, such engrams represent packets of Energy stored in the mind, via the neural network (see Mathematical Model). Such machine could be utilized as an efficient and expedient way of educating the population.

A highly educated and advanced civilization could emerge. More efficient utilization of resources would be feasible while educating individuals. PhD graduates spend around twenty years, a significant portion of their natural life, getting the advanced degree. The benefits of education for society and its population are obvious.

Science fiction movies like "The Matrix", portrait human beings 'learning' new skills by having 'programs' downloaded into their memory. According to the Conceptual computing model, only the information (I) stored by the machine needs to be updated. The Laws of Thought ('program') are time-invariant (see Cognitive/AI Architecture).

A main challenge here is determining how/where engrams are logically and physically stored inside the brain, so they can be read, recorded, edited, and/or deleted. Such challenge represents a non-trivial one. Erasing unwanted and perhaps traumatic memories would be feasible.

Furthermore, since human thoughts are physically encoded in the form of Energy, mind reading devices, and telepathic machines, are also theoretically possible. In theory, the Energy stored in the brain in the form of engrams can be copied, replicated, edited, deleted, and transferred. It would be similar to manipulating or sending an electronic computer file (a form of Energy).

Some time ago, Leibniz envisioned a Universal language for human communication (Universal Characteristic): an "algebra of thought" (see Leibniz's Philosophy of Mind [30]). In his view, the terms part of the natural language stand for complex or derivative concepts: concepts composed of, and reducible to, simpler concepts. Such language seems feasible, based on the single universal concept of Energy. Leibniz stated: "All human ideas can be resolved into a few [Concepts] as their primitives."

All concepts in physical reality can be reduced to the concept of Energy and its laws (Logos). The language part of the Conceptual cognitive architecture is consistent with his idea (see A Natural Language of Concepts). Such language is aimed to improve communication between human and machine – and also between machine and machine. His idea is also consistent with linguistic reductionism which postulates that everything can be described by a language with a limited number of core concepts and their combinations.

For instance, all physical objects are reducible to the concept of Energy: every object is a form (aggregate) of Energy. Concepts like information, thought, message, idea, sentence, Universe, and Nature are reducible as well. The universe is Energy according to physics. Nature is also reducible to the concept of Energy. It should be obvious that the natural language can be reduced (i.e. simplified) to a single concept, as far as *physical reality* is concerned.

In Leibniz's mind, "this language will be the greatest instrument of reason," for "when there are disputes among persons, we can simply say: Let us calculate, without further ado, and see who is right". The idea can be extended to groups of people and countries. A 'Peace machine' would be theoretically feasible since disputes between peoples would be resolved based on reason and logic (Logos). The idea is consistent with a 'government of reason (Logos)' which is discussed later in this chapter.

It can be argued that Occam Razor is applicable in the realm of human languages, in order to achieve simplification and reduce redundancy. If Nature can simply manage with one concept, why can't we? Why human languages seem to complicate things? For instance, information is Energy. Nature and universe can also be reduced to Energy.

Having multiple words to represent the same entity adds color and variety to the *natural* language which seems to be beneficial, as long as it is understood that those words represent the same thing. In agreement with reductionism, detecting and reducing redundancy of concepts in human languages should bring forth simplicity and better communication – in science and elsewhere. By the same token, Occam's razor opposes redundancy.

Like the rest of science, Biology can be reduced to the concept of Energy and its laws (Logos). Cells, DNA, enzymes, and so forth represent composite forms of Energy (i.e. aggregates). Based on faith, and as part of his theory of evolution, Darwin acknowledged the existence of a Creator. For him, there is no contradiction between creation ("God's works") and evolution of species. In his own words, Life was originally "breathed by the Creator". Darwin quoted Francis Bacon in his seminal book:

"To conclude, therefore, let no man out of a weak conceit of sobriety, or an ill-applied moderation, think or maintain, that a man can search too far or be too well studied in the book of God's word, or in the book of God's works; divinity or philosophy; but rather let men endeavour an endless progress or proficience in both." Francis Bacon

"Have we any right to assume that the Creator works by intellectual powers like those of man?" Charles Darwin

"To my mind it accords better with what we know of the laws [Logos] impressed on matter [Energy] by the Creator, that the production and extinction of the past and present inhabitants of the world should have been due to secondary causes, like those determining the birth and death of the individual." Charles Darwin

"There is grandeur in this [natural selection] view of life, with its several powers, having been originally breathed by the Creator into a few forms or into one; and that, whilst this planet has gone cycling on according to the fixed law of gravity, from so simple a beginning endless forms most beautiful and most wonderful have been, and are being evolved." Charles Darwin

According to the following scientists, it is mathematically improbable that anything as complex as proteins, living cells, the brain, or let alone human beings be produced by chance. The probabilities are astronomically small.

Astronomer Fred Hoyle and Professor Chandra Wickramasinghe calculated the probabilities of randomly producing the required enzymes for a simple living cell around 1 in $10^{40,000}$. Fred Hoyle also compared the random emergence of the simplest cell to the likelihood that "a tornado sweeping through a junk-yard might assemble a Boeing 747 from the materials therein."

The eminent mathematician and physicist Roger Penrose calculated the probabilities of a life-supporting universe happening by chance around 1 in $10^{10^{123}}$. Carl Sagan, who happens to be an evolutionist, estimates even greater probabilities against the simplest of life forms being created by chance:1 in $1*10^{\wedge 2,000,000,000}$.

In harmony with reductionism, Rolf Landauer agrees that computer science can be reduced to physics. He asserts that information is physical, which is in harmony with the Conceptual model. He also criticizes several of the abstractions relied upon by computer scientists and mathematicians for lacking realism – in particular, Turing machines with infinite memory [33].

"Computation is inevitably done with real physical degrees of freedom, obeying the laws of physics, and using parts [Energy/Atoms] available in our actual physical universe." Rolf Landauer

The computation (information processing) performed by the Conceptual mind is done in agreement with Landauer's views, using the universal concept of Energy. The conceptual model of the mind $(A=(f(m),I))$ overcomes his criticisms by relying exclusively on realistic 'parts' available in our actual physical universe. Information comes in the form of messages (m): *finite* aggregates or packets of Energy. Computation is done by processing information (Energy) based on the laws (Logos) of physics (see Physical Foundation).

Many philosophers and physicists assert that the abstractions of time and space are not real: not part of the physical universe (see Time [30]). Using a similar argument to Landauer's, we can argue that traditional models in physics rely on artificial abstractions or illusions: time and space. Such abstractions are not part our physical universe (i.e. nature).

This introduces a 'conceptual paradox' (Einstein's paradox): it is contradictory, for physics, to rely on concepts or abstractions that do not exist in physical reality. In other words, if time and space do not exist, how can they bend? Notice that these concepts are conspicuously missing from the Turing-complete model of the mind $(A=(f(m),I))$, although they can be part of the concepts created (i.e. fabricated) inside the mind: modes by which we think (see Physical Foundation).

Realism asserts that reality exists independent of the observer and that the truth of a representation is determined by how it corresponds to reality (The Correspondence Theory of Truth [30]).

"Time and space are modes [concepts] by which we think and not conditions in which we live." Albert Einstein

Energy is *the* real thing. In agreement with Occam's razor and reductionism, the introduction of redundant abstractions, as part of science models, must not be allowed. Per previous remarks, Mother Nature is simple and does not multiply a thing; that she makes use of the universal concept of Energy, and its law(s), for producing all her effects.

For many years, Einstein searched for a theory of everything able to unify all the forces of nature. Since everything in the universe is Energy, it can be argued that a theory of everything must be a theory of Energy. In other words, all physical phenomena are reducible to the concept of Energy and its laws (Logos). Let us hypothesize about the structure of such theory. What comes next is highly speculative.

It should be stated that scientific *models* do not need to be exact in order to be valid, but approximately true (see Models in Science [30]). Multiple valid models of the same natural phenomena are also feasible. Consider the Gravity models, for instance. Newton's model and Einstein's model are both valid models in physics. On the other hand, it can be argued that they are both 'incomplete' in the sense that they both leverage unrealistic concepts ('illusionary') as Einstein and many others clearly state it. If we accept that time and space do not exist in nature, they cannot bend.

Newton could never explain how gravity works: "I frame no hypothesis". He was uncomfortable with the 'mystical' idea of action at a distance: it is not logical for a body to "act where it was not". Therefore, what is needed to deal with the aforementioned conceptual paradox, is a model that exclusively relies on realistic concepts found in the physical universe. This is a direct consequence of Occam's razor applied in the context of a conceptual paradigm – and its associated way of thinking.

Consider a blue butterfly, flying over a pond of water. One of her delicate wings touches the surface of the water. Such phenomena can be totally described by the interactions of Energy. The atoms touched by the wing start moving which produces a wave effect. If we look closely, the physical phenomena just described can be modeled based on the interaction of two atoms (particles of Energy) repeated over and over again through the whole process.

The interaction between two particles is governed by physical laws (Logos). Each particle has a sphere of influence. When the particle moves it interacts with all the adjacent atoms (part of its sphere of influence). The process is repeated over and over again producing the concentric circular waves on the surface of the water.

Now consider holding one end of a pen in your hand, you can move the pen in any direction. In order to completely describe the physical phenomenon, you need to consider all the particles (aggregates of Energy) and their interactions: the particles part of your hand, the pen, and the air around the pen. Again, the whole physical phenomenon can be understood based on the interaction of two adjacent particles repeated over and over again. Intuitively, the atoms in your hand push adjacent atoms in the pen, which in turn push their adjacent atoms, and so on. A chain effect is produced.

Notice that there is no action at a distance. The particles at the other end of the pen are 'pushed' by the adjacent particles. The source of movement – and Energy – can be traced back, along the chain, to the particles in your hand. This is similar to the effect produced by the butterfly's wind which is propagated to the particles located around the boundary of the pond. Obviously, the particles in the pen are connected which keep the pen as a unit. To be accurate, we should understand that the pen consists of a group of particles: similar to the particles of water. Energy is transferred between adjacent particles and the law (Logos) of conservation of Energy applies.

The key of the theory is finding the Energy laws (Logos) governing the interaction between two arbitrary particles which can then be extrapolated (i.e. generalized) to the whole process (physical phenomena): all the interactions involved.

Discovering and understanding the atomic laws, in a comprehensive fashion, is not a trivial exercise that should probably keep scientists busy for a long time to come. *Conceptually*, the proposed theory is straightforward: it involves the single universal concept of Energy and its laws.

Consider a chain of people holding hands. The sphere of influence of each person consists of two people: one to the left and one to the right. Each person is able to push or pull an adjacent person (to the right or left) which generates movement. The action is propagated throughout the chain. Particles of Energy behave in a similar way at a much smaller scale. Actually push or pull, and in general the concept of force, are reducible to the concept of Energy. When we push or pull, we are actually transferring Energy. The concept of attraction is also reducible.

Now consider the game of rope pulling (Tug of war). Two teams compete against each other by pulling a rope placed in between. You can think about a new version of the game in which multiple lines of people are placed on each side. They are pulling a net instead of a rope. This modality could be viewed as a two-dimensional version of the original game.

The combined Energy transferred to the first person of each line, can be traced back through the net, to the individuals on the other side of the net. Intuitively, the amount of Energy transferred is directly proportional to the number of individuals pulling the net and inversely proportional to the size of the net (its area). Again, force is reducible to the concept of Energy and transference thereof. The Energy transferred to each individual involved in the game can be modeled and calculated.

The game of rope pulling can be used as a metaphor or analogy to explain multiple physical phenomena and the transference of Energy involved: participants in the game represent individual particles. From a realistic perspective, an object consists of a collection of Energy particles. Also, objects are connected with each other through a collection of Energy particles – like a mass of air for instance. This can be viewed as a three-dimensional version of the game.

There is a mesh or 'cloud' of particles of Energy (MP) that connects objects and serves as an 'Energy carrier'. The Energy transferred to each particle, part of either object, can be traced back to the collection of particles that belong to the other object – through the mesh (cloud) of particles in between.

Let us consider the phenomenon of magnetism in which a magnet attracts a piece of metal. Initially, it may look like an action at a distance. Clearly, a realistic model must consider all the particles of Energy involved in the phenomenon, which include the invisible particles of air between the magnet and the piece of metal. Again, each particle has a sphere of influence (SI) to consider.

The Energy transferred to a specific particle (metal) can be traced back to a collection of magnet particles through the air particles. The air consists of a mesh or 'cloud' of relevant particles (MP): group of particles that carry the Energy being transferred. The combined transference of Energy (magnetic effect) between all the particles involved makes the metal change position.

There is no action at a distance in this theory. Energy, ruled by its laws (Logos), is the only concept necessary to model the process (physical phenomena). In reality, it is a very dynamic process because each time the metal moves, a new state or configuration of Energy (SE) is produced requiring new calculations. In other words, SI and MP change dynamically as the piece of metal moves. For instance, particles of air are displaced and the piece of metal may rotate as it moves closer to the magnet.

Clearly, in order to achieve realistic correspondence, all particles and interactions of Energy must be modeled in a comprehensive fashion. The internal forces that keep the magnet and the piece of metal together must be considered also. Notice that transference of Energy (magnetic effect) will not happen if a finger is appropriately placed between the magnet and the metal which seems to clearly indicate that air particles are an integral part of the chain effect.

Particles of a thin piece of fabric or plastic, on the other hand, seem to carry it. Several pieces of metal can be chained together. The Energy (magnetic effect) will be transferred through the chain to the piece of metal farthest from the magnet. In this scenario, the mesh (MP) also consists of particles of metal which carry the Energy (magnetic effect).

The ideas just discussed can be generalized to gravity. A General Gravity theory (GG's theory) can be proposed. GG also happens to be the name of the blue butterfly that inspired it. In agreement with reductionism and Occam's razor, gravity is reducible to the concept of Energy and its physical laws (Logos). In other words, *gravity is reducible to Energy and transference thereof.*

Consider Newton's apple that falls from a tree. In order to explain the physical phenomenon in a comprehensive fashion, the complete collection of Energy particles involved must be modeled: apple, air, and earth. The Energy transferred to the participles part of the apple can be traced back to the earth particles, through the cloud (mesh) of air particles. Such transference causes the apple to move (fall). Although Newton was unable to explain gravity, he believed that his theory was compatible with a fluid-based and mechanical explanation [65]. Most of such theories relied of some sort of substance or ether filling space.

Michael Faraday believed in the existence of a relationship between gravity and magnetism. In agreement with reductionism (to Energy), there is a clear relationship. The apple and the earth represent two aggregates of particles which interchange Energy through a cloud of particles (air).

A similar scenario applies to magnetism, where two aggregates of particles interchange Energy. Both scenarios are conceptually isomorphic based on the single concept of Energy. Movement in both cases can be explained by transference of Energy: like every physical concept, *movement* is reducible to the concept of Energy and transference thereof.

Einstein's theory of general relativity predicts gravitational waves of Energy. Such prediction is in agreement with General Gravity. These invisible waves are similar to the visible ones produced on a pond or body of water. They are also similar to the invisible waves produced when you talk or pull a pen. On the other hand, general relativity explains gravity through the curvature of space and time: reduction through geometry. In contrast, General Gravity relies exclusively on the concept of Energy and transference thereof.

Intuitively, objects fall because Energy is transferred from earth particles (in waves) causing movement. This is consistent with the law of conservation of Energy: Energy can be neither created nor destroyed; only transformed from one form to another. In consequence, the Energy

214

that causes the object to fall must have a source: Energy waves (gravitational waves) coming from earth particles through air particles.

It should be stated that knowledge of atomic particles and their interactions was very limited/incomplete when Einstein and Newton proposed their theories of gravity. Clearly, in agreement with reductionism, a complete and unified theory – like General Gravity – must explain gravity at the atomic level. From a realistic perspective, the earth, Newton's apple, and the air, are made of a collection of atomic particles – similar to the rope pulling metaphor.

In modern physics, it is widely accepted that the effect of gravity applies to two adjacent particles although so far it has not being possible to measure it empirically. In Newtonian physics, an object is viewed as a unit, which can be construed as a model 'simplification' lacking realistic correspondence and therefore incomplete. In agreement with Occam's razor, realism, and reductionism, the unified theory of Energy being discussed presents the following advantages:

a) **Simplicity.** Conceptual and theoretical simplicity are achieved by relying on the universal concept of Energy, in harmony with Occam's razor. The unrealistic concepts (abstractions) of time and space are redundant and therefore removed from the theory and physics.

b) **Realism.** Realistic correspondence is a fundamental aspect in the realm of science, theory, and scientific models. The proposed theory only includes concepts part of physical reality: Energy. There is no need for additional abstractions or dimensions beyond the three ones that can be experienced through direct observation.

From a realistic perspective, we must realize that every physical object consists of a mesh (aggregate) of individual particles of Energy. By the same token, Energy is transferred between adjacent particles (physical principle of locality).

c) **Unity.** Unification of all of science based on the single concept: unification though Energy in agreement with reductionism. Einstein unified the concepts of Energy and Mass. He also searched for the unification of physics through geometry (geometrization of gravity).

However, Energy incorporates additional aspects (information) beyond geometry that are part of physical phenomena. In the case of gravity, the transference of Energy through the intermediate cloud of atomic particles needs to be realistically modeled – in a comprehensive fashion.

d) **Locality.** The effect of Energy is always local which eliminates the 'mystical' idea of action at a distance. Energy does not act where it is not. The principle of locality helps explain gravity. GG's theory is a strictly local theory, which is consistent with principle of locality in physics: gravitational waves of Energy are transferred through adjacent particles (sphere of influence).

e) **Consistency.** Solves the conceptual paradox (Einstein's paradox) associated with the illusions of time and space – not being part of physical reality. By removing time, several potential paradoxes associated with it are eliminated from science.

f) **Applicability.** The theory should be applicable uniformly and consistently to both, the very large cosmic universe and the small atomic world. A unified theory of Energy would be applicable to every form of Energy (Theory of Everything). Actually, arbitrary objects within the known universe represent aggregates of particles of Energy. The same Energy laws that apply to one particle and its interaction with other particles are applicable to large cosmic bodies and arbitrary physical phenomena.

In other words, the same Energy laws that apply to two particles can be consistently applied to physical phenomena which consist of vast amounts of particles. Of course, there may be differences depending on the multiple forms of Energy (class of particle) and their interactions: for instance, the differences between magnetism and gravity. There are several types of Energy particles and interactions – usually discussed in terms of force between particles. Like gravity, all physical forces are reducible to the concept of Energy and transference thereof.

g) **Causal Deterministic.** The proposed theory and the concept of Energy follow causal determinism: in harmony with Laplace's idea (see Causal Determinism [30]), the behavior of Energy appears to be deterministic and follow precise and timeless physical laws (Logos). At the macroscopic level, Energy can be observed to behave in such a manner.

The above is just a brief cursory presentation of the advantages exhibited by the proposed theory, which is again, speculative. Although *conceptually* simple, there are several challenges associated with the proposed theory:

a) **Atomic Laws of Energy.** The theory requires in-depth knowledge of how two particles of Energy interact with each other (laws of Energy); in particular, for the cases of magnetism and gravity. Such knowledge can then be applied to the entire physical phenomenon.

b) **Mathematical Formalization.** The theory requires a precise mathematical formalization (model). In other words, the interaction between particles (Energy transference) and its extrapolation to larger physical phenomena (gravity, magnetism, etc) need to be formalized mathematically. Such formalization is left for future efforts. If we can formalize the 3D game of rope pulling (without considering gravity), a similar mathematical formalization would be applicable to other physical phenomena: including gravity and magnetism. In summary, such universal law(s) of Energy (theory of everything) would formalize mathematically, the transformation of Energy associated with any arbitrary physical phenomena.

Conceptually, the mathematical formalization needs to realistically model and calculate the Energy transferred between two objects, which can be planets in the case of General Gravity. Newton's straightforward equation of universal gravitation is probably a good *starting point,* although several mathematical formalisms could potentially be leveraged: the gravitation force between any two objects is directly proportional to the product of their masses and inversely proportional to the distance between them. In particular, Newton's equation is straightforward, based on a three-dimensional reality, and verifiable through empirical experiments. Per earlier remarks, force is reducible to the concept of Energy.

On the other hand, distance is a redundant abstraction. In other words, distance is not a primary direct cause – Energy is. Thus, distance must be removed from the mathematical equation. Thereby, the associated singularity is also removed.

The following 'oversimplified' equation (preliminary/rough form) based on the law of conservation of Energy, contains the main factors involved. A similar equation would apply to the game of rope pulling and the magnetic effect.

$$E' = E - E_{MP} = \sum\nolimits^{i=M1, j=M2} e_{ij} - E_{MP} \approx GG * M1 * M2 - E_{MP}$$

E': Effective gravitational energy transferred to the apple which causes it to move.

E: Gravitation energy contributed by earth particles (directly proportional to the number of particles involved). This represents the summation of the energy contribution of each particle (e_{ij}). M1 and M2 represent the number of particles part of the earth and the apple respectively. e_{ij} represents the energy contributed (transferred) to the apple particle (j) from the earth particle (i). GG is a constant that represents an approximate average contribution of gravitational Energy (e_{ij}). Perhaps, it could be used to calculate a good approximation of the gravitational energy transferred (similar to the constant G). However, a robust mathematical formalization needs to calculate e_{ij} in a very accurate fashion.

E_{MP}: Gravitation energy transferred to the cloud/mesh of relevant air particles (MP) which does not reach the apple: it does not contribute to its movement. This factor needs to be deducted from E.

General Gravity helps explain Newton's gravitational equation and law - at least intuitively, in terms of atomic particles. Based on intuition, the gravitational Energy transferred is approximately proportional to the number of individual particles involved (M1*M2) and decreases depending on the distance abstraction as an indirect cause.

The game of rope puling can be used to visualize these relationships. The greater the number of air particles (MP), the less gravitational energy that reaches the apple and contributes to its movement – due to the law of conservation of Energy. In other words, as the number of air particles increases, so does E_{MP}.

In agreement with reductionism to Energy and Occam's razor, notice that the distance abstraction has been removed from the gravitation energy equation as an indirect cause: a bigger distance simply implies more air particles (direct cause), provided that the air density remains the same. Air density has an indirect influence: higher air density implies more air particles.

c) **Combinatorial Challenge**. The theory can be readily applied while the number of particles is small. It becomes difficult as the number of particles and interaction increases (combinatorial explosion/challenge). Think about the game of rope pulling with billions or trillions of individual participants.

Typical physical phenomena consist of a vast number of independent particles interchanging Energy. Consider that the state of Energy (SE) changes dynamically at each step of the process, requiring recalculation. Heuristics, approximations, model simplifications, and statistical methods will probably be required as the number of particles and interactions increases.

However, we should realize that in order to achieve close realistic correspondence, all Energy particles and interactions need to be accurately modeled. A magnet interacting with a piece of metal should be a manageable scenario.

Quantum mechanics (QM) has successfully modeled a variety of physical phenomena. A mathematical formalism based on QM could potentially be applied to General Gravity in order to model and calculate the gravitational wave (transference of Energy). In particular, considering the vast number of particles and interactions of Energy involved. It would unify gravity and QM theory. On the other hand, Einstein, a pioneer of quantum mechanics, considered it incomplete. Paul Dirac, another of the main figures linked to theory, considered it "provisional" [66]. Quantum mechanics represents *a model* of the world – in this case, a *'probabilistic' model*.

"I am, in fact, firmly convinced that the essentially statistical character of contemporary quantum theory is solely to be ascribed to the fact that this [theory] operates with an incomplete description of physical systems."
Albert Einstein

Erwin Schrödinger, one of the fathers of Quantum mechanics, also recognized the limitations of the model. He proposed the cat paradox (Schrödinger's cat paradox); against the prevailing Copenhagen interpretation [30] which proposes that the cat can be dead and alive at the same time. Obviously, this represents a contradiction in terms of physical reality. Quantum mechanics is limited to predicting the probabilities of both outcomes. Instead of providing precise answers about the state of a system, QM deals with probabilities of outcomes.

Part of the problem comes from our inability of measuring precisely at the atomic level – related to the measurement problem in quantum mechanics (see Measurement in Quantum Theory [30]). The associated Heisenberg's uncertainty principle states that one cannot determine the location and velocity of a particle at the same time.

Schrödinger expressed his feelings about QM:"I don't like it, and I'm sorry I had anything to do with it". Roger Penrose has also recognized the issues associated with Quantum mechanics [66] in terms of realism and determinism.   Conceptual difficulties plague QM, despites its impressive applicability. Richard Feynman stated "I think I can safely say that nobody understands quantum mechanics."

According to John S. Bell, QM is "unprofessionally vague and ambiguous. Professional theoretical physicists ought to be able to do better. Bohm has shown us a way." Broglie-Bohm theory attempts to address multiple QM challenges by proposing a deterministic theory. Their theory consists of particles with well-defined position and velocity guided by a pilot wave. Therefore, the wave-particle duality vanishes by explaining the wave behavior as a scattering of particles which assume the form of a wave.

"This idea seems to me so natural and simple, to resolve the wave-particle dilemma in such a clear and ordinary way, that it is a great mystery to me that it was so generally ignored." John S. Bell

Consider rolling a dice, as an analogy. A probabilistic model can give you the probabilities of getting a specific number. For instance, the probability of getting each number is one in six. Quantum mechanics works in a similar fashion. In reality, it should be obvious that rolling dice produces only one of the possible outcomes after each role. Only one possibility will be true.

In other words, no parallel universes are created (one for each possibility):per Schrödinger's paradox, the cat cannot be dead and alive at the same time – in two parallel universes (or worlds). Believing otherwise would violate everything we know about the physical world. To summarize, Einstein wrote "Quantum mechanics is very impressive …", however, "God does not place dice".

"Probability is expectation founded upon partial knowledge. A perfect acquaintance with all the circumstances affecting the occurrence of an event would change expectation into certainty, and leave neither room nor demand for a theory of probabilities." George Boole

"Concern for man himself and his fate must always form the chief interest of all technical endeavors, concern for the great unsolved problems of the organization of labor and the distribution of goods--in order that the creations of our mind shall be a blessing and not a curse to mankind. Never forget this in the midst of your diagrams and equations." Albert Einstein

Economics is the *science* concerned with the process or system by which goods and services are produced, sold, and bought. Since economics is a science, it is reducible to the concept of Energy. Actually, economics is the social science that most closely resembles the natural sciences. Economic concepts like "resources", "goods" and "services" are reducible to Energy. Since Aristotle, economics has been associated with concept of managing a household.

Mainstream economic models are based on the idea of self-interest. Homo economicus (economic human) is self-interested, individualistic, rational (Logos), perfectly informed, in competition to maximize gains. Such models have been criticized or deemed incomplete by leading economists and researchers. Periods of severe economic crisis have reemphasized the urgent need for new theoretical models and practical approaches to economics. "Keynes's characterization – a condemnation – of capitalism as based on the 'Love of Money' echoes the biblical statement: 'the love of money' is the root of all evil" [64].

The Homo reciprocans (reciprocal human), as opposed to Homo economicus, is cooperative and motivated by improving the surrounding environment [64]. Nash equilibrium demonstrates that individuals are better served when the interest of their group is taken into account (see Game Theory [30]). Physiologically, the human body works as a unit, a 'marvel' of design in terms of energy processing, distribution, consumption, and economy. All cells work in cooperation to accomplish a collective goal.

In the specific case of the logical mind: logical processing of information (Energy). In order to accomplish their work, cells require Energy which is produced and distributed by sophisticated biological mechanisms part of integrated systems. Each cell receives an allotment of Energy according to its needs and specific function.

In consequence, we can theorize about a Natural Economic Model (NEM) which mimics the model leveraged by living organisms, and the human body in particular – based on the single concept of Energy. What benefits the group or society of individuals as a whole, also benefits each individual part of the group. Conceptually speaking, the economy of the body is isomorphic with the economy of a family, a community, a country, and the world.

Nature's economic model presents unparalleled qualities: highly unified (one from many), cooperative, harmonious, just (fair), stable (resilient), efficient, parsimonious, rational, environmentally friendly, and effective. In agreement with Biomimetics, these qualities can be mimicked by an economic model part of human society. Energy is the currency (resource) of the body and the brain, so to speak. Individuals and cells can be viewed as Energy processors, part of a larger group or society (household).

Because of all the outstanding qualities listed above, it can be argued that the healthy human body represents the ideal and rational (logical) economic model that economist has been striving for. Mainstream economic models often assume that people are rational and deal with perfect information. NEM presents outstanding levels of rationality (Logos), simplicity, parsimony, and objectivity. In agreement with Occam's razor, all redundant abstractions (i.e. concepts) have been removed (shaved away). NEM also represents an application of Biomimetics to the realm of economics.

Scarcity of resources is a concept prevalent in traditional economic models. It also serves as justification for competition. On the other hand, the earth and the universe are made of abundant Energy; enough Energy to meet the needs of every human being, provided that we learn how to tap into it. The fact is that there is sufficient Energy to sustain everyone in the planet in terms of food and land [67]. By polluting the planet, typical economies are dangerously contributing to the potential creation of severe future scarcity.

It should be fairly obvious that nature, as exemplified by living beings, provides a distinct economic approach based on unity, cooperation, and the universal concept of Energy – as opposed to self-interest and competition. Each individual cell has a specific function or purpose to fulfill within the overall logical organization of the body.

Darwin's theories have been employed to justify unbridled capitalism based on competition: the survival of the fittest (see Herbert Spencer [30]). Such argument can be rebutted based on the fact that rational human beings and societies thereof, must not emulate the behavior of primitive species with limited logical abilities.

In other words, it is illogical to expect advanced societies of humans to behave like groups of primitive animals with limited rational abilities. It also contradicts a fundamental economic precept: individuals being highly rational, since primitive animals do not meet the criteria. David Sarnoff said "Competition brings out the best in products and the worst in [people]." It can be argued that intelligence (of individuals, groups, species, and civilizations) can be measured based on the knowledge, understanding, and mastery of the universal concept of Energy and its law(s).

The rationality of the concept of competition is in question, which seems like a contradiction given the rational nature pursued by traditional economic models. Therefore, a fundamental concept of traditional economic theory is being undermined. It can be argued that cooperation provides a better, more rational, and more efficient approach at many levels [67]: what benefits the group or society of individuals as a whole, also benefits each individual part of the group. Multiple publications and empirical studies have documented the case for cooperation [67].

Similar to traditional economic models, the natural one puts an emphasis on logic and rationality (Logos). An obvious difference between NEM and traditional models – as exhibited by the human body – is the fact that human beings have free will, which individual cells do not exhibit. However, it may be agued that both entities can be governed by reason as part of a larger society that pursues the common good of both: society as a whole and the individual.

Although a 'government of reason (Logos)' should sound idealistic and utopian, leading political thinkers have envisioned such government as feasible and beneficial. It makes sense for people to accept such government after grasping the logical benefits for the societal group which they are part of. It is a win-win proposition for society and the individual where there are no losers (no competition).

Stoicism has been influential in the realms of philosophy, physics, and logic. Stoics advocate living according to nature and reason as the main purpose (telos) of human life. A government of laws is a concept in high regard.

"My hope [is] that we have not labored in vain, and that our experiment will still prove that men can be governed by reason [Logos]." Thomas Jefferson

"The idea of establishing a government by reasoning and agreement, [the monarchists] publicly ridiculed as a Utopian project, visionary and unexampled." Thomas Jefferson

It can be argued that the qualities exhibited by cooperative economic model, mimicked from nature, are in better agreement with the desires and aspirations of a free democratic society in terms of harmony, liberty, unity, justice, and common welfare.

"We the People of the United States in Order to form a more **perfect Union**, establish **Justice**, insure domestic **Tranquility**, provide the common defense, promote the **general Welfare**, and secure the **Blessings of Liberty** to ourselves and our Posterity, do ordain and establish this Constitution for the United States of America." Preamble to the U.S. Constitution

Achieving the level of organization, unity, rationality, and excellence in overall 'design' exhibited by nature's economic model should prove to be a major endeavor and human challenge, requiring the investment of significant effort. A gradual transition will probably be required.

However, the human body serves as a model and example that it can be *realistically* accomplished, if we learn how to mimic nature and master the concept of Energy. It also requires a major shift in terms of thinking and economic paradigm: from selfish individualistic competition to rational cooperation within the realm of a unified society governed by reason (Logos). Education of the population must change as well in favor of rational cooperation.

Related economic models need to be mentioned. Capitalism "is not a realm of harmony and mutual benefit" (see Karl Marx [30]). Karl Marx envisioned a different economic system based on economic equality, social justice, and reduction of scarcity: from each according to his/her ability, to each according to his/her need. Nature's economic system presents similar elements: it requires a high level of organization and planning.

224

On the other hand, there are marked differences. In a healthy body, each cell receives an allocation of Energy according to its function within the body: *to each according to his/her function (purpose)*. One's function (purpose/telos) determines and justifies one's needs. For instance, a carpenter needs a hammer while a writer needs a pen (or computer) depending on their function within society.

The natural approach provides theoretical simplicity, based on a single concept: Energy. There is a biological and physiological (natural) inspiration. In consequence, there are highly rational, organized, efficient, and unparalleled mechanisms for the production and distribution of Energy.

Each cell must work and be productive to fulfill its purpose/function within the overall design and organization of the body's economy. *Depending on the specific function (purpose/telos)* to be performed, each type of cell will have different Energy requirements to be met. Distribution of Energy is based on highly unified, rational, and sophisticated systems which are quite unique.

"The imagination of nature is far, far greater than the imagination of man." Richard Feynman

"Look into Nature and you will understand everything better." Albert Einstein

To be consistent with Occam's razor, the concepts of money and wages should be examined carefully since they do not exist in nature. Eventually, such concepts conceived by the human imagination, might be shaved away altogether. However, they will probably be part of the economic system, and associated models, for a long time to come. A similar argument can presented for the concept of greed. In pragmatic terms, wages must always meet minimum sustenance requirements.

A higher level of rationality and organization results in the gradual elimination of competition in favor of cooperation between individuals, entities, and systems. There is less overlapping of activities among cooperative entities and individuals as opposed to competitive ones fighting over market share and/or resources – therefore, a more efficient utilization of Energy resources. In summary, it can be hypothesized that by carefully mimicking nature's economic model, a better "organization of labor" and "distribution of goods" will ensue.

"No business which depends for existence on paying less than living wages to its workers has any right to continue in this country." Franklin D. Roosevelt

The golden rule (Logos), is arguably a gem of logic: "Do unto others as you would have them do unto you." It seems clearly illogical (paradoxical), at the very least, to expect better treatment from others than the one we are willing to give. The golden rule is associated with what Aquinas's first moral principle: love one's neighbor as oneself (see Aquinas' Moral, Political, and Legal Philosophy [30]), part of the Decalogue – also derived from Logos. The concept of reciprocity (golden rule) is part of all major faiths.

According to Aquinas, all moral principles and norms can be inferred from the first principle (see Aquinas' Moral, Political, and Legal Philosophy [30]). The Concept of war is illogical, diametrically opposed to the golden rule. In other words, the concept of war defies logic; in particular, when engaging people of faith, who are under the golden rule: an obsolete concept reserved from a more primitive times and species. In von Neumann's terms, MAD: mutual assured destruction. Eleanor Roosevelt is quoted of saying: "Anyone who thinks must think of the next war as they would of suicide."

Logos is an awesome concept: universal, omnipresent, immutable, all-encompassing – responsible for ruling Energy and therefore the entire physical universe, our logical minds, and our moral behavior. A government of reason would be one of peace and justice. For his work, Landauer used the modern definition: "thought of as constituting the controlling principle of the universe" [33]. He also used following scripture verse to explain the concept of Logos, from the Greek.

Based on faith, it seems to make perfect sense. According to John 1.1, there is no separation between God, and Logos (reason): no division or contradiction between God and science, which is based on reason. They are one and the same. Logos (God) is the ruler of Energy, and therefore of the universe. Also, according to scripture, God is Love. In 'mysterious' ways, most of the scientists from the past named in this chapter, were people of faith.

In the beginning was the Logos, and the Logos was with God, and the Logos was God. John 1.1

226

23. ACKNOWLEDGEMENTS

Reviews, comments, and corrections are truly appreciated; in particular, recommendations to leverage relevant interdisciplinary theories and research related to the mind as a theoretical/empirical foundation for the Conceptual computing model. The list of comments includes the following:

"The [Conceptual] approach is very interesting, relevant, and can be applied to several different CS topic areas/courses."
"Applying Biomathematics and Philosophy to software engineering models and programming languages is a novel concept."

"… It's fascinating. You have clearly put an enormous amount of thought and effort … your topic is one that spans many [areas] from a software engineering perspective…."

"Interesting and provocative approach."

REFERENCES

1. Boole, G. *An Investigation of the Laws of Thought on Which are Founded the Mathematical Theories of Logic and Probabilities.* Macmillan. Reprinted with corrections, Dover Publications, New York, NY, 1958.

2. Galvis, A. *Messaging Design Pattern and Pattern Implementation.* 17th conference on Pattern Languages of Programs - PLoP 2010.

3. Turing, A. *Computing Machinery and Intelligence.* Mind 1950.

4. Galvis, A. *Process Design Pattern and a Realistic Information Model.* 18th conference on Pattern Languages of Programs (writers' workshop) - PLoP 2011.

5. Galvis, A. *Messaging Design Pattern and Live or Animated Objects.* 18th conference on Pattern Languages of Programs (writers' workshop) - PLoP 2011.

6. Lamport, L. *The implementation of Reliable Distributed Multiprocess Systems.* Computer Networks. 1978.

7. Hewitt, C. E. *Viewing Control Structures as Patterns of Passing Messages.* MIT. Artificial Intelligence Laboratory. A.I. Memo 410, December 1976.

8. Galvis, E. A. and Galvis D. E. *Conceptual Computing Model (A=(f(m), I)).* Submitted for publication.

9. Gregor Hohpe and Bobby Woolf. *Enterprise Integration Patterns: Designing, Building, and Deploying Messaging Solutions.* Addison-Wesley, 2004.

10. Galvis, E. A. *Jt - Java Pattern Oriented Framework, An application of the Messaging Design Pattern.* IBM Technical Library, 2010.

11. Gamma, E. et al. *Design Patterns: Abstraction and Reuse of Object-Oriented Design.* ECOOP '93 Proceedings of the 7th European Conference on Object-Oriented Programming.

12. Fielding, R. T. Architectural Styles and the Design of Network-based Software Architectures. Ph.D. Dissertation. University of California, 2000.

13. Bih, J. *Service Oriented Architecture (SOA) a new paradigm to implement dynamic e-business solutions.* ACM ubiquity, August, 2006.

14. Henning, M. *Rise and Fall of CORBA*. ACM queue, June, 2006.

15. Loughran S. et al. *Rethinking the Java SOAP Stack.* IEEE International Conference of Web Services (ICWS) 2005. Orlando, USA, 2005.

16. Schneider, F. B. *Implementing fault-tolerant services using the state machine approach: A tutorial.* ACM Computing Surveys. 1990.

17. Michael B. et al. *BPELJ:BPEL for Java.*BEA Systems Inc. and IBM Corp.USA, 2004.

18. *BRAIN 2025 Report, A Scientific Vision.* U. S. National Institute of Health (NIH). June 2014.

19. Turing, A. *On Computable Numbers, With an Application to the Entscheidungs problem.* Proceedings of the London Mathematical Society, Series 2, Volume 42, 1936.

20. Goth, G. *Critics say Web Services need a REST.* IEEE distributed systems online. Vol. 5. No. 12, 2004.

21. Sowa, J. *Cognitive Architectures for Conceptual Structures,* Proceedings of ICCS 2011, Heidelberg: Springer, 2011, pp. 35-49.

22. Roberts, S. on George Boole. *The Isaac Newton of logic.* The Globe and Mail. March 27, 2004.
http://www.theglobeandmail.com/life/the-isaac-newton-of-logic/article1129894/?page=1

23. Von Neumann, J. *First Draft of a Report on the EDVAC.* 1945.

24. Chen, P. *The Entity-Relationship Model--Toward a Unified View of Data.* In Communications of the ACM, 1(1).1976.

25. Newell, A. and Simon, H. *Computer Science as Empirical Inquiry: Symbols and Search.* In Communications of the ACM, 19 (3).1976.

26. Backus, J. *Can Programming Be Liberated From the von Neumann Style?* 1977 Turing Award Lecture.

27. Sowa, J. *Conceptual graphs for a database interface.* IBM Journal of Research and Development, vol. 20, no. 4, pp. 336-357. 1976

28. Nilsson, N. *The Physical Symbol System Hypothesis: Status and Prospects.* In M. Lungarella, et al., (eds.), 50 Years of AI, Festschrift, LNAI 4850, pp. 9-17, Springer, 2007.

29. Milner, R. *Elements of interaction,* ACM, 36(1), January 1993.

30. *Stanford Encyclopedia of Philosophy*. http://plato.stanford.edu/

31. Tegmark, Max. *The Mathematical Universe*. Foundations of Physics 38 (2): 101–150. 2008.

32. Newell, A. *Unified Theories of Cognition*, Harvard University Press. 1994.

33. Landauer, R. *The physical nature of information*. Physics Letters A 217, 1996.

34. Johnson-Laird, P. *Mental models: Towards a cognitive science of language, inference, and consciousness*. 1983.

35. Anderson, P. W. *More is different*. Science, August 1972.

36. Dodig-Crnkovic, G. *Significance of Models of Computation, from Turing Model to Natural Computation*. Minds and Machines, May 2011.

37. Chidamber S. and Kemerer C. *A metrics suite for object-oriented design*. IEEE Trans. on Software Engineering, June 1994.

38. Basili, V. et at. *A Validation of Object-Oriented Design Metrics as Quality Indicators*. IEEE Trans. on Software Engineering, October 1996.

39. Rosenberg, L. et al. *Risk-based object oriented testing*. Twenty Fourth Annual Software Engineering Workshop, NASA, 1999

40. Tegarden, D. et al. *A software complexity model of object-oriented systems*. Decision Support Systems: The International Journal, January 1993.

41. Lorenz, M. et al. *Object-oriented software metrics*, Prentice-Hall. 1994.

42. Lie, W. et at. *Object-oriented metrics that predict maintainability*. Journal of Systems and Software. February 1993.

43. Wooldridge, M. *Multiagent Systems: Introduction (2nd Edition)*. John Wiley & Sons. 2009.

44. Krueger, C. W. *Software reuse*. ACM Computing Surveys, 24(2), June 1992.

45. Savage, J. E. *Models of Computation*. Addison-Wesley, 1998.

46. Nenad Medvidovic and Richard N. Taylor. *Exploiting Architectural Style to Develop a Family of Applications. IEE Proceedings Software Engineering*, October 1997.

47. *Application Architecture Guide (Patterns & Practices)*, Microsoft. September 2009.

48. Culler, D. et al. *LogP: Towards a Realistic Model of Parallel Computation.* ACM SIGPLAN Symposium on Principles and Practice of Parallel Programming, May 1993.

49. Skillicorn, D. and Talia, D. *Models and Languages for Parallel Computation.* ACM Computing Surveys, June 1998.

50. Xu Liu et al. *Optogenetic stimulation of a hippocampal engram activates fear memory recall.* Nature, April 2012.

51. Nirenberg, S., Pandarinath, C. *Retinal prosthetic strategy with the capacity to restore normal vision*, Proceedings of the National Academy of Sciences (PNAS), 2012.

52. *Internet Encyclopedia of Philosophy.* http://www.iep.utm.edu

53. Fodor, J. *The Language of Thought*, Harvard University Press. 1975.

54. Ferrucci, D. et al. *Building Watson: An overview of the DeepQA Project.* AI Magazine. Fall, 2010.

55. Karen L. Myers et al. *A Cognitive Framework for Delegation to an Assistive User Agent.* AAAI 2005 Fall Symposium on Mixed-Initiative Problem Solving Assistants. November, 2005.

56. *MIT Encyclopedia of Cognitive Science.* http://ai.ato.ms/MITECS/Entry/sloman.html

57. *Survey of the State of the Art in Human Language Technology.* Cole R. Editor. 1997.

58. McCarthy, J. *From Here to Human Level AI.* Stanford CS Department Technical Report, 1996.

59. Anderson, J.R. et al. *An integrated theory of the mind.* Psychological Review, Vol. 111, No. 4, 2004.

60. Cambria, E. et at. *Jumping NLP Curves: A Review of Natural Language Processing Research.* IEEE Computational Intelligence Magazine. May, 2014.

61. Vernon D. et al. *A survey of artificial cognitive systems: implications for the autonomous development of mental capabilities in computational agents.* IEEE Transactions on Evolutionary Computation. April 2007.

62. Chong, H. Q. et al. *Integrated cognitive architectures: a survey.* Artificial Intelligence Review, 2007.

63. Darwiche, A. Y. et al. *A Symbolic Generalization of Probability Theory*. AAAI, 1992.

64. Skidelsky, R. *Keynes: The Return of the Master*. PublicAffairs, 2009.

65. Clegg, B. *Gravity*. St. Martin's Press, 2012.

66. Kruglinski S., Chanarin, O. Roger Penrose Says Physics Is Wrong, From String Theory to Quantum Mechanics. Discover, 2009.

67. Kohn, A. No Contest: The Case against Competition. Houghton Mifflin Company, 1992.

APPENDIX

A. Related Approaches of Software Reuse

"William of Occam opposed the proliferation of entities, but only when carried beyond what is needed --procter necessitatem! ... But computer scientists must also look for something basic [information/Energy] which underlies the various models; they are interested not only in individual designs and systems, but also in a *unified theory* of their ingredients." Robin Milner [29]

Realism (realistic correspondence), reductionism, and Occam's razor have had a prominent impact on science and scientific models [30, 29]. Realism asserts that reality exists independent of the observer and that the truth of a representation is determined by how it corresponds to reality (The Correspondence Theory of Truth[30]).

"I believe computer science differs little from physics, in this general scientific method, even if not in its experimental criteria. Like many computer scientists, I hope for a broad *informatical* science of phenomena- both manmade and *natural*- to match the rich existing physical science." Robin Milner [29]

As a general rule of thumb, if the technology or approach is not based on the precise Turing-complete mathematical formulation $(A=(f(m),I)/C)$, then it is clearly different. Furthermore, if the underlying model consists of more abstractions than the ones proposed, there is redundancy that should be 'shaved away' according to Occam's razor and the concepts exhibited by the natural mind. Redundant abstractions bring forth unnecessary complexity.

Krueger introduces the following taxonomy of different approaches of software reuse based on the central role played by abstractions [44]: High-Level Languages, Software Components (including OO) ,Software Schemas, Application Generators, Transformational Systems and Software Architectures. The mathematical Conceptual computing model is related to software components and software architectures.

Design patterns also represent a related approach to software reuse [11]. However, notice that these approaches of software reuse do not represent mathematical models which make them different from the start. They are also based on traditional computing models and therefore inherit their characteristics: qualities and limitations (see Model Evaluation and Metrics).

As mentioned earlier, the terms object and component are used interchangeably. From an information perspective, the fundamental aspect is whether the object or component is able to process information in the real world. If so, the object or component is represented and implemented using a Live/Animated component $(A=(f(m),I))$. The term 'component' should not be confused with how it is used (precise semantics) in the context of component-based software engineering (CBSE) and related technologies. A discussion about the CBSE approach can be found later in this section.

OO/Component technologies do not represent mathematical models of computing. The Turing-complete Conceptual computing model is different in several aspects including mathematical foundation, abstractions, simplicity (Occam's razor), Turing-complete information machine $(A=(f(m),I))$, single information primitive, single concept construct (C), reductionism based on natural concepts (information/Energy, messaging, information machine), and degree of realistic correspondence.

In agreement with reductionism and expressed by the Turing-complete mathematical model, computing can be reduced (unified/simplified) to the concepts of *information* (Energy), messaging, and information machine/processor $(A=(f(m),I))$. Such reduction is in agreement with Occam's razor applied in the realm computer science (see Physical Foundation).

Furthermore, most entities in the world around us should be realistically represented using the concept construct (C) because they are unable to process information. Adding information processing capabilities to these entities is artificial, unrealistic, and not beneficial/required.

For discussion purposes the following quote should also be carefully considered:

"We can note in passing that one of the biggest problems in the development of object-oriented SW architectures, particularly in the last 25 years, has been an enormous over-focus on objects and an under-focus on **messaging** (most so-called object-oriented languages don't *really* use the looser coupling of messaging, but instead use the much tighter gear meshing of procedure calls – this hurts scalability and interoperability)." Alan Kay et al.

Tighter gear meshing of procedure calls has also been characterized as "The complex machinery of procedure declarations" while discussing problems associated with traditional APIs [26].

"The complex machinery of procedure declarations including elaborate naming conventions, which are further complicated by the substitution rules needed in calling procedures. Each of these requires a complex mechanism to be built into the framework so that variables, subscripted variables, pointers, file names, procedure names, call-by-value formal parameters, call-by-name formal parameters, and so on, can all be properly interpreted." [26].

Furthermore, traditional component APIs usually rely on tighter gear meshing of procedure calls which is the source of a variety of issues including the ones mentioned above: coupling, interoperability limitations, and scalability limitations. Such issues apply to implementations based on components/objects and design patterns.

Consider a bank application dealing with accounts, bank statements, transactions, and so on. All of these entities can be represented as using the concept construct (C) because they are only able of conveying information. The banking system via a Live/Animated component, like a teller component, is the only entity that needs to process information in the form of the aforementioned concepts. All the other entities can be represented using the single concept construct (C).

As a consequence of the Conceptual model, a complex system can be specified, in a highly realistic fashion, using very few components with information processing capabilities. Obviously, the Conceptual model provides realism and simplicity among other advantages.

235

Now consider all the entities contained in an arbitrary database. They only contain information without processing capability whatsoever. All the entities inside a database can be represented using a single concept construct (C) for processing purposes.

Such conceptual representation also results in the significant reduction of the number of *real* components required for system implementation. In the scenario of the banking example discussed above, all the required entities (accounts, transactions, statements, etc)   can be stored and manipulated using a single abstraction: concept construct (C).

Since the concept construct (C) represent pure information – independent of computer language, technology, platform, and protocol – they can be freely interchanged between heterogeneous systems, applications systems, and components. In contrast, traditional objects or components that *artificially* couple information and processing mechanism, as a single entity, are unable to provide this degree of interoperability.

By classifying entities into two groups, the number of components necessary for implementation is significantly reduced: a few encapsulated Animated/Live components, able to process information, dealing with all the other entities represented using the concept construct (C).

The Conceptual computing model also eliminates unrealistic abstractions, artifacts, and primitives which are ultimately redundant. Overall system simplification is achieved. As an additional consequence, the complex web of tightly coupled and unrealistic component/object interdependencies is also eliminated. Artifacts are in direct conflict with natural concepts. Tight gear meshing of procedure calls (artifact) must never be confused or mischaracterized as real messaging. The natural concept and the artifact are *different*.

Traditional objects consist of a fixed number of attributes. On the other hand, the concept construct (C) is a dynamic entity which does not have a fixed number of associations. Instead, associations can be created dynamically. A sentence, for instance, can have a variety of structures (and associations). In this sense, objects are more concrete than concepts.

In turn, every physical object can be represented using the concept construct (C).

Design patterns do not represent mathematical models of computing. They are typically applicable to a specific context and focus on finding trade-offs or drawbacks associated with their utilization in such context. In contrast, the Turing-complete Conceptual computing model is applicable to the implementation of arbitrary information technologies; in particular, the comprehensive implementation of design patterns [2, 4, 5].

The model is also different in several aspects including mathematical foundation, abstractions, simplicity (Occam's razor), Turing-complete information machine $(A=(f(m),I))$, single information primitive, single concept construct (C), reductionism based on natural concepts (information/Energy, messaging, information machine), and degree of realistic correspondence.

Concepts are more general than design patterns. Notice that there is a large variety of design patterns. In agreement with reductionism, all design patterns are reducible to the concepts part of the Turing-complete Conceptual model: information (Energy), messaging, and information machine. In consequence, these concepts can be leveraged for the implementation of arbitrary design patterns [2, 4, 5].

Carefully consider that nature and natural processes already have an inherent design to them – based on the concept of Energy and processing thereof. In order to achieve true correspondence and realism [30], we must mimic it as part of the software design. Obviously, there is no point in 'reinventing' a design that already exists as part of natural creation. This realization will result in additional key differences between the Conceptual computing model and the related abstractions in terms of design approach, identification of trade-offs/drawbacks, context, and so forth.

Aristotle defined the idea of perfection based on three associated concepts: as that which is complete, that which is so good that nothing could be better (unequaled), and that which has attained its purpose (effective). Arguably, idealized natural concepts meet the criteria and are therefore flawless; in particular Energy to which all natural concepts are reducible to (see Physical Foundation). Information is reducible to the concept of Energy. The Conceptual model helps understand why trade-offs and drawbacks are not found.

Natural concepts are extracted from reality in the form in which they exist. For instance, consider the concepts of Energy and Messaging. Trying to find trade-offs and drawbacks associated to these concepts is probably a futile undertaking. Improving upon nature just seems unrealistic. The Designer of nature obviously seems to have a true knack for perfection. Also, natural concepts are unique and there are no similar entities that can be used for comparison purposes.

It is best to view and study the information family from the perspective of concepts – as opposed to design patterns. In general, while studying concepts, it is not necessary to specify or look for trade-offs/drawbacks. Concepts should be modeled, mimicked, and implemented as they exist in the real world (verbatim).

In terms of the perfection of natural creation, many theologians, philosophers, and scientists would be able to argue the subject based on faith and careful observation of the wonders of nature. "It is the *perfection* of God's works that they are all done with the greatest simplicity". – Isaac Newton.

Our best effort is limited to studying and mimicking such concepts in order to achieve a realistic representation and the associated software improvements. Going back to the taxonomy proposed by Krueger, software architectures represent reusable software frameworks and subsystems that capture the overall software design. There are key distinctions between these and the Conceptual approach. Software frameworks/subsystems do not represent mathematical models of computing. They tend to focus on *specific* application domains and are usually tied to a specific computer language [11].

238

Framework implementation usually relies on traditional APIs, gear meshing of procedure calls, multithreading, and distributed artifacts. Therefore, they inevitably inherit the limitations discussed earlier: complexity, coupling, interoperability, and scalability. It is a common practice to represent every entity using the object abstraction, with associated information processing capabilities.

In contrast, the Conceptual approach represents a Turing-complete mathematical computing model, applicable to the implementation of arbitrary information technologies; in particular, the comprehensive implementation of software architectures and reusable frameworks [2, 4, 5]. The model is also different in several aspects including mathematical foundation, abstractions, simplicity (Occam's razor), Turing-complete information machine ($A=(f(m),I)$), single information primitive, single concept construct (C), reductionism based on natural concepts (information/Energy, messaging, information machine), and degree of realistic correspondence.

The Turing-complete Conceptual approach recognizes that natural processes already have an inherent architecture and design based on a realistic set of concepts that need to be extracted, through conceptualization, as part of the software effort. Concepts are language/platform agnostic. No artificial components/objects, primitives, or abstractions are added to a realistic implementation based on natural concepts (physical concepts).

The universe of abstractions (i.e. entities) is realistically and unequivocally divided into two main categories depending on the ability to process information: Live/Animated entity (information machine) or concept construct (C). As a consequence, a reusable Conceptual framework can be implemented with only two core classes: Animated/Live component and concept construct (C).

A total of 12 key classes (NKC = 12) are required to implement a comprehensive framework, reusable in arbitrary application domains, and able to naturally handle complex real-world challenges such as distributed component/service access, security, interoperability, fault tolerance, concurrency, and scalability [2,4,5,10] (see Model Evaluation and Metrics).

Software architectures and abstractions that focus on specific application domains are typically more concrete than concepts. For example, consider a framework for the domain of banking applications similar to the one discussed earlier. It would consist of specific domain abstractions such as Account, Transaction, Statement, and so forth. Like every other abstraction found in reality, these also represent information (concept construct (C)).

In other words, they are more concrete entities part of the broader concept of information. By recognizing this, a *single* reusable software component, part of a conceptual framework, may encapsulate the functionality required to store and retrieve arbitrary pieces of information (C). Such component would mimic the human memory which is able to store and retrieve arbitrary concepts (C).

Therefore, high levels of reusability are accomplished by relying on the concept construct (C) instead of the more concrete entity (see Memory or Information Repository). In other words, the general solution applicable to the concept construct (C) is also reusable and applicable to the concrete entity (special case).

Multiple technologies and implementations fall under the umbrella of component-based software engineering (CBSE), including EJB, CORBA, and COM+. CBSE technologies do not represent mathematical models of computing or focus on mathematical foundations. Like the Conceptual model, component communication is accomplished through well-defined interfaces.

Typical CBSE technologies rely on distributed artifacts, multithreading and traditional APIs based on gear meshing of procedure calls. Therefore, they inevitably inherit limitations and drawbacks that have been studied and documented in the technical literature [13, 14, 15, 20]: complexity, interoperability, coupling, versioning, and proprietary limitations. Alan Kay's comments in terms of coupling, interoperability, and scalability also apply to typical CBSE technologies and components.

In contrast, there is a single Conceptual computing model based on a realistic approach and precise mathematical foundation (Turing

240

complete). The Conceptual approach is distinctly different in several aspects including mathematical foundation, abstractions, Turing-complete information machine ($A=(f(m),I)$), single information primitive, single concept construct (C), reductionism based on natural concepts (information/Energy, messaging, information machine), unequivocal separation between component and concept construct (C), simplicity (Occam's razor), and degree of realistic correspondence. Founded on natural concepts and realism, messaging is the *single communication interface*.

Per earlier remarks, the concept of messaging must never be mischaracterized or confused with gear meshing of procedure calls. Solutions based on the Conceptual approach can readily interoperate regardless of technology, platform, protocol, and/or computer language (including CBSE technologies). The computing model inspired by nature, also contributes to the resolution of the aforementioned software engineering challenges in straightforward and natural ways: improved coupling, interoperability, and scalability.

C2 is a component-and-message based architecture style for GUI software [47]. Like the Conceptual approach, it puts emphasis on messaging between components, independent processing mechanism, and the support for component heterogeneity – all of which present desirable qualities in software. C2 does not focus on mathematical foundations. It separates computation (components) from interaction (connectors). All communication between C2 components is achieved through asynchronous message passing between components via C2 connectors.

A C2 component consists of the following abstractions: a) dialog which receives notifications and requests mapping them into internal object operations. b) internal object c) domain translator used to resolve incompatibilities between communicating components. Additional C2 abstractions include layering, substrate independence, domain translation, top/bottom domains, and implicit invocation of the component's internal object.

In contrast, the Conceptual approach represents a mathematical computing model (Turing complete). The approach is distinctly different in several aspects including mathematical foundation, abstractions, Turing-complete information machine $(A=(f(m),I))$, single information primitive, single concept construct (C), reductionism based on natural concepts (information/Energy, messaging, information machine), unequivocal separation between component and concept construct (C), simplicity (Occam's razor), and degree of realistic correspondence.

In agreement with Occam's razor, no additional abstractions, primitives, and/or APIs are necessary. It also provides a straightforward mathematical foundation for every abstraction, at every level of organization – including component and architecture. An architecture simply consists of a group of information machines (Live/Animated entities) working cooperatively ($\{A_1, \dots, A_n\}$). All forms of messaging are supported in a natural fashion including synchronous and asynchronous.

Nature already provides *one unified* model, architecture, and design for information processing based on a complete and straightforward collection of natural concepts – in agreement with Occam's razor.

"If a thing can be done adequately by means of one [concept], it is superfluous to do it by means of several; for we observe that nature does not employ two instruments [concepts] where one suffices". St. Thomas Aquinas.

All implementations of the Conceptual model must be based on the same unified mathematical foundation (A/C) which makes them fully interoperable regardless of technology, protocol, platform, and/or computer language. As part of the Conceptual approach, there is also an unequivocal separation between component (computation) and concept construct (pure information) not studied by C2.

Most entities should be realistically represented using the single concept construct (C) with no information processing capabilities; therefore, substantially reducing the number of *real* components required for implementation. Assigning 'component behavior' to unanimated entities lacks realistic correspondence and brings forth redundant complexities. Most of the aforementioned differences also apply to other CBSE approaches, besides C2.

Conceptually, connectors are needed for a realistic representation in certain scenarios, but not always. The concept of Messaging between components can assume several forms in the real world. Both scenarios can be encountered: with or without connectors as participants.

Moreover, it may become unnecessarily cumbersome to employ C2 connectors/components and asynchronous messaging for the interaction between local components within an application – where synchronous messaging and plain local components/objects are sufficient. In agreement with Biomimetics and Occam's razor, the following quote is applicable to software architectures:

"The architect of the future will build imitating Nature, for it is the most rational, long-lasting, and economical of all methods." A. Gaudi

B. Related Models and Approaches

"William of Occam opposed the proliferation of entities, but only when carried beyond what is needed --procter necessitatem! ... But computer scientists must also look for something basic which underlies the various models; they are interested not only in individual designs and systems, but also in a *unified theory* of their ingredients." Robin Milner [29]

"I believe computer science differs little from physics, in this general scientific method, even if not in its experimental criteria. Like many computer scientists, I hope for a broad *informatical* science of phenomena- both manmade and *natural-* to match the rich existing physical science." Robin Milner [29]

The Conceptual approach represents a *mathematical model of computing*. This appendix discusses related models of computing, including the Actor model. Related approaches of software reuse have been discussed earlier: OO, CBSE including C2, and Design Patterns (see appendix on Related Approaches of Software Reuse). As discussed in the model evaluation section, multiple models of computing have been proposed: operational, applicative, and von Neumann models (see Model Evaluation and Metrics).

Relevant ideas such as realism (realistic correspondence), reductionism, and Occam's razor have had a prominent impact on science and scientific models [30, 29]. The Conceptual computing model can be applied to the implementation of arbitrary computing/information technologies. Consider that the Turing-complete mathematical model applies to all levels of organization: component, process, application, system, computer, architecture, and arbitrary groups of these entities.

However, it should be stated that all related models, technologies, and approaches are distinctly different because of their mathematical foundations. As a general rule of thumb, if the model, technology, or approach is not based on the Turing-complete mathematical formulation $(A=(f(m),I)/C)$, then it is clearly different. Furthermore, if the underlying model consists of more abstractions than the ones proposed, there is redundancy that should be 'shaved away' according to Occam's razor and the concepts exhibited by the natural mind. Redundant abstractions bring forth unnecessary complexity.

Actor model. In regards to the Actor model, it should be stated that the model was initially created during the 70's, which obviously puts it at a disadvantage. A lot of software technology advances have come to pass since that time; specifically in the areas of object-oriented/component methodologies, design patterns, and software modeling. More than 40 years later, there is a better understanding of software models, principles and abstractions. On the other hand, the Actor model provides a rigorous theoretical framework for asynchronous messaging.

The Actor model relies on several abstractions, assumptions, primitives and implementation aspects that do not mimic reality. The model makes the assumption that the message delivery is guaranteed (fairness). As a consequence, mailboxes are infinite. Such assumption has been the source of criticism, in terms of realistic correspondence – a key aspect in the context of scientific models and their evaluation. Fairness assumptions pose challenges that may have hindered the applicability of the Actor model.

Every single entity is modeled as an actor in the context of the Actor model. Even messages are artificially represented using actors, which has been criticized as dogmatic and the source of complexity. The original Actor model was not studied and specified from a modern OO perspective, unavailable at the time of its conception.

The Actor model uses the concept of *behavior*. Each time an Actor accepts a message, a replacement *behavior* is computed. Behavior is already handled by the component functionality provided by its internal functions or methods. In other words, the component will behave according to the information received (inputs), its internal state, and its collection of functions or methods. In reality, the concept of behavior is already an intrinsic aspect associated with an object or component. No separate abstraction and associated set of primitives need to be modeled and implemented.

Another example would be the required use of the *acquaintance* abstraction which fits reality within a specific set of scenarios. On the other hand, an accurate representation needs to recognize that for most messaging scenarios, an additional *acquaintance* abstraction is not really necessary. In the context of a complete distributed component/service model, acquaintances and their associated primitives are not required.

245

The Actor model relies on several additional abstractions and associated primitives: *receptionist, mail address, cell, continuation, future, task,* etc. For instance, the Actor model requires the concept of *receptionist* which is also useful for a specific set of applications. On the other hand, this abstraction and associated primitives should not always be required. The model also uses the concept of *mail address* to interchange messages between actors. An actor may obtain the target's mail address from one of three sources:

a) It was known to the actor from the start, when the actor was first created.

b) It came within a message sent to the actor.

c) It was defined by the actor when it created another actor.

The original Actor model acknowledges open issues regarding its implementation, specifically in terms of the messaging mechanisms [7]. Pure Actors are based exclusively on asynchronous communication. Typically, Actor implementations can readily interoperate with technologies based on the same model and associated set of abstractions.

The Conceptual computing model is distinctly different in terms of mathematical foundation, abstractions, simplicity (Occam's razor), Turing-complete information machine *(A=(f(m),I)),* single concept construct (C), single information primitive, degree of realistic correspondence, reductionism based on natural concepts (information/Energy, messaging, information machine), and overall realistic approach mimicked from the conceptual mind. Founded on natural concepts and realism, the model/implementation does not rely on redundant abstractions, primitives, or APIs.

The Conceptual model is founded on a modern understanding of software engineering models and principles. All modalities of messaging are accommodated including synchronous, asynchronous, streaming, local/distributed messaging, two-way messaging, secure messaging, and combinations of these forms.

246

Animated/Live components can send messages to any other component (local or remote) without restrictions. Other application components may provide the directory services required to locate distributed components. Any straightforward naming mechanism can be utilized depending on the requirements of the application being implemented. For instance, services provided by Animated/Live components can be accessed by using the URL associated to the target component. Distributed Animated/Live components may be accessed without the need for a *receptionist*. From the perspective of realistic correspondence, a message can be sent directly to an Animated/Live component without the need of intermediaries.

Process Algebras (Process Calculus). These approaches focus on the process abstraction, communication, and related operations as part of their mathematical models. Aspects such as model realism based on natural concepts (including Live/Animated entities), are not part of their scope. There are several process algebras. In contrast, there is only one Conceptual model.

The Conceptual computing model is distinctly different in terms of mathematical foundation, abstractions, Turing-complete information machine $(A=(f(m),I))$, single information primitive, single concept construct (C), biomimetics motivation, reductionism based on natural concepts (information/Energy, messaging, information machine), and overall realistic approach mimicked from the mind. Abstractions, primitives, and implementation are in correspondence as well.

The approach is able to provide a straightforward mathematical foundation for every level of organization – including the process level. A process is modeled by a group of information machines (Live/Animated entities) working concurrently (in parallel) and communicating via messaging: ($\{A_1, \dots , A_n\}$ where $A_i = (f_i(m), I_i)$). From the perspective of realistic correspondence, information machines/processors are ubiquitous entities – part of countless processes in the real world.

The Conceptual approach is not limited to a specific problem domain, area of application, or level of organization: an object/component, a service, a process, an application, a system, a computer, and arbitrary groups of these entities can be realistically modeled by the approach. It provides a Turing-complete mathematical foundation for every level of organization: in agreement with reductionism, the same mathematical concepts (i.e. natural concepts) are applicable to every level which avoids the need for redundancy in terms of abstractions (constructs), primitives, artifacts, or APIs.

"To solve nearly any problem, we must both reduce [conceptualize] the problem to its component parts [concepts], and then provide a solution to the problem as a whole. In doing so, we use both reductionism and holism in partnership." Chris Masterjohn

"It is necessary to remark that there is an ongoing synthesis of computation and communication into a **unified** process of *information processing*. Practical and theoretical advances are aimed at this synthesis and also use it as a tool for further development. Thus, we use the word computation in the sense of *information processing* as a whole. Better theoretical understanding of computers, networks, and other information processing systems will allow us to develop such systems to a higher level. " Mark Burgin

Through the years, additional general-purpose approaches of *parallel computation* have been proposed [46]: PRAM (parallel random-access machine), BSP (Bulk synchronous parallelism), and LogP.

PRAM. The Parallel Random Access Machine (PRAM) is a straightforward extension of the Random Access Machine (RAM), which consists of a set of processors connected to a shared memory [46], [29]. Like the Conceptual computing model, PRAM seeks to achieve simplicity. Typically, PRAM does not focus on aspects such as realistic correspondence or asynchronous communication. In the context of PRAM, there is the possibility of read-write conflicts, in which two or more processor try to access the same memory location concurrently.

"Once the memory is no longer at the behest of a single master, then the master-to-slave (or: function-to-value) view of the program-to-memory relationship becomes a bit of a fiction. An old proverb states: *He who serves two masters serves none.*" [29]. In contrast, the Conceptual model

248

does not require shared memory. The information stored in memory (I) is under control of single information machine (Animated/Live component). Also, the Conceptual model is different in several aspects: mathematical foundation, abstractions, information machine ($A=(f(m),I)$), single concept construct (C), single information primitive, degree of realistic correspondence, and asynchronous communication capabilities.

BSP is a distributed-memory approach, tightly synchronized, which consists of the following abstractions [53], [46]:

a) Processor/memory components

b) An interconnection network

c) A synchronizer which performs barrier synchronization through the superstep abstraction. Each superstep consists of a computation phase operating on local variables only, followed by a global interprocessor communication phase. BSP does not focus on mathematical foundation, software construction methodology [53], and interoperability. Like BSP, the Conceptual model seeks to provide a bridge between hardware and software - or theory and practice. However, BSP typically assumes special hardware support to synchronize all processors at the end of a superstep. Such synchronization hardware may not be available on many parallel machines [52]. BSP does not propose a software development methodology and typically relies on a programming environment in which algorithms are designed for the PRAM model and simulated on BSP [52], [53].

In contrast, the Conceptual model provides architecture independence and compatibility with the von Neumann machines/languages. Standard software construction methodologies, like the ones associated with CBSE, OO, and SOA, are fully compatible with the Conceptual approach – although modifications are proposed based on conceptualism and realistic correspondence.

The Conceptual model is different in several aspects: mathematical foundation, abstractions, Turing-complete information machine, degree of realistic correspondence, simplicity (Occam's razor), and architecture independence. Standard software construction methodologies and interoperability are readily accommodated by the Conceptual model.

Due to its simplicity, versatility, and Turing-completeness, the information machine is fully implementable using existing parallel and/or networked hardware.

LogP extends the BSP model [52], [53]. However, LogP does not require an overall barrier synchronization. Like the Conceptual computing model, LogP seeks realism, architecture independence, and performs all synchronization through messaging. However, LogP is based on asynchronous messaging.

In contrast, the Conceptual model is different in several aspects including mathematical foundation, Turing-complete information machine, single information primitive, single concept construct (C), and *unified* approach based on natural concepts (Biomimetics inspiration) applicable to every level of organization (component/object, computer, and architecture). All forms on messaging are accommodated including synchronous and asynchronous messaging.

Petri nets [29] focus on the mathematical modeling of distributed/concurrent systems based on several abstractions: places, transitions, and arcs. Aspects such as interoperability and realistic correspondence are not part of the scope. The Conceptual approach is different in terms of mathematical foundation, Turing-complete information machine $(A=(f(m),I))$, single information primitive, single concept construct (C), *unified* approach based on natural concepts (Biomimetics inspiration), and degree of realistic correspondence.

Several related technologies, systems, and architectural styles have been proposed: Multi-agent systems, REST, MOM technologies (including JMS), Smalltalk, and Event technologies (Event driven systems). Again, the conceptual approach represents a unified *mathematical model of computation*. These *technologies, architectural styles,* and *systems* do not represent *mathematical models* which makes them different from the start. Therefore, a comparison is not completely relevant to the current section; especially, considering their number and wide variety. Only a brief discussion of such approaches will be presented hereafter.

Their mathematical formulations are usually not part of the scope or distinctly different. In many cases, they target specific application/problem areas and/or rely on traditional artifacts, like gear meshing of procedure calls. Abstractions, primitives, and APIs that do not mimic realistic concepts (lack realistic correspondence) are ultimately redundant.

Multi-Agent systems. These systems do not represent mathematical computing models. Multi-Agent systems focus on a specific area of agency. There is no universally accepted definition of the term agent although there has been debate and controversy on the subject [43]. In general, an agent represents a computer system that is capable of independent action on behalf of its user or owner (i.e. autonomous) [43].

Historically, the concept of agent can be traced back to the Actor model. Multi-Agent *systems* do not focus on providing a unified mathematical formulation or realistic representation based on the mind's conceptual framework. Multiple perspectives, agent definitions, and implementations are feasible under the umbrella of Multi-Agent systems.

System implementation usually relies on traditional APIs, gear meshing of procedure calls, multithreading, and distributed artifacts. In contrast, there is a single Conceptual model based on a realistic approach mimicked from the mind and precise Turing-complete mathematical foundation: information machine abstraction (Animated/Live entity), information primitive, and single concept construct (C).

Due to Turing completeness, the Conceptual model can be leveraged for the implementation of Multi-Agent systems: the Animated/Live entity, which has a precise mathematical definition, can readily implement the agent abstraction, regardless of the definition being employed. Implementations of the Conceptual approach must be based on the same unified mathematical model and concepts making them fully compatible and interoperable regardless of technology, platform, protocol, and/or computer language.

Smalltalk. Object-oriented technology that implements messaging. Smalltalk does not represent a mathematical model of computing. Smalltak messaging is influenced by the Actor model. Many of the differences mentioned previously also apply to Smalltak: unified mathematical foundation, abstractions, information machine $(A=(f(m),I))$, single concept construct (C), single information primitive, overall realistic correspondence, and conceptual framework mimicked from the mind. There are also distinct differences between the abstractions involved (see appendix on Related Approaches of Software Reuse).

Event Technologies. These *technologies* do not represent mathematical models of computing. They focus on the transference of events, usually as part of GUI applications. In contrast, the Conceptual approach represents a Turing-complete mathematical computing model applicable to arbitrary information technologies. Therefore, the approach is not restricted to a specific application domain and/or category of messaging.

Also, keep in mind that implementations of typical event technologies usually rely on APIs based on traditional artifacts like gear meshing of procedure calls and multithreading. The artifact should never be confused with the real concept of messaging. Event technologies can be implemented by levering the Turing-complete Conceptual approach.

MOM technologies. A similar situation occurs with message-oriented middleware technologies (MOM), like JMS. EJB message beans are based on JMS. These *technologies* do not represent mathematical models of computing. They focus on transferring messages between distributed applications in the context of Enterprise Application Integration (EAI).

MOM APIs are usually proprietary, platform/language/vendor dependent, and based on traditional artifacts like gear meshing of procedure calls. The overhead required for these technologies is considerable which makes them unsuitable for the implementation of messaging within OO and component technologies – local messaging, in particular. In other words, it is not practical to employ MOM technologies as the basis for typical messaging within object/component architectures. They mainly focus on the enterprise application level (EAI) as opposed to the object/component level.

In contrast, the Conceptual approach represents a Turing-complete mathematical computing model applicable to arbitrary information technologies – including comprehensive OO/component technologies. The model is based on single Animated/Live component (information machine), information primitive, and single language construct (C). No artificial abstractions, primitives, or APIs are incorporated. MOM technologies can be readily implemented using the straightforward Turing-complete Conceptual approach.

Representational State Transfer (REST). Most of the distributed component/service technologies, including SOA related technologies, rely on gear meshing of procedure calls and distributed artifacts. An alternative approach called REST[12] has been proposed. REST represents a style of software architecture for distributed systems, instead of a mathematical computing model.

Aspects such as object/component orientation and mathematical foundations are not part of the main scope. REST is tightly coupled with the HTTP semantics. It is based on several abstractions including Resources and State Representations. REST presents several advantages when compared with distributed component/service technologies based on distributed artifacts: 1) simplicity, 2) generality of interface, 3) scalability. The generality of interface discussed by REST appears to be a sound idea with a variety of benefits, although the approach is mainly focused on distributed communication (SOA).

The Conceptual computing model shares the advantages of REST in terms of simplicity, scalability, and generality of interface. In contrast, the Conceptual approach is technology agnostic, founded on natural concepts. Messaging is identified as the single realistic interface (natural concept) able to provide an accurate representation of the real world (i.e. correspondence): local and distributed Live/Animated components $(A=(f(m),\ I))$ use messaging in order to communicate with each other. All forms of messaging are seamlessly accommodated, which include both local and distributed communication.

The Conceptual approach is different in several other aspects, including: mathematical foundation, abstractions, degree of realistic correspondence, simplicity (parsimony), Turing-complete information machine $(A=(f(m),I))$, single information primitive, single concept construct (C), reductionism based on natural concepts (information/Energy, messaging, information machine), and unified model applicable to arbitrary information technologies – at every level of organization. In agreement with Occam's razor, no additional abstractions or APIs are necessary.

253

C. Related Theories, Studies, and Research

"Theory, modeling and statistics play at least four key roles in our effort to understand brain dynamics and function. ... Finally, formal theory seeks to infer general principles of brain function that unify large bodies of experimental observations, models, and simulation outcomes. The brain computes stably and reliably despite its construction from billions of elements that are both noisy, and constantly adapting and re-calibrating. Elucidation of the general principles underlying this remarkable ability will have a profound impact on neuroscience, as well as on engineering and computer science". BRAIN 2025 Report [18]

The study of the conceptual mind is a multidisciplinary endeavor. Multiple related disciplines have made significant contributions to its understanding: physics, psychology, biology, neuroscience, computer science, mathematics (logic), philosophy, and so forth. The Conceptual architecture/model in correspondence and/or supported by a wide variety of disciplines, theories, and relevant research. Such relevant disciplines, theories, and research have been referenced earlier. This appendix summarizes the principal ones.

In agreement with reductionism, they offer multiple perspectives and invaluable clues that together give us a more complete/unified picture (mosaic) of the conceptual mind. Specifically, in the form of a unified mathematical theory/model able to explain/mimic the conceptual mind in terms of cognitive abilities: $A=(\beta(m),I)$.

Conceptually, the logical mind is designed for a single purpose or function: *logical processing of information.* According to George Boole's remarkable assertions, the laws of thought are mathematical in their form [1]. Boole's remarkable conclusions, regarding the mathematical (logical) nature of thought, are in harmony with modern logic and recent research in the area of cognition.

"Thought was still wholly intangible and ineffable until modern formal logic interpreted it as the manipulation of formal tokens."
 - Allen Newel and Herbert Simon [25]

Logic comes from the Greek Logos, which is a concept with broad polyvalent meaning: word, to reason, to speak, law, rule, and so on. The modern definition speaks about the power of the concept [33]: "thought of as constituting the controlling principle of the universe". The name of multiples disciplines is derived from Logos: logic, biology, physiology, neurology, psychology, information technology, theology, etc.

The Turing-complete Conceptual architecture and model are supported by the mathematical assertions above. From a conceptual perspective, reasoning (or *logical* reasoning) literally means "to form conclusions, judgments, or inferences from facts or premises". Logical processing of information (i.e. reasoning) is the fundamental concept implemented by the Conceptual machine/architecture $(A=(\beta(m),I))$. Consider that most of mathematics is reducible to logic (see Philosophy of Mathematics – Logicism [30]).

Boole's conclusions are in agreement with ideas presented by Hobbes and Leibnitz that view reasoning as computation (see Thomas Hobbes [30]). They are also in agreement with the Computational Theory of Mind (CTM) which views the mind as an information processing system (see Concepts and Computation Theory of Mind [30]). CTM encompasses the Representational Theory of Mind (RTM) and the Language of Thought Hypothesis (LOTH).

From the perspective of cognitive psychology, information processing and CTM are at the core. In agreement with the Conceptual approach, cognitive psychology views the human mind as an information processor, like a modern computer, interacting with its environment [25]. Such view has also become the dominant view in modern psychology. Several authors have suggested the need for new models more adaptable, flexible, reliable, interactive, and natural – founded on information processing and natural computation [36], [29].

"Present account of models of computation highlights several topics of importance for the development of new understanding of computing and its role: *natural computation* and the relationship between the model and physical implementation, interactivity as fundamental for computational modeling of concurrent *information processing systems* such as living organisms and their networks, and the new developments in logic needed to support this generalized framework. Computing understood as *information processing* is closely related to natural sciences; it helps us recognize connections between sciences, and provides a *unified* approach for modeling and simulating of both living and non-living systems." Gordana Dodig-Crnkovic [36]

According to psychological associationism, intelligent behavior is the result of associative learning (see Behaviorism [30]). Associations allow the mind to acquire knowledge about the "causal structure" of the world. An association refers to the connection between conceptual entities: pairing between a perceptual experience (message/energy) and the information (thoughts/memories) already contained in the mind which is mimicked by the Conceptual cognitive architecture (see Conceptual Cognitive Architecture).

The Conceptual architecture and model are in agreement with neuroscience research. According to implementation connectionism the brain neural network implements a symbolic processor $(A=(\beta(m),I))$ at a higher and more abstract level. Their research is aimed at figuring out how symbolic processing can be accomplished on a foundation of a neural network [30]. The evolutionary biologist Richard Semon proposed the idea that experience is encoded on a specific web of brain neurons. He coined the term 'engram'. Recent empirical studies on animals have showed that memories are physically encoded inside the brain [50].

By activating a small cluster of neurons through ontogenetic, the animal subject is forced to recall a specific memory. By removing these neurons, the subject would lose that memory. It is highly likely that human brain functions in the same way [50]. Many basic principles of neural organization and function are conserved across animal species.

"This is the rigorously designed 21st-century test of Canadian neurosurgeon Wilder Penfield's early-1900s accidental observation suggesting that mind is based on matter [Energy]....The main significance here is that we finally have proof that memories (engrams, in neuropsychology speak) are *physical* rather than conceptual."

The empirical findings from neuroscience are in close agreement with the Turing-complete Conceptual computing architecture: information (I) is stored in memory as a group of Energy packets or chunks. UTC and the PSSH have been very influential in the realm of cognition [61]. The Conceptual architecture and model are in close correspondence with both of them.

The Turing-complete Conceptual architecture represents a physical symbol system like human and computers; therefore, according to the PSSH, capable of *general intelligent action* [25]. The Conceptual architecture provides a precise Turing-complete mathematical

256

foundation/formalization $(A=(\beta(m),I))$ for PSSH, which has been very influential in the realm of cognitive architectures and AI. As mentioned earlier, PSSH generalizations primary rest on empirical evidence and *further formalization is left for future efforts* [25]. Having a solid mathematical formalization/foundation is of key importance in the realm of research and science; specifically, in the context of scientific theories and models [36, 26].

Several researchers have emphasized the importance of finding unified theories of cognition (UTC) [32, 42]. In agreement with reductionism, the Conceptual architecture provides a unified mathematical foundation based on the single concept of information (Energy).

"Psychology has arrived at the possibility of unified theories of cognition – theories that gain the power by positing a single system of mechanisms that operate together to produce the full range of human cognition. I do not say they are here. But they are within reach and we should strive to attain them." Allen Newell [32]

According to UTC, the mind functions as a single system. The Conceptual cognitive architecture can be characterized as a valid UTC candidate because it mimics/explains key cognitive abilities in a unified fashion: operates as a single unified system $(A=(\beta(m),I))$. On the other hand, the Conceptual architecture is based on a *precise mathematical Turing-complete model*: $A=(\beta(m),I)$. In a unified fashion, the architecture models, mimics, and explains several key cognitive abilities including logical reasoning, language/symbol manipulation, memory, learning, and goal (procedure) oriented behavior (P).

The concept of learning literally means acquiring new knowledge which can be mathematically modeled using set theory, a Boolean algebra. Problem solving means using generic or ad hoc methods (procedures (P)), in an orderly manner, for finding solutions to problems.

According to Turing, having time-invariant rules is a necessary condition that a *realistic* machine and associated computing model must meet [3]. This represents a tough challenge to overcome by any cognitive architecture while mimicking/explaining the mind's conceptual abilities. Thus, this aspect is important in regards to realistic correspondence which is a key evaluation aspect in the realm of scientific models – and part of the UTC evaluation criteria.

"My contention is that machines can be constructed which will simulate the behavior of the human mind very closely." Alan Turing

"The idea of a learning machine may appear paradoxical to some readers. How can the rules of operation of the machine change? They should describe completely how the machine will react whatever its history might be, whatever changes it might undergo. The rules are thus quite time-invariant. This is quite true. The explanation of the paradox is that the rules which get changed in the learning process are of a rather less pretentious kind, claiming only an ephemeral validity. The reader may draw a parallel with the Constitution of the United States." Alan Turing [3].

The Conceptual cognitive architecture addresses the Turing's learning 'paradox' in a realistic fashion. Using his analogy, Boole's algebra of logic represents the U.S. Constitution that provides the machine with abilities of logical reasoning: "Laws of Thought", which are time-invariant. On the other hand, the information (I) learned in the form of chunks of information and concepts (C), is ephemeral – including learned procedures (P) to solve problems or perform tasks. The Turing-complete mathematical formulation clearly shows it: $A=(\beta(m),I)$. In agreement with how Turing envisioned it, the 'child's conceptual mind' features "little mechanism and lot of blank sheets" [3]. His views are in agreement with Piaget's cognitive constructivism [61].

The Mathematical Universe Theory [31] asserts that *everything* in the universe is governed by mathematical laws [Logos] – which obviously includes the mind (*logical mind*).

Finally, relevant ideas such as realism (realistic correspondence), reductionism, and Occam's razor have had a prominent impact on science and scientific models [30],[29]. Such ideas have significant relevance to the Turing-complete Conceptual cognitive architecture(see Physical Foundation). It is widely accepted that simplicity is a theoretical, scientific, and engineering virtue [30]. Conceptually, the logical mind is an entity of beautiful and mathematical **simplicity**; responsible for a single function or purpose: logical processing of information $A= (\beta(m), I)$.

"We are to admit no more causes of natural things than such as are both true and sufficient to explain their appearances." Isaac Newton

"Nature does not multiply things [concepts] unnecessarily; that she makes use of the easiest and simplest means [concepts] for producing her effects; that she does nothing in vain, and the like." Galileo Galilei.

D. Related Cognitive/AI Models

It should be stated that the Conceptual approach can be applied to logical reasoning, conceptual processing (C), and related *conscious* cognitive abilities, because they can be modeled, understood, and explained by a precise mathematical formulation $(A=(f(m),I))$. However, the approach is general and flexible enough to be extended to other cognitive areas. The following comparison will be based on the scope just defined. I should also state that this area of application is still work in progress. The improvements derived from the application of the model to software engineering in general can be evaluated and measured in quantitative terms (see appendix on Model Evaluation and Metrics).

The specific cognitive/AI area represents only one among multiple areas of application. Consider that natural concepts are ubiquitous and extend beyond a specific area of application. Natural concepts represent mathematical entities with wide applicability. For instance, the concept of messaging, like the mathematical concepts of number and set, has wide applicability. Notice that similar to other mathematical entities, the exact same mathematical concept takes a variety of forms in the real world.

Unified Theories of Cognition (UTC) focus on the specific areas of cognition and artificial intelligence. UTC does not focus on providing a unified mathematical formulation based on the mind's conceptual framework, or integrated information model founded on natural concepts and applicable to arbitrary information/software technologies. According to UTC, the mind functions as a single system. The conceptual paradigm can be characterized as a valid UTC candidate because it models key cognitive abilities. It also operates as a single unified system $(A = (f(m), I))$.

In contrast with UTC, the Conceptual approach is based on a precise mathematical Turing-complete model: information machine $(A = (\beta(m), I))$. The conceptual paradigm, naturally and holistically explains several key cognitive abilities including logical reasoning (Boole's β-function), symbol utilization (C), memory, learning of conceptual/non-conceptual information, goal (procedure) oriented behavior (P) and knowledge representation (I/C). Motor control can also be realistically accommodated.

260

For instance, the mind communicates with other components of the body using messaging although no conceptual information is exchanged. Such components can also be modeled using the same natural/mathematical concepts and formulation: $A = (f(m), I)$. Notice that information, as expected, is a fundamental concept part of all conscious cognitive abilities.

From a logical and mathematical perspective, the conceptual paradigm is founded on a solid footing: Boole's algebra of logic which he characterized as 'The Laws of Thought". His remarkable conclusions, as applied to the conceptual model, are logical and demonstrable via formal mathematical proof (see demonstration of the Conceptual Deductive Approach). The timeless contributions of Boole's brilliant and *logical* mind, far ahead of his time, should be weighed [22].

Boole's conclusions are in agreement with ideas presented by Hobbes and Leibnitz that view reasoning as computation (see Thomas Hobbes [30]). They are also in agreement with the Computational Theory of Mind (CTM) which views the mind as an information processing system (see Concepts and Computation Theory of Mind [30]). CTM encompasses the Representational Theory of Mind (RTM) and the Language of Thought Hypothesis (LOTH).

From the perspective of cognitive psychology, information processing and CTM are at the core. In agreement with the Conceptual model, cognitive psychology views the human mind as an information processor, like a modern computer, interacting with its environment [25]. Such view has also become the dominant view in modern psychology.

From a conceptual perspective, reasoning literally means "to form conclusions, judgments, or inferences from facts or premises". Logical processing of information (i.e. reasoning), the fundamental concept implemented by the machine $(A=(\beta(m),I))$, has been mathematically formalized by Boole's algebra of logic (Laws of Thought). This should also give you a sense of the expressiveness, conciseness, accuracy, and power of the natural language as the ultimate tool for transferring information (i.e. concepts) – a match for the conceptual mind that hosts it. Human languages have evolved for ages and become highly precise and 'logical' tools for transferring concepts.

The concept "logical processing of information" can be utilized to express an otherwise complex idea in an accurate, concise, and logical fashion - perhaps almost mathematical, in terms of accuracy and precision, when looked at from a conceptual standpoint. Let us not forget the tight connection between human languages and the formal mathematical language. Both are symbolic representations of the same reality and are governed by the same logical rules expressed by Boole's algebra of logic. Both seek a realistic and accurate representation.

The concept of learning literally means acquiring new knowledge which can be mathematically modeled using set theory, a Boolean algebra. Problem solving means using generic or ad hoc methods (procedures (P)), in an orderly manner, for finding solutions.

"My contention is that machines can be constructed which will simulate the behavior of the human mind very closely." Alan Turing

"The idea of a learning machine may appear paradoxical to some readers. How can the rules of operation of the machine change? They should describe completely how the machine will react whatever its history might be, whatever changes it might undergo. The rules are thus quite time-invariant. This is quite true. The explanation of the paradox is that the rules which get changed in the learning process are of a rather less pretentious kind, claiming only an ephemeral validity. The reader may draw a parallel with the Constitution of the United States." Alan Turing [3]

Boole's algebra of logic (β-function) represents the Constitution that provides the machine with abilities of logical reasoning: The Laws of Thought, which are time-invariant. On the other hand, the information (I) learned in the form of concepts (C), is ephemeral – including learned procedures (P) to solve problems or perform tasks. The mathematical formulation clearly shows it: $A=(\beta(m), I)$. An important point is the alleged existence of rules that are time-invariant, innate if you will.

The Mathematical Universe Theory should also be mentioned [31]. If such theory is true, *everything* in the Universe is governed by mathematical laws, including the mind.

In summary, the Conceptual approach is consistent with several related perspectives: UTC's view of the mind as a single unified system (UTC Candidate), mathematical/logical perspective represented by Boole's Laws of Though, Computational Theory of Mind (CTM), cognitive psychology, psychology, philosophical conceptualism/realism, Turing's ideas ('constitution of thinking'), Biomimetics, and conceptual perspective.

It should be clear from observation of reality that the same natural concepts (mathematical entities) leveraged by the conceptual machine apply to the mind. The Conceptual approach is also in agreement with Occam's razor. Indeed, the simplest and easiest concepts: logical processing of information $(A=(\beta(m), I))$.

"Nature does not multiply things [concepts] unnecessarily; that she makes use of the easiest and simplest means [concepts] for producing her effects; that she does nothing in vain, and the like." Galileo Galilei.

"Rudiments [Concepts] or principles must not be unnecessarily multiplied." Immanuel Kant.

On the other hand, the Society of the Mind (SOM) presents an alternative approach:

"The functions performed by the brain are the products of the work of thousands of different, specialized sub-systems, the intricate product of hundreds of millions of years of biological evolution." Marvin Minsky.

The agent abstraction is introduced to refer to the simplest individuals that populate such society of the mind:

"No single one of these little agents knows very much by itself, but each recognizes certain configurations of a few associates and responds by altering its state. " Marvin Minsky.

Having multiple subcomponents part of the brain is consistent with ongoing research including the Society of the Mind. Based on the Conceptual approach, a group of information machines can be readily accommodated – living inside the mind, interchanging information via messaging, and performing multiple functions: $\{A1, A2, \dots, An\}$ where $A_i=(f_i(m),I_i)$.

Consider that the mind performs functions besides the ones associated with logical reasoning. Think that the whole body consists of a set of associated organs (components) interchanging information through the same natural concepts. They can also be modeled using a group of information machines: $\{A1, A2, \dots, An\}$ where $A_i=(f_i(m),I_i)$.

The Society of the Mind also focuses on the specific area of cognition and artificial intelligence. It does not focus on providing an integrated model based on natural concepts (i.e. mathematical entities), unified mathematical formulation, or unified model for that matter. In contrast, the Conceptual approach provides a Turing-complete mathematical foundation able to model and naturally explain a wide variety of cognitive/AI functions including logical reasoning, learning, memory, and language processing.

Founded on natural concepts and the mind's conceptual framework, it is applicable to arbitrary information/software technologies. In agreement with Occam's razor, instead of multiple SOM agents only one conceptual machine is strictly necessary for performing logical processing of information (reasoning): "Nature does not multiply things [concepts] unnecessarily;"

In contrast with the SOM agent, a conceptual machine is a single 'intelligent' entity (unit) capable of logical reasoning, self-sufficient, able to communicate/learn arbitrary amounts of concepts (C) including procedures to solve problems, and as powerful as a computer in terms of processing power (Turing complete).

Other components/functions of the mind can be simply modeled using information machines. Consider that the difference between Boole's conceptual machines $A=(\beta(m), I)$ and information machines $A=(f(m), I)$ is the ability to process conceptual information in a logical fashion. Such

264

organization would explain the widely accepted belief that only a single thought can be consciously entertained at any given time.

The same applies to conversations and performing tasks: it is also widely accepted that we can focus on doing one thing at a time. However, switching from task to task can be done very rapidly which gives the sense – probably an illusion – of multiple tasks being done concurrently.

Ongoing research supports the 'popular' beliefs grounded in common sense. For instance, Earl Miller, a neuroscientist at MIT, says that "for the most part, we simply can't focus on more than one thing at a time." By the same token, if only one thought or task can realistically be performed at any given time, *only one* conceptual machine is necessary as part of the mind, communicating with less 'intelligent' components $(A=(f(m), I))$ responsible for performing other brain functions.

Your personal computer and smartphone are capable of performing only one task at a time. The Central Processing Unit (CPU) executes one instruction at any given time although the speed of processing gives the illusion of multiple tasks being performed simultaneously.

Based on concepts, symbols, and algebra of logic, the conceptual approach is clearly different from connectionism. Conceptually, logical reasoning, entity recognition, and motor skills are different from each other: separate concepts altogether.

The way in which you carry a *logical* argument is different from the function of recognizing a face/symbol, or riding your bike. The former skill can be completely explained in logical and conceptual terms: Mary married Mr. Boole; that is how we reason that she became his wife.

In contrast, entity recognition and motor skills cannot be reasoned in the same fashion, so to speak. However these functions are complementary and work cooperatively. For instance, you may rely on certain aspects of logical reasoning to help face/symbol recognition: He looks like my friend because of the green eyes and black hair. The round shape looks like the letter O.

"Which approach is best to pursue? That is simply a wrong question. Each has virtues and deficiencies, and we need integrated systems that can exploit the advantages of both." Marvin Minsky

"Most serious of all is what we might call the Problem of Opacity: the knowledge embodied inside a network's numerical coefficients is not accessible outside that net. This is not a challenge we should expect our connectionists to easily solve." Marvin Minsky

The aforementioned views are consistent with implementation connectionists who hold that the brain neural network implements a symbolic processor at a higher and more abstract level. Their research is aimed at figuring out how symbolic processing can be accomplished on a foundation of a neural network [30].

It is not very difficult to visualize and/or theorize about straightforward ways in which the web (graph) of information/knowledge (I = {C1, ..., Cn}), part of the conceptual machine $(A=(\beta(m), I))$, could be mapped onto the brain's neural network. Both structures are isomorphic.

In theory, the biological neural network is perhaps just an ultrafast information superhighway designed to store/transport non-conceptual and conceptual knowledge (C). No much more would be required, at the bio-neural level, to support the straightforward conceptual computing model. On the other hand, notice that the same natural concepts apply to all aforementioned skills: information, messaging, and processing of information. Actually, empirical findings strongly suggest that each memory (i.e. engram) is encoded on a specific web of brain neurons.

Ponder that a neuron, like the mind, can be completely specified using the same mathematical concepts: $A=(f(m), I)$. A neuron is an analog information machine or information processor (mini-machine). Obviously, the 'implementation' is different although the concepts are the same: function $(f(m))$, information stored (I), and message (m).

The BDI (Belief-Desire-Intention) model developed by Bratman is based on folk psychology [30]. BDI does not focus on providing a formal mathematical foundation. Beliefs, desires, and intentions represent concepts as well (see Concepts [30]) and can be modeled by the Conceptual approach which is general, and able to accommodate arbitrary concepts.

In summary, the Conceptual approach is distinctly different from other AI/Cognitive approaches in several aspects including Mathematical formulation, Turing-complete information machine, conceptual machine $(A=(\beta(m), I))$, single information primitive, single concept construct (C), realistic approach based on natural concepts, conceptual framework mimicked from the mind, applicability to arbitrary computing technologies, and single unified/realistic implementation.

E. Related Natural Language Processing Approaches

"There is in my opinion no important theoretical difference between natural languages and the artificial languages of logicians; indeed, I consider it possible to comprehend the syntax and semantics of both kinds of languages within a single *natural* and *mathematically* precise theory"   Richard Montague

Since language/symbol manipulation *is a cognitive area, it is being researched in the context of related cognitive architectures as opposed to separately (stand-alone). In agreement with UTC, all cognitive abilities are tightly intertwined (unified).* Like Montague, we believe that it is possible to understand the syntax and semantics of both languages – logical and natural – within a single natural and mathematically precise theory: *a conceptual theory and model.* After all, both, 'the natural language and fundamental areas of mathematics/logic seek to express the same physical reality – founded upon the natural concept of Energy and governed by the laws of nature (Logos).

Similar to Montague's semantics, the Conceptual approach is also based on the principle of compositionality [30].   On the other hand, Montague's approach has no psychological or cognitive claims. There is a perceived gap between the propositional approach found in the model and psychology [30]: several researches have also questioned the notion of propositions and the abstraction of 'possible worlds' [30, 57].

Montague's model mainly considers sentences in isolation which present challenges while dealing with anaphora and discourse [30]. Multiple Montague-derived approaches have been proposed including Discourse Representation Theory (DRT) And Dynamic Semantics [57, 30].

The Conceptual approach is distinctly different from Montague-derived approaches in several aspects including mathematical foundation, Turing-complete conceptual machine $(A=(\beta(m),I))$, simplicity (parsimony), psychological/cognitive motivation, *single* primitive for logical processing of information, single concept construct (C) for knowledge representation, information (I) stored in memory that represents all forms of conceptual information (discourse, pronouns, context, etc.), degree of realistic correspondence, and conceptual framework mimicked from the mind.

268

Several related approaches to Natural Language Processing have been proposed including [60]: Bayesian networks, ontology web language (OWL), and Cyc. The issues associated with these approaches have been studied and documented in the research literature [60, 63]: difficulty determining probabilities, limited expressiveness, difficulties representing temporal-dependent knowledge, need for knowledge engineers, or expertise on a formal logical language. Additionally, several related approaches have been proposed including semantic networks, WordNet, and the Open Mind Common Sense Project (ConceptNet) [60].

A semantic network is a graphical notation for representing knowledge in patterns of interconnected nodes and arcs. WordNet is a popular and widely used semantic resource comprising of a database of words (nouns, adjectives, verbs, etc.) linked by a small set of semantic relations (synonym, 'is-a', 'part-of'). WordNet is most suitable for lexical and word comparison processing. Like NATURAL, ConceptNet represents knowledge in the natural language: no need for expert engineers or formal logical language.

The Conceptual approach is distinctly different from the aforementioned approaches in terms of mathematical foundation, abstractions, Turing-complete conceptual machine $(A=(\beta(m),I))$, theoretical simplicity (parsimony), mathematical rules of probable cause and effect (common sense knowledge), psychological/cognitive motivation, single concept construct (C) for knowledge representation, linguistic reductionism based upon three elementary/primary concepts (building blocks) extracted from physics, and degree of realistic correspondence.

NATURAL is capable of mimicking a typical dictionary and represent knowledge (symbol definitions) using the natural language (see Language Examples): L consists of a finite set of symbols (building blocks) and their associated definitions: L = {(symbol1, Definition (symbol1)), ... , (symboln, Definition (symboln))}. Discourse, pronouns, and context can be accurately modeled via the concept construct (C) and information associations.

A large number of common sense facts can be represented and a rich context-aware inferences made based on the rules of probable cause and effect, which are similar to Polya's patterns (see Language Examples). NATURAL mimics the human language and no numerical values are required for knowledge representation and reasoning. However, precise numerical probabilities can be used when available. Intuitively, people can make inferences based on exact numerical probabilities; or without them, if they are not available (often difficult to determine [60, 63]). The latter scenario is realistically more likely. For instance, a person, perhaps a researcher, may know that $P(Fly\ (x) \mid x \in Birds) = .9$.

Several well-known mathematical and logical formalisms are being leveraged: algebra of logic, set theory, probabilities, and plausible reasoning. Multiple examples of concepts (building bocks), part of NATURAL, have been provided (see Language Examples). Consider that most of mathematics is reducible to logic (see Philosophy of Mathematics – Logicism [30]). Set theory represents a Boolean algebra. Reduction brings forth theoretical simplicity (Occam's razor), unification, and elimination of redundancy, gaps, or contradictions.

There is tight connection between probability and logic. Some influential mathematicians consider their work on probability part of logic itself (see Logic and Probability [30]). There are several potential interpretations for probabilities. Keynes and Carnap advocated a logical interpretation which is consistent with the Conceptual approach and associated NATURAL language, based on algebra of logic: probabilities are to be objective logical relations between propositions (or sentences).

It should be emphasized that the unified Conceptual cognitive architecture and associated computing model holistically explain/mimic key cognitive abilities beyond natural language processing/production, in a unified fashion: memory, logical reasoning, learning of conceptual/non-conceptual information, and goal (procedure) oriented behavior.

Human-machine communication represents a complex area, intimately intertwined with *all* of the aforementioned cognitive abilities [60]. Therefore, a comprehensive solution is probably bound to require a unified cognitive architecture able to realistically mimic human capabilities. This view is supported by widely accepted theories of

270

cognition (Unified Theories of Cognition) which advocate for a unified approach [32].

"Psychology has arrived at the possibility of unified theories of cognition – theories that gain their power by positing a single system of mechanisms that operate together to produce the full range of human cognition. I do not say they are here. But they are within reach and we should strive to attain them."

Allen Newell

F. Reference Implementation (Requirements and Setup)

Jt is a reference implementation of the Conceptual computing model. The software is included. It represents only one of the many potential implementations of the model. The main framework functionality requires a single Jar (Jt.jar) with small memory signature of about 512K. To utilize the Jt framework, install the software according the packaged instructions. Source code distribution and accompanying materials for this book can be downloaded from the following URL:

https://sites.google.com/site/conceptualparadigm/documents/Jt.zip?attredirects=0&d=1

The distribution includes the latest version of the framework, examples, and working applications. The distribution has been archived using the .zip format. To extract the files, you will need a de-compression program such as WinZip. You will find a Readme file in addition to installation instructions. Feel free to employ your favorite IDE. Eclipse and Java 2 platform version 1.5 or better are recommended. A build.xml file for Ant is also included.

G. Software Examples (Conceptual Framework)

G.1 Messenger

The reference implementation of Messenger is responsible for transferring messages between Live/Animated components ($A=(f(m),I)$ – from component sender to the receiver. All modalities of messaging are supported including synchronous, asynchronous, distributed, and secure messaging. Messenger delegates responsibility to other framework components for the implementation of security, encryption, authentication, and authorization of the messaging being exchanged.

For convenience, a `sendMessage()` method is provided:

Method	Description
`sendMessage(Object object, Object message)`	Send a message to the specified component. The `object` parameter can be either a reference to the component or the component `id`.

Also for convenience, the following attributes control the behavior of Messenger:

Attributes	Description
`synchronous (boolean)`	Specifies whether asynchronous or synchronous messaging should be employed. Synchronous messaging is the default.
`encrypted (boolean)`	Enables or disables encrypted messaging. By default, no encryption is performed.

The methods above are provided mainly for readability and convenience. The same functionality can be accomplished via the information primitive. The following software example illustrates the use of Messenger.

The concept construct (C) is represented by the framework class JtConcept. Messages can be of arbitrary types (Object). On the other hand, a separate class is often employed for representing messages: JtMessage. For convenience and readability reasons, the framework defines a class named JtMessage, which inherits from JtConcept.

Also for convenience, a message ID can be readily specified during the creation of the message. For instance, the following statement creates a new message and specifies its message ID:

```
msg = new JtMessage (JtComponent.JtREAD);
```

Messenger is also able to handle distributed messaging via framework Proxies. Such proxies need to specify a way of locating the distributed component; for instance, component URL and class need to be provided to locate components via a HTTP Proxy.

```
/**
 * Demonstrates the JtMessenger functionality
 */

public static void main(String[] args) {

    JtMessenger messenger = new JtMessenger ();
    WeatherService weather;
    JtPrinter printer = new JtPrinter ();

    JtConcept reply;
    JtHttpProxy proxy;
    JtFactory factory = new JtFactory ();
    String url =
        "http://localhost:8080/JtPortal/JtRestService";
    JtMessage msg;
    JtConcept ctx;

    weather = new WeatherService ();

    // Send a message via the framework messenger

    reply = (JtConcept) messenger.sendMessage(weather,
                        new JtMessage
```

274

```
                              (JtComponent.JtREAD));

   printer.processMessage(reply);

   // Asynchronous messaging is supported

   messenger.setSynchronous(false);

   messenger.sendMessage(weather,
        new JtMessage (JtComponent.JtREAD));


// Distributed messaging. Create
// an instance of the remote Proxy

messenger = new JtMessenger ();

proxy = (JtHttpProxy) factory.createObject
        (JtHttpProxy.JtCLASS_NAME);

// Specify URL and class name for the remote component

proxy.setUrl(url);
proxy.setClassname
            ("Jt.examples.WeatherService");


// Send the message (Read) to the distributed
// component that provides the Weather service.
// Weather information is retrieved.

reply = (JtConcept) messenger.sendMessage (proxy,
                            new JtMessage
                            (JtFactory.JtREAD));

if (reply instanceof JtError) {
     System.out.println
        ("Exception detected:");
     printer.processMessage(reply);
} else
     printer.processMessage (reply);


// Distributed messaging (encrypted and authenticated)

proxy = (JtHttpProxy) factory.createObject
        (JtHttpProxy.JtCLASS_NAME);

proxy.setUrl(url);
proxy.setClassname ("Jt.examples.service.BankTeller");

ctx = new JtConcept ();
factory.setValue(ctx, "username", "jt");
factory.setValue(ctx, "password", "messaging");

messenger = new JtMessenger ();
messenger.setContext(ctx);
```

```
// Specify that secure/encrypted messaging should be used.
// The Bank Teller component requires it.

messenger.setEncrypted(true);

// Send the message to the distribute bank teller component
// to retrieve account information. A concept (account)
// or an exception is returned.

msg = new JtMessage (JtComponent.JtREAD);
factory.setValue (msg, BankTeller.ACCOUNT, "12345678");

reply = (JtConcept) messenger.sendMessage (proxy, msg);


if (reply instanceof JtError) {
  System.out.println ("Exception detected:");
  printer.processMessage(reply);
} else
  printer.processMessage (reply);


// Remove the proxy and all remote references.
// The remote component should be ready to be
// garbage collected after this operation.

factory.removeObject(proxy);
}
```

G.2 Factory

Factory (`JtFactory`) is responsible for manufacturing and updating framework components and concept constructs (C) – including messages. It also provides reusable Singleton and Prototype functionality: the Factory is able to manufacture 'one of a kind' and make copies (i.e. clones) of arbitrary components.

The framework Factory interfaces with a Registry subcomponent (Singleton) to keep track of active system components. Components can be registered and located based on component ID. Factory provides methods for the manipulation of the concept construct (C) and its associations.

During creation, components and concepts are configured by Factory with the assistance of the Resource Manager (RM). The framework RM is responsible for managing resources found in the properties file or stream. Factory implements the following main messages as part of its conceptual interface (CI):

Message ID	Description
JtCREATE	Create an instance of the specified class (CLASSNAME) and return it. If an id is provided (INSTANCE_ID), the new instance is added to the framework registry. Null is returned if the entry (INSTANCE_ID) already exists unless the message includes additional directives: a) If RETURN_IF_ALREADY_EXISTS is specified, the existing entry is returned. b) If REPLACE_IF_ALREADY_EXISTS is specified, the entry is overridden. Null is returned if the operation fails.

JtREAD	Retrieve the specified instance (INSTANCE_ID) from the framework Registry. Null is returned if the instance cannot be found.
JtGET_VALUE	Retrieve the value of an attribute or association. A reference to an Object is returned.
JtSET_VALUE	Set the value of the attribute or association. String values are automatically converted to the appropriate type by the framework.
JtDELETE	Delete the specified instance (INSTANCE_ID) from the framework Registry.

The messages above have additional modalities. For instance, Singleton functionality is implemented via the SINGLETON directive (see Singleton handling in this section). Mainly for convenience, JtFactory supports the following methods which provide comparable functionality to the messaging interface just described:

Method	Description
`createObject` `    (String classname)`	Create a component of the specified class (`classname`) and return it.

`createObject`
`    (String classname,`
`     Object id)`
	Create a component of the specified class and return it. Also, the component (id) is added to the framework Registry. It can be later retrieved from the framework Registry based on component ID.

`setValue (Object object,`
`        String attribute,`
`        Object value)`
	Set the value of the attribute or association(`attribute`). String values are automatically converted to the appropriate type by the framework. The `object` parameter can be either a reference to the component or the component ID (`id`) .

`getValue (Object object,` `        String attribute)`	Retrieve the value of an attribute or association . A reference to an Object is returned. The `object` parameter can be either a reference to the component or the component ID (`id`).
`lookupObject (String id)`	Retrieve a component from the framework Registry using its id and returns a reference to it. Null is returned if the component (`id`) is not found in the Registry.
`removeObject (String id)`	Remove the component (`id`) from the framework Registry. Returns true if the component is removed; false otherwise. After removing the component from the Registry, it becomes ready to be collected by the standard garbage collection mechanism.

The methods described previously are provided mainly for readability and convenience. The same functionality can be accomplished via the information primitive. The framework Factory is responsible for providing Singleton functionality: class restricted to having a single instance. The following table of messages defines the conceptual interface (CI).

Message ID	Description
JtCREATE (SINGLETON)	Create a Singleton of the specified class (CLASSNAME) and return it. SINGLETON has to be included (WHAT attribute) as part of the message. The new component (Singleton) is added to the framework Registry. Null is returned if the Singleton cannot be created. Further attempts to create a component of the same class will result in the Singleton being returned.
JtREAD (SINGLETON)	Retrieve the Singleton of the specified class. Null is returned if a Singleton for the specified class is not found.
JtDELETE (SINGLETON)	Delete the Singleton associated to the specified class.

The framework Factory is also responsible for proving Group (G) functionality. It relies on the `JtGroupFactory` support class for the implementation of such functionality (see Group Factory). A realistic implementation of the Prototype functionality is provided by the framework Factory. It 'manufactures' copies of any arbitrary component or concept construct (C) by processing the CLONE message:

JtCLONE	Build a clone of the specified component or concept construct (INSTANCE).

The following example creates and manipulates several components and concept constructs (C) via the framework Factory. The manipulation of Singletons is also demonstrated.

```java
/**
 * Framework component implementation of Factory Method.
 * It creates and manages framework.
 * The Concept construct is implemented via a factory
 * (Factory Method pattern). Concepts can also be
 * implemented using compiler capabilities
 * (Conceptual language) which is more concise
 * and clear. Such implementation would be similar
 * to the implementation of the object abstraction.
 */

    public static void main(String[] args) {

        JtFactory factory = new JtFactory ();
        JtMessage msg;
        JtConcept Concept;
        JtPrinter printer = new JtPrinter ();
        Integer Int;
        String str;
        WeatherService weatherComponent;
        Object obj;


        // Use the factory to manipulate a
        // concept construct (information associations)

        Concept = new JtConcept ();
        factory.setValue(Concept,
                WeatherService.summary, "Sunny");
        factory.setValue(Concept, WeatherService.maximum,
                new Integer (80));
        factory.setValue(Concept, WeatherService.minimum,
                new Integer (67));

        factory.setValue(Concept,
                WeatherService.precipitation,
                new Float (5.0));

        printer.processMessage(Concept);

        // Retrieve associations

        Int = (Integer) factory.getValue(Concept,
                WeatherService.maximum);

        System.out.println(WeatherService.maximum + ":" +
            Int);

        Int = (Integer) factory.getValue(Concept,
            WeatherService.minimum);

        System.out.println(WeatherService.minimum + ":" +
            Int);

        str = (String) factory.getValue(Concept,
            WeatherService.summary);

        System.out.println(WeatherService.summary + ":" +
            str);
```

```
// Create a framework component.
// Properties are loaded automatically
// from the properties file.

obj = factory.createObject
        (WeatherService.JtCLASS_NAME);

// A component can be added to the
// component Registry during creation.
// A component ID (name) is assigned to it.
// The Registry allows components to
// find each other using a component ID.

obj = factory.createObject
        (WeatherService.JtCLASS_NAME,
         "my component");

// Use the factory to retrieve the
// component from the registry.

obj = factory.lookupObject("my component");

// Remove component from the registry

factory.removeObject("my component");

// Demonstrate the handling of singletons (via
// JtFactory). It handles concurrency.

msg = new JtMessage (JtFactory.JtCREATE);
factory.setValue(msg, JtFactory.SINGLETON, new
    Boolean (true));

// Specify the classname as part of the message.
// Any arbitrary class may be specified.

factory.setValue(msg, JtFactory.CLASSNAME,
                WeatherService.JtCLASS_NAME);

// Create the singlenton.

weatherComponent = (WeatherService)
factory.processMessage (msg);


// Retrieve the Singleton

msg = new JtMessage (JtFactory.JtREAD);
factory.setValue(msg, JtFactory.SINGLETON,
    new Boolean (true));
factory.setValue(msg, JtFactory.CLASSNAME,
    WeatherService.JtCLASS_NAME);

weatherComponent = (WeatherService)
    factory.processMessage (msg);
```

282

```java
if (weatherComponent != null)
  System.out.println("Singleton (JtREAD): GO");
else
  System.out.println("Singleton (JtREAD): FAIL");

// Attempt to create another instance of
// the singleton class. The singleton
// instance is returned. No new instance is created

obj = factory.processMessage (msg);

if (weatherComponent == obj)
      System.out.println
        ("create singleton (JtCREATE): GO");
else
      System.out.println
        ("create singleton (JtCREATE): FAIL");

// Delete the Singleton

msg = new JtMessage (JtFactory.JtDELETE);
factory.setValue(msg, JtFactory.SINGLETON,
  new Boolean (true));
factory.setValue(msg, JtFactory.CLASSNAME,
  WeatherService.JtCLASS_NAME);

factory.processMessage (msg);

msg = new JtMessage (JtFactory.JtREAD);
factory.setValue(msg, JtFactory.SINGLETON,
  new Boolean (true));
factory.setValue(msg, JtFactory.CLASSNAME,
  WeatherService.JtCLASS_NAME);

weatherComponent = (WeatherService)
  factory.processMessage (msg);

if (weatherComponent == null)
      System.out.println
        ("Singleton (JtDELETE): GO");
else
      System.out.println
        ("Singleton (JtDELETE): FAIL");


}
```

G.3 Live or Animated Component

`JtComponent` is the reference implementation of Live/Animated components $(A=(f(m),I))$ for Java and Android. This framework class hides the complexities associated with managing asynchronous messaging and traditional multithreading. It can be readily reused, through inheritance, by every Live/Animated component in the system which improves overall complexity, software reusability, and quality (see Model Evaluation and Metrics). All forms of messaging are accommodated including synchronous, asynchronous, and streaming. Information and messages are represented using the concept construct (C).

`JtComponent` needs to maintain a queue of messages which are processed one at a time, in the order in which they are received. The message queue is a common resource that can be accessed by several threads of execution concurrently. Such access needs to be controlled in order to avoid race conditions. Several control mechanisms are feasible. Java and Android manage this situation via thread synchronization.

Instances of `JtComponent` use their independent thread of execution. In order to do so, they implement the Runnable interface. The run method of the class is called after the thread is started.

The following are the main *internal* methods implemented by the reference framework class:

Internal Method	Description
`activate ()`	Responsible for creating, configuring, and starting an independent thread of execution. It is invoked when the first message is received by the Live/Animated component.

`run ()`	After the independent thread is started, this method is invoked. It consists of a loop which is constantly extracting messages from the queue and processing them using the information primitive *(f(m))*.
`dequeueMessage ()`	Extracts the next message from the queue.
`suspendThread ()`	Suspend the component by calling `wait()` when the message queue is empty. Once a new message arrives, `notify()` is called and the component resumes processing messages.
`resumeThread ()`	Resume an idle component by calling `notify()` once a new message arrives for processing.
`requestStateTransition()`	Manage the life cycle of the component which consists of several states: inactive, active, idle and stopped.

The life cycle of a JtComponent instance consists of several states:

State	Description
INACTIVE	Before the independent thread of execution is started. No messages have been sent to the component at this point.
ACTIVE	After the independent thread is started and while messages are being processed. The component thread is first started and configured once the first message arrives.

IDLE	The message queue is empty and the component is waiting for new messages to arrive. Once a new message is received, the component will become active again.
STOPPED	The component is not longer needed and has been stopped. Housekeeping is performed as a result.

Depending on the information technology being used, other implementations of the Live/Animated entity ($A=(f(m),I)$) are feasible. On the other hand, the main concepts part of the Turing-complete Conceptual model, will still apply: information (Energy), messaging, and information machine.

The following example illustrates the use of the Live or Animated Entity. A timer component is implemented which keeps track of the time and runs using its own independent thread of execution. The timer simply inherits most of the required functionality from the framework `JtComponent` superclass.

The main component sends a message (`JtACTIVATE`) to start the timer. A standard framework message (`JtREMOVE`) tells the Live/Animated component to stop processing messages and perform housekeeping operations in preparation for the component to be discarded. The main functionality is inherited from the framework superclass (`JtComponent`).

```
/**
 * Timer implementation based on the Live or Animated
 * Components. The timer runs using its own independent
 * thread of execution. Most of the asynchronous messaging
 * and threading functionality is implemented by the
 * Conceptual framework and reused.
 */

public class TimerComponent extends JtComponent {

  private static final long serialVersionUID = 1L;
  public static final String JtCLASS_NAME =
    TimerComponent.class.getName();
  public static final String UPDATE_TIME = "UPDATE_TIME";
  private long tstart = 0L;        // t0
  private long tend;               // t1
  private double time;             // Elapsed time in seconds (delta)
  private JtFactory factory = new JtFactory ();
  private JtLogger logger = null;  // Logger component

  public TimerComponent() {

  }

  // Locate the framework Logger.

  private JtLogger locateLogger () {

    // Locate the framework Logger
    logger = (JtLogger) factory.lookupObject(JtFactory.jtLogger);

    // Create an instance if it cannot be found
    if (logger == null)
      logger = new JtLogger ();

    return (logger);

  }


  /**
   * Retrieve the time attribute
   */

  public double getTime () {
    return (time);
  }
  /**
   * void operation
   *
   */
  public void setTime (double time) {

  }
```

```java
private void updateTime () {

  if (tstart == 0L)
    tstart = (new Date()).getTime ();

  tend = (new Date ()).getTime ();
  time = (tend - tstart)/1000.0;

}


// Verify type of messaging

private boolean isSynchronous (Object message) {
  Boolean Bool;

  if (message == null)
    return (false);

  Bool = (Boolean) factory.getValue(message,
      JtMessage._SYNCHRONOUS);

  if (Bool == null)
    return (true);

  return (Bool.booleanValue());
}

// Process component messages

public Object processMessage (Object message) {

  Object msgid = null;
  JtMessage msg = (JtMessage) message;

  if (msg == null)
    return null;

  // locate Logger component
  if (logger == null)
    logger = locateLogger ();

  msgid = factory.getValue(msg, Jt.concept.JtMessage.ID);

  if (msgid == null)
    return null;

  // Add asynchronous messages to the message queue
  if (!isSynchronous (message)) {
    enqueueMessage (message);
    return null;
  }
```

```java
    // Start/Update the timer

    if (msgid.equals (TimerComponent.UPDATE_TIME) ||
        msgid.equals (JtComponent.JtACTIVATE)) {


      updateTime ();

      // Another UPDATE_TIME request is added to the message queue
      enqueueMessage(new JtMessage (TimerComponent.UPDATE_TIME));


      return (null);
    }


    // Let the superclass handle JtREMOVE (housekeeping is
    // performed)

    if (msgid.equals (JtComponent.JtREMOVE))
      return (super.processMessage (message));


    logger.processMessage (new JtError ("Invalid message:" +
     msgid));
    return (null);


}

static private char waitForInputKey () {
  char c = ' ';

  try {

    c = (char) System.in.read ();
    while (System.in.available () > 0)
      System.in.read ();

  } catch (Exception e) {
    e.printStackTrace ();
  }

  return (c);
}


public static void main(String[] args) {

  JtFactory factory = new JtFactory ();
  JtMessenger messenger = new JtMessenger ();
  TimerComponent timer;


  // Create the Timer component

  timer = (TimerComponent) factory.createObject
    (TimerComponent.JtCLASS_NAME);
```

```java
System.out.println ("Press any key to start the timer ....");
waitForInputKey ();
System.out.println ("Timer started ....");

// Start the timer component (Live/Animated Component).
// The framework is responsible for implementing
// the processing or threading mechanism. This message is
// processed asynchronously via a message queue.

messenger.setSynchronous(false);


messenger.sendMessage (timer,
    new JtMessage (JtComponent.JtACTIVATE));

System.out.println ("Press any key to stop the timer ....");
waitForInputKey ();
System.out.println (timer.getTime() + " second(s) elapsed.");

// Stop the timer

messenger.sendMessage (timer,
    new JtMessage (JtComponent.JtREMOVE));


    }


}
```

G.4 Registry

Animated/Live component responsible for maintaining the framework registry. This component also implements a naming mechanism to uniquely identify each component being added to the registry. It allows framework components to locate and cooperate with each other; in particular, in the context of distributed and concurrent applications. The framework Registry also supports the implementations of the Singleton pattern.

The following are the main *internal* methods implemented by the reference Registry:

Internal Method	Description
add ()	Add an entry to the framework Registry using a unique id (key).
update ()	Updates a registry entry.
lookup ()	Retrieves an entry from the framework Registry using its associated key. Null is returned if the entry is not found.
remove ()	Removes the specified entry from the framework Registry.

The framework Registry properly handles concurrent access (i.e. synchronized). All framework components interface with the same Registry instance. Such access is mainly performed indirectly via the framework Factory. The Registry class may be reused for general-purpose distributed/concurrent applications. The following conceptual interface (CI) and associated messages are provided.

Message ID	Description
JtCREATE	Add a new entry to the Registry (INSTANCE attribute) using the specified key (KEY). A framework error is returned if the entry already exists – unless the message includes additional directives: a) If RETURN_IF_ALREADY_EXISTS is specified, the existing entry is returned. b) If REPLACE_IF_ALREADY_EXISTS is specified, the entry is overridden. An appropriate framework error is also returned when the operation fails.
JtREAD	Retrieve the entry associated with the specified key (KEY). Null is returned if the entry does not exist.
JtUPDATE	Update the registry entry associated with the key (KEY) using the specified instance (INSTANCE). A framework error is returned if the entry does not exist or the operation fails.
JtDELETE	Delete the registry entry associated with the key (KEY). A framework error is returned if the entry does not exist or the operation fails.

G.5 Logger

Logger provides built-in logging capabilities. The framework can be configured or directed to log all the messages interchanged between components which facilitates debugging, testing, and implementation efforts. It can also automatically log all framework operations. Problems can be quickly identified and resolved by checking the messaging being automatically logged.

For convenience, the following attributes are provided by the framework Logger:

Attributes	Description
logging (boolean)	Logging flag which specifies whether logging is enabled or not. Thus, the feature can be enabled and disabled at will.
logLevel (integer)	Log messages can be assigned a level and selectively logged. This attribute specifies the current log level: messages of level below the specified level are not logged. Valid values are between the constants: a) `JtMIN_LOG_LEVEL` b) `JtMAX_LOG_LEVEL` The default value is `JtDEFAULT_LOG_LEVEL`. If the current log level is equal to `JtMIN_LOG_LEVEL`, all messages are logged.
logFile (String)	Logging information can be sent to a file. This attribute specifies the path of the file to be used for logging purposes.

Messages sent to the Logger are processed (i.e. logged) depending on message type:

Message Type	Description
String	Logs the message specified by the String parameter. The default log level is employed (JtDEFAULT_LOG_LEVEL).
JtLogMessage	Logs a message. JtLogMessage is a subclass of JtConcept. Optionally, the JtLogMessage instance may contain the log level (LEVEL).
JtError	Logs an error message. JtError is also a subclass of JtConcept. Error messages (instances of JtError) are always logged regardless of the current log level.
JtWarning	Logs a Warning (JtWarning). JtWarning is also a subclass of JtConcept. Warning messages are always logged regardless of the current log level.
JtConcept	Logs the concept construct (C) using the XML format. The default log level is employed (JtDEFAULT_LOG_LEVEL).

For convenience, the framework Logger is able to handle instances of any class. If the class is not contained in the table above, the instance is converted to XML and logged – similar to what is done with the concepts construct (JtConcept).

The reference implementation consists of the following internal methods:

Internal Method	Description
`log ()`	Logs an entry. A logging level is specified. For clarity and readability the XML format is employed when appropriate. `processException()` and `processError()` rely on this method.
`encodeInstance ()`	Encode entry using the XML representation.
`processException ()`	Log a Java Exception.
`processError ()`	Log a framework error (`JtError`).

In general, all application components should share the same Logger responsible for the central management of logging information. The framework creates and registers a 'central' Logger which can be located via the Factory. Components that wish to use the framework Logger can retrieve it by using the following snippet:

```
// Locate the framework Logger
logger = (JtLogger)
    factory.lookupObject(JtFactory.jtLogger);
```

The following example demonstrates the use of Logger based on its specification.

```
/**
 * Provides logging capabilities for
 * the Conceptual framework. It is able
 * to log framework concepts and objects.
 */

public static void main(String[] args) {

        JtLogger logger = new JtLogger ();
        logger.setLogging(true);
        JtConcept reply;
        JtConcept weatherInformation;
```

295

```
JtFactory factory = new JtFactory ();


// Log a message

logger.processMessage("Log message");

// Log a message using explicit log level (default)

logger.processMessage (new JtLogMessage
   ("Log message (default level - explicit)",
   JtLogger.JtDEFAULT_LOG_LEVEL));

// The following message should not be logged
// because it uses the minimum log level.

logger.processMessage
     (new JtLogMessage (
                "This message should not be logged",
                JtLogger.JtMIN_LOG_LEVEL));

// Change the log level (minimum level)

logger.setLogLevel(JtLogger.JtMIN_LOG_LEVEL);

logger.processMessage
     (new JtLogMessage (
         "Log message (minimum level - explicit)",
         JtLogger.JtMIN_LOG_LEVEL));

// Change the log level (maximum level)

logger.setLogLevel(JtLogger.JtMAX_LOG_LEVEL);

logger.processMessage
     (new JtLogMessage (
         "This message should not be logged."));


// Log an error message

logger.processMessage
   (new JtError ("Log this error"));


// Log an exception

try {

   // generate an internal JtException

   throw new Exception ("Log this exception");

} catch (Exception e) {
   reply = (JtConcept) logger.processMessage (e);
}

logger.processMessage(reply);
```

296

```
// Log a warning message

logger.processMessage
  (new JtWarning ("Log this warning"));


logger.setLogLevel(JtLogger.JtDEFAULT_LOG_LEVEL);

// Log a concept

weatherInformation = new JtConcept ();
factory = new JtFactory ();

factory.setValue(weatherInformation,
            WeatherService.summary, "Sunny");
factory.setValue(weatherInformation,
            WeatherService.maximum,
            new Integer (80));
factory.setValue(weatherInformation,
            WeatherService.minimum,
            new Integer (67));
factory.setValue(weatherInformation,
            WeatherService.precipitation,
            new Float (5.0));

logger.processMessage(weatherInformation);

// Locate the Logger component

logger = (JtLogger)
  factory.lookupObject(JtFactory.jtLogger);
}
```

G.6 Exception Handler

Framework component responsible for handling exceptions and errors. The built-in Exception Handler forwards errors and exceptions to the framework Logger. A custom exception handler can be easily incorporated by registering it. The reference implementation of the Exception Handler is able to process two types of messages:

Message Type	Description
Java Exception (`Exception`)	Forward the exception to the framework Logger.
JtError	Forward the error to the framework Logger.

In general, all application components should share the same handler responsible for the central management of exception and error information. The framework creates and registers a 'central' handler which can be located via the Factory. Components that wish to use the framework Exception Handler can retrieve it by using the following snippet:

```
// Locate the framework Exception Handler

exceptionHandler = (JtExceptionHandler)
        factory.lookupObject(JtFactory.jtExceptionHandler);
```

The example below demonstrates the use of the framework Exception Handler.

```
/**
 * Demonstrates the messages processed by the framework
 * Exception Handler.
 */

public static void main(String[] args) {
```

```java
JtExceptionHandler exceptionHandler =
        new JtExceptionHandler ();
JtFactory factory = new JtFactory ();


// Locate the exception handler


exceptionHandler = (JtExceptionHandler)
  factory.lookupObject
    (JtFactory.jtExceptionHandler);

if (exceptionHandler == null) {
        System.err.print
          ("Unable to locate the Exception Handler");
        System.exit(1);
}

// Java Exception

exceptionHandler.processMessage
    (new Exception ("my exception"));


// Framework error

exceptionHandler.processMessage
    (new JtError ("my error"));


}
```

G.7 Printer

Framework component responsible for printing capabilities. It is able to print detailed information about a concept construct (C) or component. The XML format is usually employed since the entity being printed may represent a complex hierarchy. Printer provides additional convenience while building, testing, and debugging applications. The standard output stream (stdout) is utilized.

Messages sent to the Printer are processed (i.e. printed) depending on message type:

Message Type	Description
String	Print the message specified by the String parameter.
JtConcept	Print the specified concept construct (C) using the XML format. Each one of the concept associations is printed.
Object and its subclasses	Print the specified object using the XML format. Each object attribute is printed.

The reference implementation of Printer consists of the following *internal* methods:

Internal Method	Description
`encodeInstance ()`	Encodes instance using the XML representation. For clarity and readability XML is employed when appropriate.
`printBuffer ()`	Prints a buffer (`byte[]`). XML representation is not required.

For convenience, Printer is able to handle instances of any class. The following example demonstrates the use of Printer.

```
/**
 * Framework component responsible for printing the content of
 * components and concepts (C).
 */
public static void main(String[] args) {

    JtFactory factory = new JtFactory ();
    JtPrinter printer;
    HelloWorld hello = new HelloWorld ();
    JtConcept weatherInformation;

        printer = new JtPrinter ();

    weatherInformation = new JtConcept ();


    // Create a concept construct

    factory.setValue(weatherInformation,
                WeatherService.summary, "Sunny");
    factory.setValue(weatherInformation,
                WeatherService.maximum, new Integer (80));
    factory.setValue(weatherInformation,
                WeatherService.minimum, new Integer (67));
    factory.setValue(weatherInformation,
                WeatherService.precipitation,
                new Float (5.0));

    // Print the concept construct

    printer.processMessage(weatherInformation);

    // Print an Object

    hello.setGreetingMessage("Hello World");

    printer.processMessage(hello);

    // Print a String

    printer.processMessage("Print this string.");


    }
```

G.8 Resource Manager (Properties File)

The Resource Manager is responsible for configuring components and concept constructs (C) when they are created. Attributes are read from the framework properties resource file. The mechanism provides a consistent way of customizing applications without having to hard code attribute values. Moving to a new platform or environment becomes a matter of replacing the resource file with one appropriate for the new environment.

The following are the main internal methods implemented by the reference Resource Manager:

Internal Method	Description
`loadResourcesFromStream()`	Read resource entries from the input stream associated with the framework properties file (`Jt.properties`).
`parseEntityResource()`	Parse input line containing a resource entry that corresponds to a specific component or concept.
`parseClassResource()`	Parse input line containing a resource entry associated with a class.
`loadComponentResources()`	Initialize component using its associated resources.
`loadConceptResources()`	Initialize concept (C) using its associated resources.

The Resource Manager is based on pure Java and able to transparently run on every Java platform. No platform-dependent APIs are employed for its implementation. It also facilitates localization and internationalization of framework applications. Several software features are usually configured via the Resource Manager. Among them:

-   Application context (Application name, platform, locale, etc)
-   Logging capabilities
-   Data Sources including SQLite Adapter
-   JDBC driver
-   Security and Encryption features (Cypher, KeyStores, etc.)
-   JMS configuration parameters
-   Web service adapters (SOA)

The Factory implementation relies on the Resource Manager to initialize component/concept attributes during creation. A resource entry applies to a class, component, or concept construct (C). The following is the syntax employed:

className.attribute:value

or

~entityID.attribute:value

entityID represents the concept or component ID. When an entity with the specified ID or class is created by the Factory, the attribute is initialized with the value found in the properties file. A complete example of the resource file is shown below:

```
! Resource properties file

! Application Context
```

```
~jtContext.applicationName:myapplication


! Logging paramenters

!Jt.JtLogger.logging:true
!Jt.JtLogger.logLevel:0
!Jt.JtLogger.logFile:log.txt


! Hello World demo application

Jt.examples.HelloWorld.greetingMessage:Hi there ...


! The attribute can also be initialized by using the
! component ID instead of the class.

!~helloWorld.greetingMessage:Hi there ...


! Graphical User Interface

~commandDialog.message:Enter keyboard input . . . .
~commandDialog.positiveButtonLabel:OK
~commandDialog.negativeButtonLabel:Cancel

~exitDialog.messsage:Are you sure you want to exit?

~addUrlDialog.message:Add web page bookmark
~addUrlDialog.positiveButtonLabel:OK
~addUrlDialog.negativeButtonLabel:Cancel


! JDBC adapter (MySQL settings)

Jt.jdbc.JtJDBCAdapter.user:root

Jt.jdbc.JtJDBCAdapter.password:123456
Jt.jdbc.JtJDBCAdapter.driver:com.mysql.jdbc.Driver
Jt.jdbc.JtJDBCAdapter.url:jdbc:mysql://localhost/test
!Jt.jdbc.JtJDBCAdapter.datasource:datasrc


! Java Mail Adapter

Jt.mail.JtMail.server:serve.mydomain.com
Jt.mail.JtMail.username:user
Jt.mail.JtMail.password:password
Jt.mail.JtMail.port:587

! JNDI Adapter

Jt.jndi.JtJNDIAdapter.factory:weblogic.jndi.WLInitialContextFactory
Jt.jndi.JtJNDIAdapter.url:t3://localhost:7001
```

G.9 Distributed Proxy

The Conceptual framework provides transparent access to distributed components and services via reusable Proxies (see Distributed Conceptual Environment). Framework Proxies hide the complexities associated with distributed and secure access (see Figure below). The same Proxy can be *reused* to access arbitrary components remotely. It is responsible for levering the framework in order to forward messages to the target component.

Proxies usually communicate directly with a corresponding framework Adapter which is able to interface with the target technology or protocol. As the figure shows, the framework relies on a 'messaging pipeline' to transfer messaging from sender to receiver, which are Live/Animated components $(A=((f(m),I))$.

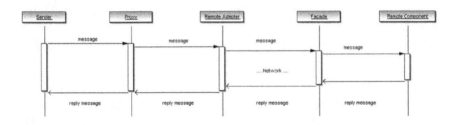

A straightforward naming mechanism is required while configuring framework Proxies to communicate with distributed components (somewhat analogous to the phone directory). For instance, computer URL and class name (or component ID) needs to be specified in order to locate the distributed component. Other mechanisms are feasible for implementation.

Secure access (encrypted and/or authenticated) is also supported. Design patterns like Proxy, Adapter and Façade are implemented based on Conceptual model (see Design Pattern implementation). The concept construct (C) can be transparently interchanged between heterogeneous systems regardless of platform, technology, computer language, protocol, data representation, and so on.

The Conceptual framework also provides built-in exception handling capabilities. Exceptions detected during distributed communication and/or execution are automatically propagated backwards, through the messaging pipeline, for handling by the sender component.

The following example demonstrates the use of the Proxy provided by the framework which supports the HTTP protocol. Several other reusable Proxies, applicable to common distributed technologies, are built-in as part of the framework – including Apache Axis, REST, and EJB. The framework can be readily extended by building custom Proxies for distributed technologies based on specific requirements.

Few additional components are required to interoperate with a new technology or protocol. Most of the needed functionality can be copied from existing framework Adapters, Proxies, and Façades. Keep in mind that the framework is mainly responsible for transferring information (messaging) between sender and receiver components. While reducing overall complexity, the Conceptual model provides the framework with a high degree of interoperability between technologies, protocols, and computer languages.

HTTP Proxies are implemented via the `JtHttpProxy` class. The reusable HTTP Proxy needs a way of locating the distributed component. In order to do so, the URL is necessary (`setURL ()`). The class of component to be accessed also needs to be provided (`setClassname ()`). The specific example deals with a distributed component responsible for providing weather information: `Jt.examples.WeatherService`.

After receiving the `JtREAD` message, the distributed component returns the information using the concept construct (C). If an exception is detected during execution, it is returned to the calling component for handling. This is possible because of the framework's built-in mechanism of propagating exceptions. Authenticated and encrypted access to distributed components is also fully supported.

By leveraging the Conceptual framework, communication with distributed components becomes straightforward – including secure access. Notice the absence of distributed artifacts and artificial primitives which add unnecessary complexity.

```java
public static void main(String[] args) {

    JtFactory factory = new JtFactory ();
    Object reply;
    JtHttpProxy proxy;
    JtConcept ctx;

    String url =
      "http://localhost:8080/JtPortal/JtRestService";
    JtMessenger messenger = new JtMessenger ();
    JtMessage msg;
    boolean bool;
    JtPrinter printer = new JtPrinter ();

    // Create an instance of the remote Proxy

    proxy = (JtHttpProxy) factory.createObject
      (JtHttpProxy.JtCLASS_NAME);

    // Specify URL and class name for the distributed
    // component

    proxy.setUrl(url);
    proxy.setClassname ("Jt.examples.WeatherService");

    // Send the message (Read) to the distributed
    // component that provides the Weather service.
    // Weather information is retrieved.

    reply = messenger.sendMessage (proxy,
                new JtMessage (JtFactory.JtREAD));

    if (reply instanceof JtError) {
        System.out.println
          ("Service Invocation (JtREAD):FAIL");
        System.out.println ("Exception detected:");
        printer.processMessage(reply);
    } else {
        System.out.println
          ("Service Invocation (JtREAD):PASS");
        printer.processMessage (reply);

    }

    proxy = (JtHttpProxy)
      factory.createObject (JtHttpProxy.JtCLASS_NAME);
    proxy.setUrl(url);
    proxy.setClassname
      ("Jt.examples.service.BankTeller");
    proxy.setRestful(false);

    messenger = new JtMessenger ();
```

307

```
// Specify that secure/encrypted messaging
// should be used. The Bank Teller component
// requires it.

messenger.setEncrypted(true);

// Authentication information

ctx = new JtConcept ();
factory.setValue(ctx, "username", "jt");
factory.setValue(ctx, "password", "messaging");

messenger.setContext(ctx);

// Send the message to the distributed
// teller component to retrieve account
// information. A concept (account)
// or an exception is returned.

msg = new JtMessage (JtComponent.JtREAD);
factory.setValue(msg,
  BankTeller.ACCOUNT, "12345678");

reply = messenger.sendMessage (proxy, msg);

if (reply instanceof JtError) {
  System.out.println
   ("Authenticated/Encrypted Service (JtREAD):FAIL");
        System.out.println ("Exception detected:");
        printer.processMessage(reply);
} else {
  System.out.println
   ("Authenticated/Encrypted Service (JtREAD):PASS");
        printer.processMessage (reply);

}

// Remove the proxy and all remote references.
// The remote framework component should be ready
// to be garbage collected after this operation.
bool = factory.removeObject(proxy);


if (bool)
        System.out.println("removeObject:PASS");
else
        System.out.println("removeObject:FAIL");


}
```

G.10 Distributed Façade

The reference implementation of Façade (JtRemoteFacade) is mainly responsible for forwarding messages to the appropriate distributed component (Live/Animated component). It is also responsible for providing access control and message security (authentication and encryption) through several support components.

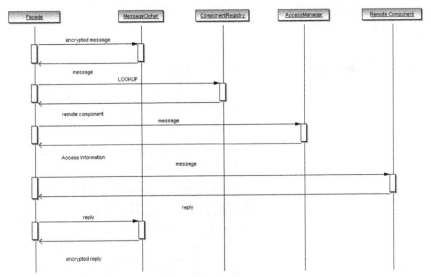

Secure access to distributed components/services based on Concepts (server side)

The following are the components involved:

Component	Description
MessageCipher	Live/Animated component responsible for decrypting the input message and encrypting the reply message. This component can be configured to use a specific encryption scheme. This component is only applicable when secure messaging is being utilized.
Registry	Allows the Façade to register and look up distributed components by ID.

AccessManager	Responsible for granting/denying access to distributed components. When needed, it authorizes and authenticates the messages received. If the Access Manager is unable to authenticate the message, it never reaches the intended receiver. An error is produced and propagated.

The following are the main *internal* methods implemented by the reference framework Façade:

Internal Method	Description
decryptMessage ()	Utilize the message cipher to decrypt secure incoming messages.
verifyAccess ()	Relies on the Access Manager for the verification of authorized access to the distributed component.
authenticateMessage()	Authenticate the incoming message.
encryptMessage ()	Relies on the message cipher to encrypt replies when secure messaging is being employed.
generateUniqueId ()	Generate unique ID for the distributed component when needed. The ID is returned to the client during the initialization of the distributed Proxy. It allows subsequent access to the distributed component via its Proxy.

The reference implementation of the Conceptual framework supports a straightforward naming mechanism for distributed components based on URL, component ID and class. As part of the conceptual interface (CI), several message types are defined to manipulate distributed components and its attributes: JtCREATE, JtSEND_MESSAGE, JtGET_VALUE, JtSET_VALUE, and JtDELETE correspondingly.

The previous messages are leveraged by framework Proxies to provide access to distributed components. Each message type is structured as follows:

Message ID	Description
JtCREATE	Create a component of a specific class (CLASSNAME) and return a generated component ID. The new component is added to the internal component registry maintained by JtRemoteFacade. This message is usually utilized by Proxies during initialization. The life span of the new component is temporal. It will exist until the distributed Proxy is discarded (JtREMOVE message). A framework error is returned if the operation fails.
JtSEND_MESSAGE	Forward the message (MESSAGE) to a distributed component (COMPONENT) for processing. The reply message is returned unless the operation fails in which case an error is returned.
JtSET_VALUE	Set the value of the component attribute (ATTRIBUTE). This message also contains component ID (COMPONENT) and attribute value (VALUE). A framework error (JtError) is returned if the operation fails.
JtGET_VALUE	Retrieve the value of the component attribute (ATTRIBUTE). This message also contains component ID (COMPONENT). If the operation fails, a framework error is returned.
JtLOOKUP	Locate a distributed component based on its component ID (COMPONENT). This message is usually utilized by Proxies during initialization. The framework Registry is checked. Null is returned if the component cannot be found. If the operation fails, a framework error is returned.

JtREMOVE	Removes the component (COMPONENT) from the internal registry maintained by `JtRemoteFacade`. A framework error is returned if the operation fails.

The conceptual interface (CI) described above is independent of platform, technology, protocol, computer language, data representation, and so forth. By leveraging the Conceptual computing model, arbitrary technology pieces can be transparently integrated into a unified and interoperable environment. The framework messaging pipeline is highly reusable: usually a single Proxy and associated Adapter is all that is required to support a new distributed technology or protocol. The bulk of the distributed information infrastructure remains unchanged.

G.11 Message Cipher

Framework component responsible for encrypting and decrypting messages, as part of secure communication between distributed components. The message cipher relies on several additional support components which have dual responsibilities (client and server side).

Support Component	Description (client)	Description (server)
Symmetric Cipher (JtAsymmetric)	Encrypt messages using a session key which can be provided or automatically generated. The symmetric cipher is responsible for generating the session key (if one is not provided). Decrypt reply messages using the same session key.	Decrypt messages using the encrypted session key passed as part of the message. The session keys needs to be decrypted beforehand as described below.
Asymmetric Cipher (JtSymmetric)	Encrypt the session key using the public key of the recipient (server). The encrypted key is sent, as part of the message, to the remote computer.	Decrypt the session key using the private key of the receiver (server). Once the session key is decrypted, it can be utilized to decrypt the message itself via the symmetric cipher.

G.12 Access Manager

The reference implementation of the Access Manager (AM) controls messaging access to distributed components. By default, no access is granted to any distributed class or component unless it is explicitly enabled via the AM configuration file. Access to distributed framework components can be enabled or disabled. It can also be configured to be encrypted and/or authenticated.

ENABLED	Enables the messaging access to a distributed component, class, or package.
ENCRYPTED	Messaging must be encrypted using the appropriate session key, in order to be processed by the distributed receiver.
	Otherwise, it is rejected by the framework because of a security violation. The session key is automatically encrypted using the framework public key.
AUTHETICATED	Messaging must contain valid authentication information like username and password. Otherwise, it is rejected by the framework because of a security violation. For tight security, authenticated messaging should be employed in conjunction with encrypted messaging.

Additional features can be incorporated as part of the Access Manager. For instance, access can be granted based on user, role, and/or group. In conjunction with the capabilities provided by the framework, distributed components may readily implement custom security mechanisms (encryption/authentication) over the messaging being exchanged. The reference implementation of the Access Manager relies on a configuration file or database which contains a group of access entries like the following:

```
<Entry>
  <classname>Jt.examples.MyClass</classname>
  <enabled>true</enabled>
</Entry>
```

The previous entry enables messaging access to the class named Jt.examples.MyClass. Access can be specified to be encrypted:

```
<Entry>
  <classname>Jt.examples.MyClass</classname>
  <enabled>true</enabled>
  <encrypted>true</encrypted>
</Entry>
```

Access can also be specified to be encrypted and authenticated:

```
<Entry>
  <classname>Jt.examples.MyClass</classname>
  <enabled>true</enabled>
  <encrypted>true</encrypted>
  <authenticated>true</authenticated>
</Entry>
```

Instead of a class name, a component ID can be specified as part of the access entry:

```
<Entry>
  <entryId>myComponent</entryId>
  <enabled>true</enabled>
  <encrypted>true</encrypted>
  <authenticated>true</authenticated>
</Entry>
```

The previous entry enables access to the component named myComponent. Messaging access is specified to be encrypted and authenticated. Finally, access can be granted to a package of classes by using wild characters. The following entry enables encrypted access to all the classes that belong to the package Jt.service.

```
<Entry>
  <classname>Jt.services.*</classname>
  <enabled>true</enabled>
  <encrypted>true</encrypted>
</Entry>
```

Configuration entries can be easily extended to deal with additional access features (roles, usernames, etc.) . The following are the main *internal* methods implemented by the Access Manager (reference implementation):

Internal Method	Description
readConfigFile ()	Read access entries from a configuration file, stream, or database.
retrieveClassAccessEntry ()	Retrieve the access entry associated to a specific class.
retrieveComponentAccessEntry ()	Retrieve the access entry associated to a specific component.

G.13 Adapter

The Conceptual computing model has been leveraged for the reusable implementation of several design pattern – including GoF Adapter (see Design Pattern Implementation). Adapter is leveraged to interface with a diverse variety of technologies. In the context of the Conceptual model, the main purpose of Adapter is the transformation of messages between sender and receiver so they can communicate. Information and messages are represented using the concept construct (C). Adapter implements the information machine abstraction (Live/Animated entity - $(A=((f(m),I)))$).

Each distributed technology or protocol requires the implementation of a suitable Adapter and corresponding Proxy to interface with the distributed information infrastructure provided by the Conceptual model. For instance, the JtHttpAdapter class is the framework Adapter responsible for distributed component communication via the HTTP protocol. For convenience, messages (C) are converted to the XML format. However, arbitrary data representations can be employed including binary and custom formats. Typically, the client application interfaces indirectly with the Adapter component through the corresponding Proxy, part of the messaging pipeline.

The HTTP Adapter is usually employed in conjunction with the HTTP Proxy as part of the framework's messaging pipeline (see JtHTTPProxy). All forms of messaging are supported including synchronous, asynchronous, and secure (authenticated and/or encrypted).

The following are the main *internal* methods implemented by the reference HTTP Adapter:

Internal Method	Description
sendRemoteMessage ()	Forwards the message (C) to a distributed component by posting it as an HTTP request via the framework's messaging pipeline.

G.15 Android Location and GPS Interface

Reference implementation of the Location/GPS functionality for Android (JtGPS class). Notice that by levering the Conceptual computing model, the implementation is straightforward: simple conceptual interface (CI) based on the following few messages. The Conceptual framework transparently handles most of the complexities associated with concurrency and asynchronous messaging. This framework class is also responsible for encapsulating ('hiding') the initialization, configuration, and housekeeping functionality required by Android – which makes the use of this class straightforward. Conceptually, the user simply needs to retrieve (read) location/GPS information from the Animated component.

Message ID	Description
JtACTIVATE	Activate component to start listening for location updates: location information is retrieved. This message consists of the following pieces of information: a) Controller component responsible for handling messages that contain location/GPS updates (REPLY_TO). b) Serial to be matched when the location update is received by the controller component (SERIAL).
JtDEACTIVATE	Deactivate component (stop listening for updates).

The following message containing a location update is forwarded to the controller component (Live/Animated component). Finally, notice that the straightforward conceptual interface provided is based on messaging as opposed to gear meshing of procedure calls.

Message ID	Description
JtGPS_LOCATION	Location update. The message consists of: a) Latitude (LATITUDE) b) Longitude (LONGITUDE) c) Altitude (ALTITUDE) d) Accuracy (ACCURACY) e) Speed (SPEED) f) Time (TIME)

```java
/*
 * Framework component for the Android Location/GPS API
 * (reference implementation). A conceptual interface
 * is implemented. This Live/Animated component can be readily
 * replaced by another platform-specific component
 * using the same conceptual interface without any
 * impact on the rest of the system. Minimum software
 * changes should be needed (if any).
 */

public class JtGPS extends JtComponent
implements LocationListener {


    private static final long serialVersionUID = 1L;
    public static final String JtCLASS_NAME = JtGPS.class.getName();
    public static final String LOCATION = "LOCATION";

    public static final String ACCURACY = "ACCURACY";
    public static final String LATITUDE = "LATITUDE";
    public static final String LONGITUDE = "LONGITUDE";
    public static final String PROVIDER = "PROVIDER";
    public static final String SPEED = "SPEED";
    public static final String ALTITUDE = "ALTIDUDE";
    public static final String TIME = "TIME";

    public static final String PROVIDER_DISABLED =
        "PROVIDER_DISABLED";
    public static final String PROVIDER_ENABLED = "PROVIDER_ENABLED";

    public static final String CURRENT_ACTIVITY = "CURRENT_ACTIVITY";
    public static final String SERIAL = "SERIAL";
    public static final String toastComponent = "toastComponent";

    private Object context;
    private JtFactory factory = new JtFactory ();
    private JtLogger logger;
    private boolean networkProviderEnabled = true;
    private boolean gpsProviderEnabled = true;
    private long minTime = 0L;
    private float minDistance = (float) 0.0;
    private Object replyTo = null; // Send reply to this component
    private String serial = null;
    private Object currentLocation =null;
    private LocationManager locationManager;
    private boolean status = false;
    private boolean repeat = false;
    private boolean synchronousMessaging = true;
    private boolean gpsDisabled = false;
    private boolean networkDisabled = false;


    public JtGPS() {

    }
```

```java
/**
 * Returns the value of the networkProviderEnabled flag
 * which specifies whether or not location updates should
 * be requested from the network provider.
 */

public boolean isNetworkProviderEnabled() {
  return networkProviderEnabled;
}

/**
 * Sets the networkProviderEnabled flag.
 */

public void setNetworkProviderEnabled
(boolean networkProviderEnabled) {
  this.networkProviderEnabled = networkProviderEnabled;
}

/**
 * Returns the value of the isGpsProviderEnabled flag which
 * specifies whether or not location updates should be
 * requested from the GPS provider.
 */

public boolean isGpsProviderEnabled() {
  return gpsProviderEnabled;
}

/**
 * Sets the networkProviderEnabled flag.
 */

public void setGpsProviderEnabled(boolean gpsProviderEnabled) {
  this.gpsProviderEnabled = gpsProviderEnabled;
}


/**
 * Returns the current location.
 */

public Object getCurrentLocation() {
  return currentLocation;
}

/**
 * void operation
 */

public void setCurentLocation(Object curentLocation) {

}
```

```java
/**
 * Returns the time (in milliseconds) between location
 * updates.
 */

public long getMinTime() {
  return minTime;
}

/**
 * Specifies the time (in milliseconds) between
 * location updates. To obtain notifications as frequently
 * as possible, set parameter to 0.
 */
public void setMinTime(long minTime) {
  this.minTime = minTime;
}


/**
 * Returns the minimum distance between location
 * updates.
 */

public float getMinDistance() {
  return minDistance;
}

/**
 * Specifies the minimum distance between location
 * updates. To obtain notifications as frequently
 * as possible, set parameter to 0.
 */

public void setMinDistance(float minDistance) {
  this.minDistance = minDistance;
}

/**
 * Specifies whether or not the component
 * should keep listening for location updates
 * after the first update.
 */

public boolean isRepeat() {
  return repeat;
}

public void setRepeat(boolean repeat) {
  this.repeat = repeat;
}
```

```
/*
 * Start listening for Location updates
 */

private Object activate (Object message) {
  Location location;
  Boolean Bool;

  replyTo = factory.getValue(message,
      JtMessage.REPLY_TO);
  serial = (String) factory.getValue(message,
      JtGPS.SERIAL);

  Bool = (Boolean) factory.getValue(message,
      JtMessage._SYNCHRONOUS);

  if (Bool != null)
    synchronousMessaging = Bool.booleanValue();

  gpsDisabled = false;
  networkDisabled = false;

  // Acquire a reference to the system Location Manager

  try {
    locationManager = (LocationManager)
    ((Context) context).getSystemService
    (Context.LOCATION_SERVICE);

    // Register the listener with the Location Manager
    // to receive location updates
    if (networkProviderEnabled)
      locationManager.requestLocationUpdates
      (LocationManager.NETWORK_PROVIDER,
          minTime, minDistance, this);

    if (gpsProviderEnabled)
      locationManager.requestLocationUpdates
      (LocationManager.GPS_PROVIDER, minTime,
          minDistance, this);

    location =
      locationManager.getLastKnownLocation
      (LocationManager.NETWORK_PROVIDER);
    logger.processMessage ("JtGPS(lastKnownLocation) ....");
    logLocation (location);
    status = true;
    return (null);
  } catch (Exception ex) {
    displayMessage ("Unable to start GPS component.");
    return (logger.processMessage (ex));
  }

}
```

```java
private void removeListener () {
  // Remove the listener previously added
  try {
    locationManager.removeUpdates(this);
    status = false;
    logger.processMessage ("removeListener");
  } catch (Exception ex) {
    logger.processMessage (ex);
  }
}

private Context retrieveAppContext () {

  Object context;

  context = (JtConcept)
  factory.lookupObject(JtFactory.jtContext);


  if (context == null) {
    logger.processMessage
    (new JtError ("Invalid Jt context"));
    return (null);
  }

  return ((Context)
      factory.getValue(context,
          JtGPS.CURRENT_ACTIVITY));
}

// Retrieve the framework Logger

private void locateLogger () {

  logger = (JtLogger)
  factory.lookupObject(JtFactory.jtLogger);

  if (logger == null) {
    System.err.println("Unable lo locate Logger");
    logger = new JtLogger ();
  }

}

// Display message via the GUI component

private void displayMessage (String message) {
  JtMessenger messenger = new JtMessenger ();
  JtMessage msg = new JtMessage
  (JtComponent.JtACTIVATE);
  Object uiComponent;

  if (message == null || message.equals(""))
    return;

  uiComponent = factory.lookupObject(JtFactory.uiComponent);
```

323

```java
    if (uiComponent == null) {
      logger.processMessage
      (new JtWarning ("Unable to locate UI component"));
      return;
    }

    factory.setValue(msg, JtMessage.MESSAGE, message);
    factory.setValue(msg, JtMessage.WHAT,
        JtGPS.toastComponent);

    messenger.setSynchronous(false);
    messenger.sendMessage(uiComponent, msg);

}

/**
 * Process component messages.
 * <ul>
 * <li>JtACTIVATE - Activate component to start listening
 * for location updates.
 * <li>JtDEACTIVATE - Deactivate component.
 * <li>JtREMOVE - Remove component.
 * </ul>
 */

public Object processMessage (Object message) {

  Object msgId;

  if (message == null)
    return (null);

  locateLogger ();

  if (!(message instanceof JtMessage)) {
    logger.processMessage
    (new JtError ("Invalid message format."));
    return (null);
  }


  context = retrieveAppContext ();

  if (context == null) {
    displayMessage
    ("Unable to start GPS component: context is missing.");
    logger.processMessage
    (new JtError ("Invalid context (null):"));
    return null;
  }

  msgId = factory.getValue(message, JtMessage.ID);

  /*
   * Start listening for Location updates
   */
```

324

```java
    if (msgId.equals(JtComponent.JtACTIVATE)) {
      if (status)
        removeListener ();
      return (activate (message));
    }

    if (msgId.equals(JtComponent.JtDEACTIVATE)) {
      removeListener ();
      return (null);
    }

    if (msgId.equals(JtComponent.JtREMOVE)) {
      removeListener ();

      // Forward the message to the
      // superclass
      super.processMessage(message);
      return (null);
    }

    return (logger.processMessage
        (new JtError ("Invalid message Id:" +
            msgId)));


}

// Log the current location

public void logLocation (Location location) {
  if (location == null) {
    logger.processMessage ("JtGPS(location): null");
    return;
  }
  logger.processMessage("Accuracy:" + location.getAccuracy());
  logger.processMessage("Latitude:" + location.getLatitude());
  logger.processMessage("Longitude:" + location.getLongitude());
  logger.processMessage("Provider:" + location.getProvider());
  logger.processMessage("Speed:" + location.getSpeed());
  logger.processMessage("Altitude:" + location.getAltitude());
  logger.processMessage("Time:" + location.getTime());
}


// Location update

public void onLocationChanged(Location location) {

  JtMessage message = new JtMessage (JtGPS.LOCATION);
  JtMessenger messenger = new JtMessenger ();

  logger.processMessage("onLocationChanged:" + location);
  if (location == null)
    return;
  if (synchronousMessaging)
    messenger.setSynchronous(true);
  else
    messenger.setSynchronous(false);
```

```
// Returns the GPS information as
// a concept (message).


factory.setValue(message,
    JtMessage.SUBJECT, JtGPS.LOCATION);
factory.setValue(message,
    JtMessage.IS_REPLY, new Boolean (true));
factory.setValue(message,
    JtGPS.LATITUDE, new Double (location.getLatitude()));
factory.setValue(message,
    JtGPS.LONGITUDE, new Double (location.getLongitude()));
factory.setValue(message,
    JtGPS.ACCURACY, new Double (location.getAccuracy()));
factory.setValue(message,
    JtGPS.PROVIDER, location.getProvider());
factory.setValue(message,
    JtGPS.ALTITUDE, new Double (location.getAltitude()));
factory.setValue(message,
    JtGPS.SPEED, new Double (location.getSpeed()));
factory.setValue(message,
    JtGPS.TIME, new Long (location.getTime()));

// Serial to be matched by the component
// requesting Location information.
factory.setValue(message, JtGPS.SERIAL, serial);

if (replyTo != null) {

  messenger.sendMessage(replyTo, message);

  if (!repeat)
    removeListener ();
}
currentLocation = message;
logLocation (location);

}

public void onProviderDisabled(String provider) {
  JtMessenger messenger = new JtMessenger ();
  JtMessage message = new JtMessage (JtGPS.LOCATION);

  logger.processMessage("onProviderDisabled:" + provider);

  if (LocationManager.NETWORK_PROVIDER.equals(provider))
    networkDisabled = true;

  if (LocationManager.GPS_PROVIDER.equals(provider))
    gpsDisabled = true;

  if (!(networkDisabled && gpsDisabled))
    return;

  // Both providers are disabled. Notify the user.

  factory.setValue(message,
      JtMessage.SUBJECT, JtGPS.PROVIDER_DISABLED);
  factory.setValue(message,
```

```
        JtMessage.IS_REPLY, new Boolean (true));


    if (replyTo != null)
      messenger.sendMessage(replyTo, message);


  }

  public void onProviderEnabled(String provider) {

    logger.processMessage("onProviderEnabled:" +
        provider);
  }

  public void onStatusChanged(String provider, int status, Bundle
extras) {

    logger.processMessage ("onStatusChanged(" + provider + "):"
        + status);

  }


}
```

INDEX

A

A = (f(m), l), 11, 23
Actor model. *See* Appendix
Android
 Conceptual framework, 95
Aristotle
 perfection, 32, 238

B

Biomimetics, 5
Boole
 Conceptual Machine, 12, 122
 Laws of Thought, 12
 Logical Engine, 143
Business Process Execution Language
 (BPEL), 34, 64, 125
Business Process Modeling (BPM), 34,
 64, 125

C

Church-Turing thesis, 121
Cognitive models, 260–327
Common Object Request Broker
 Architectures (CORBA), 240
complex machinery of procedure
 declarations, 47, 235
Complexity, 24, 25, 46, 110
Component-based Software
 Engineering (CBSE)
 Common Object Request Broker
 Architectures (CORBA), 240
 compared to Concepts, 240
 Component Object Model (COM),
 240
 Enterprise Java Beans. *See* EJB
Concept
 abstraction level, 30
 implementation, 42
 mathematical notation, 39
Conceptual computer language, 42
 information domain, 172
 Language (L), 13
 Procedure (P), 13, 171

Sentence (S), 13, 171
Conceptual framework, 26, 31, 34, 87–
 97
 core components, 93
 Exception Handler, 94
 Factory, 93
 Logger, 93
 Messenger, 93
 Printer, 94
 Registry, 93
 Resource Manager, 94
Conceptual information, 39, 40, 84
Conceptual interface, 45–60
Conceptual paradigm, 5, 32
 learning curve, 32
Conceptualism, 10
Conceptualization, 13
Concurrency, 54
Connectionism, 265
Correspondence Theory of Truth, 7, 16
Coupling, 24, 29, 46, 110

D

Data Access Objects (DAO), 85, 86
Debugging, 53
Decoupling. *See* Coupling
Deductive approach. *See* Conceptual
 computer language
Design pattern, 33, 55, 98–107
 Adapter, 99
 Bridge, 101
 Command, 101
 Data Access Objects. *See* DAO
 Decorator, 102
 Façade, 100
 Factory, 102
 Gang of Four (GoF), 98–104
 implementation, 98–107
 J2EE Business Delegate, 35, 107
 J2EE Service Locator, 109
 J2EE Session Façade, 107
 Master-Worker, 128
 Model View Controller. *See* MVC
 Prototype, 104
 Proxy, 98
 Singleton, 103

U

Unanimated object, 10
Unified Modeling Language (UML), 52
Unified Theories of Cognition (UTC), 260

Universal. *See* conceptualism

V

Versioning, 53, 240

About the Author

Mr. Galvis has had several roles over a period of more than 15 years in the computer industry. Roles include Computer Scientist at research facilities and responsibilities as a technical consultant and architect for several major corporations. He has also authored several papers published in technical conferences and journals.

Rejoice Evermore !

Rejoice evermore, God will come !
And death shall be no more
No more sorrow or darkness
No more pain
No more hate or fear
No more war
No more need or chains

Rejoice! God is near
Lord of Peace
Reign of Freedom and Justice
Perfect Union
God is Love, God is Mercy
Water of Life, infinite Grace and Wisdom
Universal *Logos*, Light to us All

Rejoice! Do Pray (Live) in Faith and Thanksgiving
May God's blessings be upon you, Always
In God put your Trust
Rejoice evermore, Love is near !